NUMBER NINE DREAM

NUMBER NINE DREAM

An Autobiography
Rob Howley

with Graham Clutton

MAINSTREAM
PUBLISHING

EDINBURGH AND LONDON

First published in Great Britain in 1999 by
MAINSTREAM PUBLISHING COMPANY (EDINBURGH) LTD
7 Albany Street
Edinburgh EH1 3UG

ISBN 1 84018 208 3

A catalogue record for this book is available from the British Library

Typeset in Garamond
Printed and bound in Great Britain by Butler and Tanner Ltd

CONTENTS

ACKNOWLEDGEMENTS

Robert and Graham would like to thank the following people for their help and support:

Ceri and Megan Howley, Brenda and David Howley, Denise Clutton, Sarah Clutton, Dave Hollins and Sacha Miller at *Wales News, The Western Mail,* the *South Wales Echo,* Neil Bennett and Alan Edmunds at *Wales on Sunday,* Reebok, Alan Evans of Cardiff RFC, Graham Henry, Colorsport, Fotosport, Les Loosemore, Huw Evans, Alex Skybinski, Julie Longden, Tim Buttimore at SCG, Derrick King, Richard Evans, Wayne Barrington, and Bill Campbell, Peter MacKenzie, Sarah Edwards and Siân Braes at Mainstream Publishing.

FOREWORD

by Graham Henry

When I first arrived in Wales, I suppose I was certain of only two things. Firstly, I understood that, because of recent results, I had a fairly big challenge on my hands. Secondly, I knew from television coverage that Robert Howley, a 27-year-old scrum-half from Cardiff, had been the national captain for the best part of a year.

Therefore, it is fair to say that I came in pretty blind. I had seen Wales performing on TV and I had watched Rob play on numerous occasions. My thoughts on Rob were quite simple: good player, good guy. Whether he was a good captain or had the makings of a good leader, I didn't know. I would have to find that out for myself. However, I am not one of these coaches who make changes for change's sake. After all, as far as Rob and the Wales captaincy were concerned, I knew as much about Rob Howley as I did about any other Welsh player.

As most people know, I organised a couple of trial games in the late summer to try and evaluate the strengths and weaknesses of the leading players I would have at my disposal. That was stage one. Stage two would be to take a close look at what was going on at club level, while stage three would be to pick my side for the forthcoming game against the Springboks.

None of that would have been possible without help, although when you have travelled blind, from the other side of the world, knocking on doors and asking opinions is not that straightforward. I had to rely on those closest to me. It was because of that need to know what was going on that I turned to Rob. I wanted to talk about the players and the coaches in Wales and to learn a little bit more about the man on whom the responsibility of captaincy had fallen following the injury to Gwyn Jones.

I was mightily impressed with Rob's attitude and I realised from the outset that I had made a wise move. He had a real enthusiasm for a game which, to be honest, at that stage was going through difficult times. He was excited about what lay ahead and despite what had gone on during the summer felt that there was a genuine opportunity for Welsh rugby to close the gap. He spoke with great knowledge and authority and, most of all, with great honesty.

Those people who know me – and many of them are back in New Zealand – know that I am a fairly straightforward guy who speaks his mind. I don't talk around a subject, I talk about it. Sometimes, perhaps, I say a bit too much for some people's liking. However, I do get a bit tired with people who are so concerned about what they are going to say that they end up saying nothing. On that occasion, I wanted Rob to give me chapter and verse. It would have been very easy for him to fudge the important issues and say nothing, but he didn't do that and I left the hotel that evening knowing that Rob Howley was a guy I could hang my hat on.

I decided very quickly that Rob would be the national captain and told him as much. Sixteen months on we are still together. Furthermore, he has grown into the role and is now an experienced captain for whom I have the utmost respect. He certainly isn't one of those captains who thinks about things and then says nothing.

As I have said to Rob on numerous occasions, you don't become a great captain overnight. However, if you have the necessary qualities to succeed, you will do so. We are sometimes far too quick to criticise our own and to knock people off their pedestals. Remember, these are the same pedestals that we put them on in the first place. Rob suffered a fair amount of criticism last season but he came through it, with the help of his senior players and the management. He is better for the experience and, as anyone can see now, he is comfortable with the job and communicates far better than he did at the outset. That is an example of how time can produce quality.

I have worked with a great many good players and captains, people like Pat Lam, Sean Fitzpatrick and Zinzan Brooke. They will all tell you how easy it is to captain a side off the field; the real test of a captain is when things go wrong on the field. It concerns how he handles certain situations, the decisions he takes and the response he gets from his players.

Rob has handled the difficult times well and he responds well to tricky situations. He is now a dictator on the pitch and that is something which has come with experience. He is a fine player too, and to have both assets is a great quality. For those who doubt that quality, I would remind them that Rob Howley has led Wales to a record number of successive Test victories. You don't achieve that without good players and good leadership. Over the past year, Welsh rugby has had both.

As a captain, I think Rob Howley has become an inspirational figure for the young players playing at grass-roots level. They look up to him as a player and a leader and we all know how important it is to have figureheads in the game. Like myself, Rob always tries his hardest to produce his very best, on and off the field. That focus is important if you are going to succeed in life, and Rob possesses that single-mindedness to succeed.

I have enjoyed working with Rob Howley both as a player and as a captain, and I hope there are many more games and victories ahead of us.

1. SECOND TIME OF ASKING

A New Wales Captain

I was no different from any other impressionable schoolboy. I would go to sleep dreaming of running out at Cardiff Arms Park and I would wake up with a warm glow having scored the winning try against England at Twickenham.

Some nights I would even be the Welsh captain, leading the side in a deafening rendition of 'Hen Wlad Fy Nhadau' before celebrating a 35-point victory over the old enemy. From the moment I first picked up a rugby ball it was always my biggest single ambition – to play for and captain my country.

Like most of my friends, I never imagined that my burning ambition would become reality. On the contrary, if anybody had suggested that one day I would lead Wales into a Five Nations Championship, on a summer tour to South Africa or into the World Cup, let alone all three, I would have laughed in their face. Such achievements were for the great players like Gareth Edwards, Mervyn Davies, Phil Bennett and Robert Jones, not Robert Howley.

But there is no harm in aiming high. At least that is what my parents told me as I battled against the odds of size and stature during my early days as a wishful thinker. The words of support were constant and in the end my parents were right, as parents invariably are. I battled against those escalating odds, both as a schoolboy and in my initial days with Bridgend. After a lot of blood, sweat and tears I finally realised my goal.

Now, as scrum-half and captain of Wales, I can reflect on the past six or seven years with great satisfaction. The hours of training on my own, the operations on my shoulder and knee, the teething problems of professionalism and the subsequent anxiety and frustration of conflicting club and country contracts have been worth it. I have even come to accept the often unnecessary criticism in certain areas of the local press!

I am not one to preach to others, nor do I take kindly to others preaching to me. As I was growing up, that was something else I learned. However, I honestly believe my experience should be a lesson to any youngster with aspirations of reaching the top. If you want something badly enough and you are prepared to work hard to achieve it, you will do so.

I longed for success from the day I first played for the school team. I wanted to be a winner, somebody who would never have to say 'if only'. Of course, there have been numerous hiccups along the way. However, at the age of 29 at least I can say that I have been there and bought the T-shirt.

Just to be spoken about in the same terms as the great scrum-halfs like Gareth Edwards, Terry Holmes and Robert Jones makes up for the veiled threats and harsh ultimatums that have often left me wondering whether I made the right decision to go professional. To have led Wales to a first victory over South Africa and to have captained my country to a record number of successive victories is something that nobody can take away. The papers, or at least one or two of them, might have tried to deny me the opportunity of leading Wales in to the World Cup with their persistent sniping, but in the end I have had the last laugh.

Perhaps it sounds a little strange for a professional sportsman to be speaking in such humble terms, but those people who know me well will understand what success means to me. I have always been taught to appreciate success and to avoid taking things for granted. I hoard my memories in dozens of scrapbooks and diaries and I can recall every moment as if it were yesterday. My first game for Bridgend, my first try, my first cap and my first victory for Wales will never be forgotten. I still remember the first training session at the Brewery Field and my first letter of selection from the Welsh Rugby Union.

However, if I had to highlight a few achievements above anything else, they would all coincide with my time as captain. I treasure the moment I captained Wales for the first time against Italy at Llanelli in 1998, and I will never forget the victories over the French in Paris and against England at Wembley and the first game at the Millennium Stadium, when we beat the Springboks for the first time. Special moments should live with you for the rest of your life, regardless of how they come about. These are all significant moments in my career and I often switch on the video to take a look. After so many years of waiting, I feel justified in a moment of self-indulgence.

What makes those moments so special is the fact that had it not been for the former Wales coach Kevin Bowring I might still be the bitter and twisted Robert Howley waiting for that elusive first cap. For that opportunity I will be eternally grateful to Kevin. Whatever anyone cares to think or say about him, Kevin was the one person who enabled me to realise my boyhood ambition.

What's more, how many coaches would have asked a player a second time to lead his country after being turned down the first time? It was a carefully guarded secret at the time, but at the end of 1996 I turned down the opportunity to captain Wales against the United States in Cardiff. Jonathan Humphreys, a good friend of mine and a player for whom I have and always will have the utmost respect, had done a great job as captain under Kevin and at that particular juncture there was never any question of him losing or relinquishing the job. Unfortunately, as you will see later in the book, nothing is ever straightforward in Welsh rugby.

Humph experienced that much during the 1996–97 season when Cardiff travelled to Brive for the semi-final of the European Cup. It was a dreadful weekend, in more ways than one. We had a precarious six-hour coach journey in the most treacherous winter conditions I have ever experienced, and when we arrived in Brive the town was under a foot of snow.

Somehow the locals and a handful of volunteers from a nearby army base worked through the night to make sure the game went ahead. Unfortunately, the snow that had been swept from the pitch provided the rather volatile locals with the perfect ammunition with which to bombard anyone in a Cardiff shirt or tracksuit. From the moment we arrived at the ground they took great pleasure in using us as target practice. I have never subscribed to the French sense of humour and I found it difficult to understand their delight when Andrew Lewis was smacked on the head by an object that resembled one of those day-night cricket balls, in both appearance and weight. It was ridiculous. Sadly, the day went from bad to worse. Brive at that time were the most complete club side in Europe, and although we fancied our chances they quickly established a lead and went on to teach us a lesson we will never forget.

Then, as so often happens in France, the game started to cut up. Surprise, surprise, Brive, who had been putting the boot in for most of the afternoon – much of it on me – started whinging to the referee. The next thing we knew, Humph had been sent off for what appeared to be a minor indiscretion in comparison to what had gone on before half-time.

As expected, we lost the game, but we then found out that due to his alleged moment of madness Jon had been suspended by the match commissioner for two weeks. It was bad enough being sent off in such a high-profile game, but when Humph realised he would miss the forthcoming international against the United States, you can imagine his disappointment.

Suddenly Kevin was faced with finding and appointing a new captain as well as a new hooker. There was a lot of talk in the press over the next few days and somehow it was deemed by everyone outside the national set-up to be a straightforward race between Swansea centre Scott Gibbs and me. I found that a bit puzzling, because I was a relative newcomer in terms of international rugby and was hardly the natural choice. But, as is so often the case, the press seemed to know something that I didn't.

Kevin rang me out of the blue and invited me to go in to Cardiff for a chat. Although I was conscious that my name had been linked with the job, I was sure he wanted to talk tactics rather than the captaincy. I certainly had no idea that he had me in mind as Jon's temporary successor.

I pulled up in the car park and went in to see Kevin.

'How are you?' he said.

'Okay,' I replied.

'Will you captain the side as a one-off against the USA?' were the next words to come out of his mouth.

My response was not as immediate as it had been 30 seconds earlier when asked about my welfare. It was a strange moment. There I was, an international baby compared to Ieuan Evans, Neil Jenkins, Scott Gibbs and Gareth Llewellyn, yet I was being asked to lead my country in a full international in two weeks' time.

Something inside me said no straight away. Not that I told Kevin, of course. I asked for a bit of time and went home to bounce the idea off my girlfriend Ceri, my parents and a few of the guys at the Cardiff club. In my own mind, I knew that I was going to stick by my initial feelings, but I wanted to gauge the reaction of others. It came as no great surprise when Ceri, Mum, Dad and Terry Holmes, who was the coach at Cardiff, said I would be 'crazy' not to accept.

It wasn't that easy, however, and although the advice was solid I was not about to allow anyone else to persuade me. I knew there was at least one other player who could do a better job than me. Furthermore, when I quizzed myself about whom I would have chosen, the answer was not Rob Howley. At that time, and considering Ieuan had already done the job, that one player was Scott Gibbs.

I was unsure about my feelings towards the job but I felt I had more to lose than gain from accepting the position in Jon's absence. I suppose from my hesitance, Kevin knew what my eventual answer would be. So, despite the urges of Ceri, my parents and one or two others, I stuck to my guns and went back to see Kevin the next day. I explained to him why I thought he would be better served looking elsewhere, he said 'Thanks' and we left it at that.

That was the great thing about Kevin. He took a fearful amount of stick from some ill-informed ex-players who thought that they knew best and he was, in my view, forced into a position at the end of the 1998 championship season where resignation was the only answer. But he was always sincere. I actually resented the way he was criticised for a so-called lack of success during his time in charge. He did not deserve that. There are several national coaches who, I am sure, would have made me pay for declining such a privileged offer of the captaincy. Kevin Bowring wasn't like that. He didn't hold grudges. However, it was always in the back of my mind that I might never again get the chance to lead my country. I need not have worried.

The countdown to the USA game continued and the press got to work on choosing their own man. For quite a few days they had no idea of my offer or my subsequent decision to say no. But they were very quick in stating that Rob Howley was 'not the man for the job'. I remember reading an article that said, 'If it comes down to a straight race between Scott Gibbs and Robert Howley, then Scott should get the vote.' Once again they were right – well, nearly, but not quite. Yes, they were right to suggest I was not the ideal candidate, but they were wrong because Scott didn't get the vote. At that time he was second best. He took his chance because I didn't want it.

As I am sure most players will testify, there are times when you want to pick up the phone and tell the journalists what is going on. Fortunately, I didn't stoop to that level then and I have never stooped that low since. Don't get me wrong – I get on with most rugby journalists, but unfortunately there are one or two who try to talk in detail about matters of which they have no real inside knowledge. My worst experience with the press came during the 1999 Five Nations and I must admit that I was close to losing my cool. I will come back to that later in the book because it hurt me. However, as far as the captaincy was concerned, on this occasion Scotty accepted Kevin's offer and Humph came back for the Five Nations Championship. The rest is history.

Little did any of us know at that stage that within a year the captaincy would change hands twice more. First, Kevin decided that Gwyn Jones, who was in the same Cardiff side as Humph and me, should take over from Jon for the six-match summer tour to North America. Gwyn did a great job on a very difficult tour and was hugely popular with Kevin and the players.

The British Lions had taken the best Welsh players to South Africa and there were numerous others, like Humph, who stayed behind because of injury. Still, Gwyn was not put off by that and as a result of his success in North America he kept the job for the start of the new season back in Wales.

He led the team to a record victory over Romania in Wrexham, to victory over Tonga in Swansea and finally in the not too disheartening defeat against the All Blacks at Wembley. But after that it went terribly wrong for Gwyn, as he was struck down by injury in the Cardiff–Swansea game. Although the full extent of the injury was not known for two or three weeks, we had a horrible feeling that Gwyn would never play again. Our worst fears were realised. Wales had not only lost one of its world-class players, it had also lost its captain.

I will talk about the Swansea game and Gwyn later in the book, for it is a subject that nobody should ignore. But it was the twist of fate that opened the door for me and gave me my chance to lead my country. That was the second decision Kevin had to make inside that 12-month period. I don't think anyone will ever understand how dreadful I felt when Kevin finally asked me to do the job. Losing Gwyn as a playing colleague was bad enough, but to see him in such a predicament was too terrible for words. It was a shocking Christmas for everyone involved with Cardiff and Welsh rugby, and although there was obviously a problem over who would fill the vacant role at number seven and as Wales captain, we all found it extremely difficult even to broach the subject.

Eventually, however, the situation had to be addressed, and once again the press had their say. As the Italy game moved ever closer, the same two names came into the equation. Scott emerged as the favourite, as he had done 12 months earlier, and that was fine by me. I was not convinced that he was the right person to assume such an important position on a permanent basis, but I was quite happy for the press to be talking him up. Don't get me wrong – I respect Scott as a player and what he has achieved in rugby union and league. I also think he has done a great job in charge of Swansea. However, Scott would far rather concentrate on his own game than anyone else's. While that is not meant as a criticism of the individual, it is an observation that confirmed to me that on this occasion I was possibly the better choice.

Scott gives the impression that he is happy to play the game but equally content to be showered, changed and in the car within ten minutes of the final whistle. The players always have a joke with him, suggesting that he leaves his car engine running while he is on the pitch in order to make a quick getaway after the game. But that is not what captaincy is all about. It is about more than the 80 minutes on the field. It is about dealing with players, coaches, team managers and the media. I know that in recent months I have done my bit to avoid attending every press conference, but at the time I felt I was ready to take up the challenge.

So, having not wanted the captaincy a year earlier, I was now on the verge of being offered it for the second time. This time I would be succeeding my best friend in the worst possible circumstances. When Kevin asked me to lead the team against Italy, I reluctantly accepted. Stupid as it might sound, I just couldn't envisage myself going into hospital and telling Gwyn that I was about to profit from his misfortune. Once again, I need not have worried. Gwyn sees very little bad in anyone and he was arguably more excited about my pending appointment then I was.

From a personal point of view, I felt as though I needed something to lift my own game as well as my spirits, having spent most of my Christmas in the Heath Hospital with Gwyn. I wasn't sure whether succeeding a man who was laid up in bed not knowing whether he would ever walk again was the right kind of tonic. But Kevin rang me at home to say he wanted a chat about the position and finished by saying it was good news.

The following afternoon I went to South Glamorgan Institute, where the Welsh Rugby Union has its Directorate, and Kevin greeted me by saying 'Congratulations, Rob'. I told him that, having felt so low after the British Lions tour when I had had to come home with a shoulder injury, it was the kick-start I needed. But all the same, I was still mindful of Gwyn's situation and equally aware that other senior players like Gareth Llewellyn, Gibbsy, Allan Bateman and Scott Quinnell would have been consulted by Kevin. I often wonder what they said about me.

Kevin's one major concern was whether I could cope with the job, having turned it down 12 months earlier. I had no problem with that as long as he was comfortable with the appointment, and so we were both happy. Little did I know that from the moment I said yes, my life would never be the same again.

So how would I tell Gwyn? That was the next big obstacle. The players who had served under Gwyn in the United States and Canada spoke of him highly. He was a captain who commanded great respect from his peers. Even when the flak was flying, Gwyn was above it all, and that was what made him such a great leader. I have never lacked confidence in my own ability, but whether I could reach the standards set by Gwyn and Humph played on my mind. I wanted to tell Gwyn myself before he heard the news from anyone else, so after plucking up enough courage to make the 20-mile journey from my home to the hospital, I walked in, told him the news and awaited the reaction. It was typically Gwyn. He simply said 'Well done' and, with a big smile on his face, added, 'Watch your back.'

He told me to be wary about team selection. He said I should keep a close eye on what was being said and done off the field and that I should stay in control of my own destiny. From that moment, Gwyn has continually given me sound advice on how to speak to players, when to speak to them and what kind of relationship I should have with the national coach, whether it was Kevin or whoever. There is no doubt that Gwyn had a major influence on the way I did the job in those early days; to be quite honest, he still does.

Once the appointment had been made and announced in the press, I had to turn my attention to keeping the position. Easier said than done in Wales. You only have to look at players like Gareth Edwards and Terry Holmes, two of the greatest players Welsh rugby has ever seen, to see that great players don't always make great captains. I remember reading an article about Gareth by his Wales half-back partner Phil Bennett, who admitted that although Gareth was a great player he was uncomfortable with the captaincy.

I think people felt the same about me. I didn't necessarily agree, although I admit that it took me some time to grow into the role. My initial difficulty, especially in the build-up to that first game, was that I found it quite awkward telling experienced players like Ieuan Evans and Neil Jenkins what I expected of them. I was like the tea-boy who had suddenly been promoted to managing director. It was a strange feeling. But I am a strong person and I have a vision of how I believe Wales should play the game. I think that tied in with Kevin's vision, and that was obviously the main reason why I got the job.

The two of us worked closely in the build-up to the game against Italy and he made me feel very much at ease. He advised me on how to deal with certain situations and on how to handle the press. Kevin didn't like the press and, in some ways, I could see why. He always felt as if they were on his back. I didn't see it quite like that, although I did share some of his views at that time. For a start, I totally disagreed with the accessibility the press had to the players.

I found that quite difficult after the Italian game. Within ten minutes of the game ending I was faced with a bunch of eager reporters asking me 'Why did this go wrong?' and 'Why was that part of the game so sloppy?'.

Then I was asked the traditional question: 'Are you pleased to win?' I felt like saying, 'No, it is the worst moment of my life!' There is a time and a place for everything. Ten minutes after a Test match is not the time to speak to the press, regardless of deadlines. That has to change.

I must admit that it was a bit of a shock. Okay, so we didn't play that well, but I had just captained my country for the first time and we had beaten a very good Italian side, something Scotland had failed to do a week or so earlier. It was a very proud night for me and I looked forward with relish to leading Wales into the Five Nations Championship.

Little did I know what was awaiting us around the corner. We had only won one game in the build-up to the competition, yet there we were shouting from the rooftops about how we would beat England for the first time at Twickenham since 1988 and hopefully sweep all before us on the way to the silverware. We were definitely the masters of our own downfall on that occasion and that was probably the first important lesson I learned. It was also a lesson to the WRU, who shoved us in front of the media on every occasion they could.

I will expand on the mistakes we made before and during that game but as far as I was concerned we got our just deserts. As a captain I learned a great deal from that episode in my life, as did a number of the senior players on duty that day. By the time Graham Henry came on to the scene we had all learned a harsh but very valuable lesson.

I believe I have been very fortunate to serve under two sincere coaches who have given me the level of support that any Welsh rugby captain requires. Kevin introduced me to the role and Graham has nurtured my development. I am indebted to both, especially Graham, who supported me long and hard under pressure from *The Western Mail*, who wanted me replaced as captain after the 1999 championship defeats by Scotland and Ireland.

The last 12 months have been a roller-coaster ride for me as captain. But I can honestly say that I have become a better person and a far more complete rugby player for the experience. Captaincy is a very special part of my game, and no matter how thick and fast the criticism comes, as long as the boss believes you are doing a good job, then who cares?

2. LOCAL HERO

Friends, Heroes and the Kitchen Roof

The words would echo around the local park, just behind Priory Avenue in Bridgend.

'Robert, it's time to come in.'

For any one of my neighbours who had lost his or her watch, my father's order meant it was Sunday night at about half past seven. Standing on the roof of the kitchen extension, he would pick me out amongst the boys playing in the park and tell me to come home. Sunday night meant homework, bath and early to bed.

Like any schoolboy or schoolgirl, I would always have a moan. After all, my father's words would invariably come at the wrong moment. I was just about to score either the winning goal for Tottenham Hotspur against Arsenal in the FA Cup final or the winning try for Bridgend against Cardiff in the Welsh Cup final at Cardiff Arms Park. As you can see, the bitter rivalry between Bridgend and the city slickers from just up the M4 was as keen then as it is now. It was Tottenham and Arsenal on an infinitely smaller scale.

When spring gave way to summer, I would swap the rugby or soccer ball for a piece of willow and a cricket ball. Don't ask me why, but when the sun shone I would be Geoff Miller, the Derbyshire all-rounder. After scoring an unbeaten century against the Aussies at the Oval, I would round off my Sunday evening by taking all ten wickets to clinch the Ashes. Then it was time to go home and reflect on a job well done. From a very early age, sport was my life.

I am not sure whether my parents could understand my obsession with the round or oval-shaped objects that cluttered up the outhouse. Neither had been particularly sporty during their schooldays, but they gave my sister Karen and me all the support we could ever have wished for.

My father always tells me that my rugby ability comes from my great-uncle Tommy. Tommy played for Ebbw Vale and the British Army during the First World War and eventually went north in 1920 to play rugby league for Wigan. He played in Wigan until the early 1930s and, according to reports, he was a half decent player.

My sister, too, was talented when it came to sport. She was a fine athlete and became the first netball international from Brynteg School. Like any brother and sister, we had our ups and downs. However, I grew up with Karen and her friends and felt more at home with the older kids than I did with those of my own age. Much of that was probably down to the fact that there simply were no kids of my age in Priory Avenue.

Not only was I the youngest in the group, I was also the smallest. Playing with the older kids meant I would have to try that bit harder to compete on level terms. It came as second nature in the end. I was so desperate to step out from my sister's shadow and prove to myself that I would go that extra inch, yard or mile to succeed. I wanted to prove that there was another member of the Howley household who had an ounce or two of sporting talent in his blood.

Like any other kid growing up in the 1970s and early 1980s, I had my heroes. When it came to soccer, there was nobody who could hold a candle to Glenn Hoddle. I would always play with my shirt out, as Glenn did, and I would always try to imitate his elegance in the midfield. In my case, it was an old T-shirt rather than a Spurs shirt and an area between the swings and slide rather than White Hart Lane. However, it felt the same when the ball struck the back fence. I would always salute the Shelf – or the local houses, to be more precise – as I peeled away from a goal made up of two dirty jumpers and an old boot-bag. Normally, my goals would be close-range tap-ins. However, by the time I was ready for bed, I would tell my father about the wonderful hat-trick of 30-yard free-kicks I had just scored.

When the rugby ball came out, I was Gareth Edwards. Although my career as a scrum-half didn't develop until a few years later, I always looked up to Gareth. He was an ambassador. I remember the first time I saw the great try he scored for the Barbarians in Cardiff; it gave me goose pimples. To be honest, it still does. I haven't told Gareth this, but I have scored a few of those in my time too. Most of them came between the swings and the slides at the Priory Avenue park, but there have been one or two in my dreams too. From a very early age, I wanted to emulate this legend of Welsh sport. I wanted to be the best, the very best.

In between holidays, I attended Oldcastle Primary School, just a short walk from my parents' house in Priory Avenue. It was a great little school and I had some good times there. But, like most of my friends at the time, I was far more concerned with playing soccer and rugby than I was with the three Rs. Don't get me wrong – I did the work and I did quite well. But I played hard too.

Being so small, it was important that I ate well and slept well. The sleep was no real problem, as I could sleep for Wales. However, at feeding times I was a bit of a handful. I wanted my food at the right time – normally to fit in with the next round of the FA Cup in the park – and I normally requested eggs, beans and chips or a healthy round of cheese sandwiches. I wasn't fussy, but I knew what I liked and didn't see any point in trying anything else. I suppose the only worry as far as school lunches were concerned was the way I went about consuming those famous cheese sandwiches. Instead of sitting down with a can of pop and a KitKat, I would bolt them down in the playground so I could get on with the next instalment on the yard. Food was to be eaten between matches, and indigestion had never been heard of. The pains in our stomachs were just a coincidence!

Because my early days at Oldcastle were spent playing with kids much older than me and much bigger, I had plenty of determination. What's more, I was so sick and tired of the teachers saying 'Are you Rob Howley, Karen's brother?' that I would try extra hard to succeed in whatever I was doing. It felt like I had something to live up to. I just wanted to prove that Rob Howley could stand on his own two feet and mix it with the best.

My first recollection of an organised game of rugby was during my time at Oldcastle. I had just turned nine and was in Standard 2. My teacher, Mr Hearing, asked me to take part in the 1st XV trial and I reluctantly agreed. The trial was held at the local Newbridge Fields, and when the shirts were handed out I ended up at full-back in the Whites team. We were the 'Possibles', while the 'Probables' were given the traditional school colours of maroon. Included in their side was a lad we used to call 'Wattsy'. I was never sure of his full name but I think most of the lads called him 'Sir'. He was huge. He was certainly not a nine-year-old to mess with.

The game was just a few minutes old when 'Wattsy' went on one of those Quinnell-like charges up the middle. He brushed past the first four or five tackles and then found himself in acres of space. All that stood between this nine-year-old giant and a try that would secure his place in Mr Hearing's 1st XV was a scrawny young full-back called Robert Howley. I thought about running for the nearby trees or pretending I had been shot by a sniper lurking in the bushes. Instead, I lined him up, remembered that I had taken many a fearful whack from boys much older than me and dumped him on the turf. Trying to mask the pain of doing so, I peeled myself off the floor and duly staggered back into position. The ball came free and one of our lads scurried back and kicked it into touch.

Mr Hearing must have been impressed, because the following day he picked the side to face our neighbours, Penybont. I hurried to the notice-board to see the name of Rob Howley next to the number 15. I was thrilled, just as I am now when Graham Henry reads out the Wales team. Whether you are nine or 90, being selected is very satisfying.

We beat Penybont and one or two other schools that season before we came up against the one team we honestly feared. Litchard Primary School invariably provided the lion's share of players in the Bridgend and District side and would often go through the season undefeated. One of their best-known players in the 1970s was Mike Hall. The match would have been a thorough examination anyway, but for me it was made all the more testing because during the first half I wore my boots on the wrong feet. I realised that something wasn't quite right but I wasn't sure what it was until one of my classmates, Jason Gibbs, starting sniggering as Mr Hearing handed out the half-time oranges. Not surprisingly, my second-half performance was much improved.

Later that year, and having worked out right from left, I won my first representative honours – for the Bridgend District Under-11s. To begin with, I played in the B side. But it was still a thrill. The eggs, beans and chips had obviously done the trick because I was bigger now and felt more comfortable in these different surroundings.

My parents were very proud, although at that stage I was still more concerned with my collection of rosettes, my Bridgend Rugby Club programmes and scoring the winning goal for Spurs before my father blew the whistle for full-time. I even found the time to do a bit of train-spotting and stamp-collecting with my friend Andrew Hill. It is not something I tend to boast about. In fact, whenever my friends remind me of how I would often spend my day at Bridgend railway station with Andrew, I always explain why: 'He was my friend and I used to follow him.'

The truth was that I would rather be on the platform taking numbers than at home staring at the four walls of my room like so many kids do these days. I understand the necessity for computers but I would rather see those kids split their time between the VDU screen and playing in the park. Anyway, as far as the stamp-collecting was concerned, I have to admit there are no excuses.

The first final for any youngster in whatever sport is always the one that sticks in the memory. For me, it was the DC Thomas Cup final against Cardiff. Unfortunately, as expected, we lost. However, it gave me a real taste of the big time – relatively speaking, of course! – and I enjoyed it so much that when the team asked my parents if I could go on tour at the end of the season, I begged them to say yes. They did.

It was an annual event which saw the A and B teams travelling to Ireland to play games against Terenure College and St Mary's College in Dublin. I was obviously excited about the prospect of touring with my friends but my parents were a little concerned because their son was not the world's greatest traveller. I had thrown up on the way to Morecambe on a number of occasions, so a journey across the Irish Sea might be a little too much to cope with.

I certainly lived up to expectations. By the time we reached Swansea, I was already being sick, and I continued to call for the brown paper bags until we arrived in Holyhead. It didn't get any better on the ferry and, to make matters worse, I had only been in Dublin for a few hours when I told one of the tour leaders that I was feeling homesick. I wanted to catch the next ferry home but was told that wasn't possible. Although I enjoyed the rugby, I was certainly glad to get home. Why I went on the same trip for the next two years, I am not sure. Perhaps it tells you just how much I was growing to love this great game of ours.

In my final year at Oldcastle, I captained the 1st XV and went on to play for Bridgend Under-11s and finally West Wales Under-11s. It was my first taste of playing with really good players and I often look back at the newspaper cuttings to see which members of that Bridgend side are still playing and where. One name that springs to mind is Nick Beal, the Northampton and England back. The other was a certain Neil Jenkins. I often remind him of the score in the DC Thomas Cup semi-final – Bridgend 36, Pontypridd 0.

On moving up to Brynteg, I came across the one person who, above anyone else, inspired me to go on and realise my ambitions. Keith Crockett was and still is the rugby master at the school and is a coach and a person for whom I have the utmost respect. He was honest and knowledgeable and, furthermore, he was the one who gave me an opportunity to play at scrum-half. By the time I first played at Brynteg I had experienced life as a full-back, hooker and blindside flanker. But I wanted to be Gareth Edwards. I wanted the number nine jersey and I was prepared to work as hard as I possibly could to earn the right.

I realised that ambition within a matter of months and have never once regretted it. Brynteg was giving me the perfect grounding and my development was hampered only by a teachers' strike when I was about 14. With no rugby on the menu, I spent a season playing soccer for a local side,

Brackla. There were no swings and slides and we had proper kits and nets. Sadly, despite playing in the centre of midfield, I was not exactly Glenn Hoddle and didn't trouble the keeper on too many occasions. However, I did enjoy the change of scenery and it certainly made me appreciate what rugby union has to offer. I realised that if I was to play at Wembley then it would have to be as a rugby player. Maybe one day Wales would have to play their home games at Wembley while a new stadium rose from the debris of the Arms Park!

By the time I reached the Upper School, I had finally emerged from the shadow of my sister and was in the school's 1st XV. I won my Wales Under-18 schools' cap and became the youngest player to play for the 1sts. We had a great season, winning all 20 games. Mr Crockett was delighted, as you can imagine, but he was less than happy with the approach made to me by Bridgend. He thought I was good enough but felt it might be a touch too early. He didn't want me to go the same way as so many had before me. Gradually, though, he warmed to the idea and when the invitation to make my first-team debut came he was as pleased as anyone. That chance was against Llantwit Major.

I had been a bag of nerves all week and when I arrived at the ground, ready to play my first competitive game for the club, I got hold of a programme and noticed that my name was there alongside Gareth Williams, John Apsee and a replacement by the name of Peter Rogers. Isn't it strange how things work out?

I felt I acquitted myself fairly well, considering it was my first taste of first-class rugby. What's more, I was sure that I would be given another chance. However, due to the amount of work that I had to do to prepare for my A levels, my opportunities were limited. In those days, when professionalism was a word which sat uncomfortably with the members of the International Board, there was always a place for a travelling reserve. Although I was still revising, I said yes when the club asked me to go as a non-playing stand-by to London Welsh. It would be good experience, whatever the outcome.

As predicted, I wasn't required, yet when I got back to the dressing-room after the game I was asked to sign a piece of paper. In return I was given an envelope. I wasn't sure whether it was some kind of apology because I hadn't played or whether it was a form to sign for the following season. However, the envelope made a strange noise, as if there was money inside. Not wanting to show my naïvety, I slipped into the car park and under a street lamp opened the envelope. Inside was £8.50, my reward for spending six hours on the bus to watch a game of rugby. How times have changed!

Having left Brynteg with A levels in maths, geography and economics, I went to Swansea University, where I really started to make some progress as a player. Unfortunately, it was during that time that I suffered my first major injury, damaging the cruciate ligaments in my knee during the UAU final against Cardiff University at Twickenham.

We had travelled to London that year with a side capable of beating anyone. Jason Ball, Paul Flood, Adedayo Adebayo, Richard Jones of Cardiff and I were all in the team and our coach Stan Addicot believed we had a great chance of winning. Sadly, not only did I leave the field early and in agony but we also lost the game and had to travel back in the knowledge that Cardiff had once again put one over on Swansea.

The injury meant that my career with Bridgend was put on hold until the beginning of the following season. However, I spent the summer building myself up, and when September came around I was in great shape. I was determined to prove that Robert Howley was good enough to go all the way.

3. PUT YOUR FAITH IN ME

Namibia, Faith Healers and Moving to Cardiff

Welsh rugby has never been short on scrum-half talent. From the days of Clive Rowlands through to Gareth Edwards, Brynmor Williams and, in more recent times, Robert Jones, Andy Moore and Rupert Moon, the national game has been fortunate to have an abundance of riches in that crucial area of the game.

I wanted to be included in the list of modern-day international scrum-halfs, although it was proving far more of a challenge than I had ever imagined. Once you have experienced international rugby at schoolboy, youth or Under-21 level, you automatically think that a senior cap will come as a matter of course. Unfortunately, it doesn't work like that. I would like a pound for every schoolboy international who has failed to swap that honour for a place in the senior Wales team. It has been a problem for many years in Wales.

However, during the latter months of the 1992–93 season I was finally beginning to make the headlines. My first cap was still proving to be elusive but my form had earned me the man-of-the-match award in the East Wales against West Wales game at the National Stadium and the Welsh Rugby Writers had voted me their Most Promising Player of the Year. I hadn't joined the aforementioned group of great inside-halfs as yet, but things were definitely looking up.

It was around the time of the East against West game that Cardiff made their first move. To be honest, I was flattered. Knowing that somebody else thought that I could play a bit was very satisfying. Alex Evans was the Cardiff coach at the time and judging by what I had heard on the grapevine he rated me and believed I would be a useful addition to the side, or the squad at least. When I finally arrived, I realised it was the latter.

With another Five Nations Championship likely to pass by without featuring the name of Robert Howley, I felt that it was time to move away from Bridgend and chance my arm with one of the game's bigger clubs. Not only would my profile improve, or so I believed, but also it would give me a chance to play alongside the likes of Adrian Davies and Mike Hall as well as two other former Bridgend boys, Mike Budd and Owain Williams. They were keen to get me on board and, to be honest, I was keen to go. For some reason, playing for Bridgend appeared to be holding me back. I was playing well but I couldn't quite make that final leap on to the international ladder. I was knocking on the door but nobody was there to open it.

I had been with Wales to the World Cup Sevens in Edinburgh but that was more of a token gesture, or so I thought at the time. After all, I came home the only player not to be selected on either one of the two summer tours. Alan Davies was national coach at the time and although we got on with each other, I am not sure he had too much time for me as a player. I asked him why I had been omitted from both squads while other scrum-halfs would be getting a chance to improve their playing fortunes. I had no problem with the fact that Robert Jones and Rupert Moon were his two scrum-halfs for the senior tour to Zimbabwe and Namibia, but I was very confused, frustrated and angry when he told me that I was 'too overdeveloped' for the Development Tour of Europe. It was baffling. How can you be too overdeveloped when you have never won a cap? In my eyes, it was the perfect tour for me, but I was beginning to think that I might never get the chance.

Then came the twist of fate which I thought might finally lead to me winning that elusive cap. When Scotland's Gary Armstrong was forced to withdraw from the British Lions tour to New Zealand due to injury, Robert Jones was called in as a late replacement. The knock-on effect meant that I got the nod to take over from Rob in the Wales squad and Rupert assumed the number one position. I was delighted that my first chance would come from Bridgend, but I had made up my mind about leaving and couldn't envisage myself changing course in the few weeks before I left. How wrong can you be?

It got to the last game of the domestic season, and although I was not playing, I did go to the Player of the Year ceremony at the club that evening. I spent a great deal of time that night with our club captain David Bryant, a player for whom I had enormous respect. He was far and away the best openside flanker in Wales and to my mind would have gone on to win a bucketful of caps had it not been for one or two serious injuries.

I watched the game, went home to get changed and then made my way back to the club with only one thing on my mind. Because of the respect I had for Dai, my intention was to have a chat, tell him of my decision and then await the response when I made public the news that I was leaving to join Cardiff.

I spoke to Dai at the beginning of the evening over a quiet beer and he told me in no uncertain terms that while he wanted me to stay for another season at least, he understood that it might be for the best if I accepted the invitation to go and play for Cardiff. I played around with the idea for the rest of the night and didn't believe that anything would alter my decision. Four hours and a few beers later, I had turned full circle. I was awarded the club's Player of the Year award and immediately felt a few pangs of guilt. So instead of spilling the beans, I changed my mind and confirmed to everyone that I would be staying for another season at least. It showed a lack of bottle on my part and no little stupidity.

Dai was amazed and I didn't blame him. At seven o'clock that night I had been ready to pack my bags and head off down the M4 to Cardiff, yet at 11 p.m., and after a few beers, I was confirming myself as a Bridgend player and telling everyone involved with the club that I was desperate to give my all for another season. Dai caught up with me a little later and said just four words before leaving me to digest his response: 'You must be mad.'

In my own mind, I felt not only that I had made the right decision but also that I would now find it easier to concentrate on my first senior tour with Wales. It was a golden opportunity for me to win my first cap and I didn't want any outside influences distracting me. If I had moved then, I am sure my mind would have been focused on playing for Cardiff and not on the fact that I was embarking on arguably my most important overseas trip to date.

The tour consisted of six games, including three Test matches – two against Zimbabwe and one against Namibia – and with Moony going as the number one scrum-half I knew that my chances would be few and far between. I would have to play the midweek games, so a cap might depend on a loss of form or an injury to Rupert. I was determined to make an impression but conscious that I might come home as frustrated as I had been when Alan Davies overlooked me for the initial party.

I played against Zimbabwe B in Harare and Stuart Davies of Swansea captained the side. He had a quiet word with all the players and made it quite clear that if we played well, Alan would have to consider playing us in the first Test against Zimbabwe later that week.

Ironically, my partner that day was a certain Neil Jenkins. I was delighted to score a try in a comfortable 64–13 victory and was content that my all-round performance had been quite impressive. I felt that I had shown enough to persuade Alan and his team manager Robert Norster that I was worthy of a place in the second Test at least. But it didn't happen and, to be honest, I was really annoyed. I was left on the bench in both games and we won easily on both occasions. I couldn't understand why Alan couldn't even give me the last five minutes. After all, we had wrapped up both matches by that time. I was pretty bitter; I had seen a Welsh cap but I couldn't lay my hands on it.

I scored in the victory over Namibia B, but although I played well once again I did feel a slight problem in my left knee. I had had a reconstruction in 1991 and although the operation had been successful, I was starting to feel a twinge. The hard grounds didn't help and as a result I had to miss a few sessions. That certainly wrecked any chance of playing in the final Test, against Namibia. Alan put me on the bench but left me there once again. I acted as a water-boy in the game against the South African Barbarians and travelled home with as many caps as I'd had when I'd left Wales – none.

I did enjoy the tour but I was bitterly disappointed with Alan's attitude and approach. I kept saying to myself that it would not have hurt to have put me on for a few minutes. We had been playing two of the minor nations, yet Moony had had to stay on until the final whistle. It was a joke.

I started the season with Bridgend and I have to admit that, with some intensive physiotherapy, the knee improved. The tour had made me more determined than ever. What's more, the responsibility of being captain for the opening games after Dai pulled up with a serious knee injury certainly helped.

The campaign began quite brightly, unlike a few others since, and we beat Cross Keys and Pontypool without too much trouble. Before I knew it, Kevin Bowring picked me for the A team against Japan and then the North of England.

It was around that time that I began to have second thoughts about staying with Bridgend. The week before the Japanese game Bridgend played Neath. We were beaten convincingly and as I sat in the dressing-room I wondered whether I had made the right decision in staying. Over the next two or three weeks I was away with Wales and had only limited sessions with Bridgend. I always turned up to watch if I could, but it was during those three weeks that I decided to leave. I played well for the A team against Japan but was once again overlooked for the senior game at Cardiff.

I turned my attentions to domestic rugby for a while and wondered whether Cardiff would still be interested. Having spurned them in the summer, I was sure they would turn around and say 'Thanks but no thanks' – after all, I wasn't exactly Nick Farr-Jones or David Kirk. I was sure they could cope without me. Still, I made a phone call to Adrian Davies to confirm my interest. His plan of attack would be to ring Mike Hall and gauge the situation. His last words were, 'I'll get back to you.'

I didn't hold my breath but within an hour, Mike rang me to say the club was still interested. For a moment, I was genuinely elated. However, I knew that my parents and my mother in particular would be less than pleased. I was right; she made it very difficult for me. She hated Cardiff and yet I was on the brink of joining them.

Once again Dai Bryant said that I was doing the right thing but this time he laid the blame squarely at the door of the club. At the end of the previous season, I had been told that certain aspects within the club would change. They hadn't, so what did they expect?

I phoned Gerald Williams, who coached the backs, to tell him of my intention. I said that I wanted to sign for Cardiff and I needed to meet with him, Clive Norling, who was the new rugby director, Ceri Townley, the forwards coach, and the chairman Huw Ceredig as soon as possible. When I told them that I wanted to move, the reaction was shocking. Initially, I was told that they wouldn't agree to the transfer immediately. I knew that would make life difficult because the ruling at the time stated that players moving during the season would be required to miss three league games. The longer they held on to the form, the longer it would be before I played my next game of rugby.

They wanted time to find a replacement. That infuriated me, as did the reaction of Clive Norling. He had only been there a matter of weeks, yet he came out and told me in no uncertain terms that the club would make it as difficult as possible for me. I was hoping that time might heal the situation and that within a few days they would reconsider their stance and realise that their attitude was not helping anyone. But nothing changed whatsoever. They held on to my transfer form and I ended up missing four or five big games.

Because of that, I was glad to get away from Bridgend, although I was still a little anxious about the whole situation of joining a club who have been hated by the rest of Welsh rugby for many years. But I felt I had no choice; I was going nowhere at Bridgend and needed to rejuvenate my career.

I suppose I should have listened to my mother, because as soon as I arrived, I found it very difficult to settle. Because of the ruling on transferred players, I spent the first few weeks holding tackle bags. It was dreadful. And although Cardiff was only 20 miles away, I found the travelling difficult. There were no incentives. I would turn up, take a hammering on the bags and go home knowing that I couldn't even play on the Saturday.

Eventually, I made my debut against Newport, and I played in three other matches before it all went horribly wrong. From the outset, I had found it impossible to break into the clique that existed within the squad. However hard I tried, I was never going to manage. But the straw that perhaps broke the camel's back came just before Christmas. The Cardiff club always stages its own carol service where players get a chance to invite their sponsors as a thank you for their support during the year. Andy Moore and Mike Rayer had organised the day and I agreed to go along. I wish that I had stayed at home.

During the evening there was a slot when the players had a chance to join in with a sponsored sing-song. One table asked Andy Moore to do a turn and he obliged. When he had finished, all the other boys just stood up and started chanting his name. It was like he was some god. What's more, he was the scrum-half that I would have to oust if I had any intention of becoming number one. There was no chance I was going to do that, was there? That got to me. I felt like a total outsider. It was as if they were doing it on purpose. Call me sensitive or paranoid, but I was convinced that they were trying to ostracise me and make a point.

Gradually, as the weeks wore on, my game deteriorated and I could see myself slipping down the international ladder. From being number three at the beginning of the season, I was now languishing down at number five behind Robert, Rupert, Andy Moore and Paul John. I suppose I didn't help myself because after the first few Cardiff matches I left straight away and drove back to Bridgend Rugby Club, where Ceri and I would have a drink. It was a big mistake on my part and slightly immature. If nothing else, I just put myself back in the firing line.

Not one to throw in the towel for any small reason, I knew that it would take a major event to convince me that my future lay elsewhere. That event came just before Christmas. Cardiff were due to play Cross Keys but the weather was shocking and the game had been in doubt for a couple of days. However, not having heard from the club, I set off along the M4 and was just about to turn into Cardiff when I heard on the radio that the game had been called off. I was seething. The media knew, yet nobody had bothered to phone me. I turned around at the next roundabout and drove straight to Bridgend, where Pontypridd were the visitors. Steve Fenwick had been named as the new chief executive at Bridgend and I told him that night that I had had a gutful at Cardiff and wanted to come back. I was totally confused but I knew that I had to get out of Cardiff.

Like so many others, they had promised so much but delivered very little. Take my company car, for example. When I first joined the club, they sorted me out with a decent car. It was an L reg car with only a few hundred miles on the clock. I thought that it was my car. But within a few weeks I was given Hemi Taylor's old car, a Sierra Cosworth with about 30,000 on the clock. It was as if they had got me there to penalise me for not coming at the first time of asking in the summer.

I decided in my own mind that I would be better off at Bridgend and all that remained was to tell Alex Evans. I went up to Cardiff with Ian Greenslade and John Purnell, one of my closest friends from school. I parked the car by the club and the boys went into town. I said that I would be back with them in half an hour. Alex had arranged the meeting, believing that I wanted to go through some moves involving the back row. I walked into the hospitality suite and told him straight that I hadn't enjoyed my time at Cardiff and wanted to leave. He told me that I couldn't do it but I said that I had made up my mind and would not be talked out of it. He made a quick exit and left me in the room on my own. I chucked my keys down on the table and left.

I was glad to be back at Bridgend and glad to be playing rugby again. Unfortunately, it was not long before the knee flared up again. I got through the season and the summer but at the beginning of the following season it was starting to get a great deal worse. I had played quite a bit of sevens in the summer and the hard grounds had taken their toll. I saw the physios at the club but to be honest there was very little improvement. That was when I turned to alternative medicine.

I knew of this guy called Alan Matthews from near Bridgend. He was a faith healer and had been recommended by a number of people, amongst them Robert Jones. Rob told me to keep an open mind and to give him a chance. I phoned Alan and agreed to meet him at the club. I ended up seeing him twice at the start of the 1994–95 season and he worked wonders.

Simon Thomas was the baggage-master at Bridgend at the time and he asked if I had any objection to him sitting in on my meeting with Alan. We were due to play Neath that night so I managed to see Alan at about 4.40 p.m., well before the boys arrived.

Alan came in and immediately took off his shoes and socks. He said that he had to feel the ground. I sat on the physio's bed and Alan put his hands on my shoulders. He said that I would feel a warmth through my body and then feel drowsy. I certainly did. Then he moved his hands down to my left knee to feel the problem. He told me that he could feel the pain going through my body. The reason why he had taken his shoes off was to allow him to earth himself. I was glad Simon was there because I don't think anyone would have believed me if I had come up with this story on my own.

Alan kept his hands on my knee for about ten minutes and to this day I have had no further problems. It was an unbelievable feeling, although it got club physio Nicola Phillips's back up. Nicola and her sister Joanne were wonderfully supportive to me, but Nicola was far from happy that I had chosen to seek an alternative cure. She had helped sort out the operation on my knee three years earlier and I was very grateful. But she didn't like what I was doing now.

All of a sudden, after I had seen Alan, the media got to hear about it and that was the turning point for Nicola. She didn't think that I had any right to go to the papers to tell them about the benefits of faith healing. In the end, she sent a stinging letter of complaint to Steve Fenwick, who gave me a slap on the wrists and told me to be careful. I agreed but expressed genuine concern that Nicola was not happy for me. However, I was at a point where any help would have been gratefully accepted.

Our relationship became very strained and still is today. It was a very awkward situation because she had done so much hard work with me and I didn't want to fall out with her. However, that was her decision and as far as I was concerned at the time I was just happy to be back playing, even if I had not yet won that senior cap.

4. CAPPED AT LAST

An International Chance

Having gone back to Bridgend, I quickly fell from grace. At one stage, I had worked myself into third place in the international pecking order. However, my loss of form and subsequent loss of confidence meant that I was now ranked no higher than number five.

It was very difficult to accept. I still had this ambition to make it on to the ultimate stage and to run out at Cardiff Arms Park, Twickenham or one of the other great stadiums in the world, yet it was looking more and more unlikely.

Nothing much changed throughout the 1994–95 season and it was no great surprise that I was barely considered for the World Cup in South Africa. Alan Davies had left the job of national coach by then and Alex Evans and Mike Ruddock were brought in with Dennis John as their assistant. Andy Moore and Robert Jones were given the two scrum-half berths in the squad and once again I was resigned to watching this ultimate rugby spectacular on the television in my front room. By that time I wondered exactly what I would have to do to convince these people that I was worthy of being given a chance.

The squad failed to reach the latter stages of the competition and although there was quite a bit of support for all three coaches, it came as no real surprise when the WRU opted for Kevin Bowring as their first full-time coach. As you can imagine, I was delighted with the appointment. Kevin had guided me through the Under-21 and A teams and if anyone was going to recognise me as a potential international, it was Kevin. Although my form had dropped during the previous season, I made up my mind to give the first half of the season my best shot. I got myself into great shape and started to play with much more authority. Then came the moment for me to prove that I was capable of making that final step.

Bridgend were playing Cardiff on a Wednesday night down at the Brewery Field and, having spent the best part of a week thinking of nothing else, I produced probably my best performance for more than a year. I was sound in every aspect of my game and came off the field with a huge smile.

I knew that Kevin was in the crowd so my post-match meal went down very nicely. There was still no guarantee that I would get the vote but I felt that I couldn't do any more. If I didn't succeed now, it was probably the end for Robert Howley as far as international rugby was concerned.

Within a matter of days, I had been chosen on the bench for the two Five Nations warm-up matches against Fiji and Italy. Andy Moore was selected for both games but I thought that Kevin was waiting for a chance to give me a go. Having got so close and having felt that Kevin was keen, I knew how important my performances over the coming weeks would be. It got to Christmas time and, although I have always kept myself in good shape, I must admit to overindulging over that particular festive period. Thankfully, I wasn't made to regret it.

We played Newbridge at the Welfare Ground on 28 December and I made a special point of getting out on to the pitch in time to have a really good stretch. The turkey was lying heavy and the booze was still swilling around. As I sprinted between the touch-lines, I looked up and saw Allan Lewis standing there. Allan and I had always got on very well and it didn't surprise me that Kevin wasted little time in asking him to become assistant coach. His knowledge is superlative and his views are particularly strong. When I saw him standing on the terrace alongside the main stand, the adrenaline started to flow.

It made my Christmas. I knew that I was close but his presence convinced me that if I could play well in front of him, perhaps my opportunity at least to be in the shakedown for a place against England would finally arrive. I was more than happy with my contribution to the game and when I got home that night I had another drink just to celebrate my performance. This time it wasn't alcoholic and, to be honest, from that moment on I didn't touch another drop – just in case.

The New Year came and went, as most of them do, without any resolutions being made, and within a week we were into the Swalec Cup. We drew Abertillery away and on that occasion it was Dave Clark, the Wales fitness coach, who was given the job of assessing my form. Throughout that period, we had a number of camps in west Wales and I became more and more familiar with what Kevin required.

He split the workload between Andy and me but I was still unsure about my chances because my time was spent partnering Arwel Thomas. I had nothing against Arwel but, like myself, I thought that he might be starting the campaign on the bench rather than in the side. Although he had played against Italy, I still had my doubts over his quality at that level and believed that Kevin would err on the side of caution by playing Jenks at ten. How wrong can you be?

It was about ten days before the game against England at Twickenham when Kevin finally put me out of my misery. The build-up to the game was coming to a head and the players knew that a press conference had been called for the following day to announce the side. As usual in the week leading up to the match, we got a chance to train at the National Stadium. We were all in the Cardiff club ground's dressing-rooms getting changed when Kevin came up to me and said, 'Can I have a quick chat?'

By that time, I was so used to rejection that I half expected him to take me outside and explain the reasons why once again Andy was being preferred. When we got outside, however, under the Cardiff stand, Kevin turned to me and said, 'I've decided to put you in.' I was speechless. I had waited for so long to hear those words.

Although at that particular stage I would have played anywhere and in any position, I had always wanted to win my first cap in the Five Nations as opposed to a touring game or a friendly international. And here I was, ten days away from playing for Wales in the Five Nations Championship against England. It was perfect.

As I walked back into the dressing-room, I tried to avoid eye contact with the players, especially Andy Moore. However, as soon as I sat down I felt myself turning my head towards him. You know the feeling when somebody says 'Don't look now, but . . .' – you just have to look. I did and so did Andy. Without changing his expression, he mouthed to me that I was in. I acted dumb and replied 'What?' and shook my head. I didn't want to tell anyone. I just wanted to hold on to my own secret until everyone had been told.

Once training was over and the boys had showered and changed, we went round to the team-room on the other side of the stadium, where Kevin announced the team. Andy Moore was actually sitting next to me when Kevin read out the side. He glanced over and pointed to Andy and me sitting next to each other. He said, 'That shows exactly what kind of team spirit we have in the squad. That proves Andy is willing Rob to do well.' I knew what Kevin was trying to say but I can't say that I agreed with him.

Although it was nice to get the congratulations from players like Ieuan and Nigel Davies, two of the more experienced members of the squad, I was desperate to get out of the room and drive back home to tell the world of my selection. It was a night that I will never forget. I was in a total daze.

As soon as I got back to Bridgend, I headed for Ceri's parents' house. I parked up and as I walked down the drive to the front door, Ceri's dad met me. He said, 'On the bench again, are you?'

'No, I'm playing,' I replied.

The look on his face was one of surprise and sheer elation. He congratulated me and after a brief chat with Ceri I left and made my way round to see my mum and dad. There were tears of joy all over the place and although I wanted to stay and talk all night, there were plenty of other people I had to tell.

Because of my love affair with Bridgend in those early days, I headed for the club where the boys had been training. I apologised for missing the session due to Wales duties and asked our backs coach Gerald Williams how things had gone. He skirted over the details and repeated the words that Ceri's dad had come out with an hour or so earlier. 'On the bench, are you, butt?' Gerald always called you 'butt' and he always had the same response: 'Yes, Gerald, I am.' Not this time. With a beaming smile I said, 'No, I'm playing.' He almost fell over.

When something like a first cap is dangled in front of you, there is always a temptation to overdo things and perhaps risk the possibility of a silly injury. Knowing my luck, I would give it a bit extra and turn my ankle walking off the bus to an extra session, or something equally daft. Obviously, I couldn't take it easy, but I was extra careful. Having got this far, I wasn't going to waste the opportunity I had been given.

The squad spent the three days before the game in Bagshot in Surrey and we trained at the army camp in Sandhurst. Our training was slightly hindered by the frosty conditions but it was nothing to worry ourselves about. The final build-up went well and by the time it came to Saturday we were ready to go.

I had breakfast with all the boys and then ran into Allan Lewis at the front of the hotel just before lunchtime. He asked me if I fancied a quiet walk to settle the nerves. I told him that although I was nervous, I had looked around the side at breakfast and realised that I was one of the more experienced members of the party. That made me feel a little more comfortable with the situation and I was just relishing the challenge.

I did ask myself that morning whether I would be fit enough to last the game and whether my skills would be good enough to survive on the ultimate stage. After all, I had nothing to compare them with. Once again, Allan provided the answers that I wanted to hear. He told me that if I went out and played as I had done over the previous four years, there would be no problem. He said all the right things and hit all the right buttons. I was very grateful. He told me that I should have been capped sooner but said that it was not the time to look back. I had to look ahead at making the position mine for some years to come.

So, having got that far, I certainly didn't envisage the dressing-room problems that subsequently threatened to ruin my first cap. The coach journey was fine, the warm-up exhilarating and Kevin's team-talk inspiring. Then, at about 2.22, I realised that one of my studs had shorn off. I hit the panic button and shouted for John Rowlands, the baggage-man. I quickly whipped my boot off as the boys were getting ready to leave the dressing-room and, with a pair of pliers, JR somehow yanked the thread from the hole in my boot and replaced the stud without any damage having been done. As I laced my boot, the players were just leaving. It wasn't the greatest start to my international career but I joined the boys in the tunnel and raced on to the field as though nothing had happened. The rest is history.

To play in my first international against the likes of Will Carling, Jeremy Guscott and Lawrence Dallaglio was unbelievable. To score on my international debut, too, was something I could scarcely have imagined. Although we lost, I looked back at the game and realised that one of my early boyhood dreams had just come true.

Despite our defeat, there was a genuine air of confidence about the squad as we prepared for the game against Scotland at Cardiff Arms Park. It would be my first cap at the National Stadium and that was something very special. I had heard plenty of players wax lyrical about the stadium, its atmosphere and the special glow that you experience on leaving the tunnel. I couldn't imagine what they meant until I experienced the magical moment for myself.

The game itself will be remembered for one crazy incident. Jenks had just kicked a penalty and as the boys prepared for the Scots to restart, Scott Hastings suddenly appeared from nowhere with a ball and took the kick-off. To say we were caught short would be the understatement of the year. We couldn't believe what was happening. The ball appeared from the touch-line – which was against the laws of the game, as you have to use the same match ball that had just been kicked for goal – and, what's more, we questioned who actually threw the ball on to the field. Was it a planned move? If so, it was certainly not in the spirit of the game.

To add insult to injury, Scotland scored straight away, and while we just looked at the referee, the crowd went berserk. We lost the game 16–14 and there was certainly a sour taste in our mouths as we grudgingly shook hands.

The trip to Dublin was special in more ways than one. While it was my first visit to the Emerald Isle, it saw the biggest single exodus of people out of Wales ever. There were thousands of people at the airport as we left on Thursday and the Irish news bulletins showed continuous pictures of the constant stream of people arriving by boat and air. Unfortunately, the weather turned on the Friday, and although we were safely ensconced in the team hotel, there were hundreds of fans stranded at the various ports and airports on mainland Britain. Many of them simply never arrived.

By the time we had been demolished by the Irish, I think most of us wished that we had been in the same boat as the frustrated supporters back at home. We were beaten fairly and squarely and had no complaints. We started badly, got worse and, despite a couple of good tries, were never in the contest. They held the upper hand at the set-piece and, with players like David Corkery and Victor Costello carrying with great purpose, never let us get into our stride.

Victor is one of the most powerful runners from the base of the scrum in world rugby and he targeted Arwel Thomas from the first minute. In typical Arwel fashion, he met the challenge head on. Unfortunately, he came off second best and ended up on his back after another barn-storming break from Victor, requiring lengthy treatment. He told the boys after the game that he had been slightly concussed but wanted to carry on. I couldn't wear that. He stayed on by choice and was therefore fit enough to carry on. You don't, or shouldn't, carry on if you have concussion.

Anyway, his decision backfired on us. He missed touch on three or four occasions over the next ten minutes and Ireland set out their stall with two tries from two separate mistakes. Arwel just couldn't find touch; it was a nightmare. Although Ieuan scored two wonderful tries – the second from my final scoring pass – we were beaten 30–17 and were facing the ignominy of yet another championship whitewash.

When you have lost three games in a row, the last thing you want is to play the French. Luckily, the French have this knack of capitulating away from home. Well, at least that had been the case on a number of occasions. They were far from cohesive at that time and we felt that there was a real opportunity to at least finish in a blaze of glory and redress the balance of another woeful season.

Jonathan Humphreys was captain at the time and before we left the hotel for the ground, he called the players together and delivered one of the most powerful performances I have ever heard. It is not really my style but it was what Humph wanted. He told us, one by one, that we had to start looking at ourselves first before blaming others. We had to take the responsibility on our own shoulders. If we did that, we would win. And win we did.

I was fortunate to score the conclusive try on the blindside of a ruck in the second half, and when Gareth Llewellyn pinched the third piece of line-out possession on their throw in the final moments, the referee called it a day. The boys were delighted, both for themselves and for Humph, who spent the first five minutes after the game kissing the three feathers on his shirt and bending down to kiss the turf.

After the calamities of Twickenham, the defeat against Scotland in Cardiff, and Dublin, it was a consolation well worth waiting for. The problems, however, were still there.

5. SIGNING ON THE DOTTED LINE

Motorway Service Stations and Airport Ultimatums

Having enjoyed the taste of international rugby, albeit belatedly, I was not about to relinquish my place in the side. However, it is not always that straightforward, and after so many seasons of disappointment I was certainly not taking anything for granted.

Despite having started all four games in the 1996 championship and, in my eyes, performing with a fair degree of success, I was still not convinced that I would be an automatic choice for the party to tour Australia in the summer. That being the case, I was desperate to make an impression in the closing few weeks of the domestic season. Perhaps I was being a bit over-cautious. However, having failed to impress previous selectors and coaches, I was in no mood to allow the final weeks of the campaign to slip by without making a real effort.

Unfortunately – or, as some might say, fortunately – there was a major distraction which would ultimately change my life. After less than a season in the Wales team, and having been the subject of severe criticism following my initial move to Cardiff, I was suddenly in demand from two of the greatest club teams in world rugby. Ironically, one of them was Cardiff.

It should have been a time to celebrate and to reflect on my first season in the big time with Wales. But there was no time for any of that. Within a matter of days I was involved in a tug-of-war between the same Cardiff club I had walked out on and Bath, arguably the best club side in the world. It was some distraction.

I am sure that many top players in Britain will agree that playing sport, especially at the highest level, can often be overshadowed by personal problems at club level. The press often ask whether those headaches affect you in the build-up to Test matches or international tours and most lads trot out the party line: 'No, we try to put it to the back of our minds.' I agree. You try – but you can't help but worry about what is happening to your bread and butter. I was certainly not unique at the time but I have to admit that I found it desperately hard to cope with the pressure.

The game was less than eight months into the new era of professionalism and here I was facing the task of shaping my own future. None of us had any experience of negotiating big-money contracts and nobody really understood what was around the corner. So when you consider that players were being offered salaries of up to four and five times more than they had been used to outside rugby, they were not decisions to be taken lightly.

At the same time that Bath and Cardiff were knocking on the front door, Bridgend offered me a contract of around £17,500 for the following season. I have to admit that I was tempted to sign and forget about the complications that another transfer could bring. However, having considered my options, I plucked up the courage to go and see Derrick King, a close friend of mine and the chairman of Bridgend Rugby Club. It was the Sunday morning two weeks before we left for Australia and clearly I had enough on my mind already.

Derrick is a person for whom I have enormous respect. His views on the game are forthright but he has a charming way of conducting his business with players. I felt he would understand my predicament and provide me with some logical and valid advice. While it was very difficult for Derrick to accept that his captain was leaving the club for a second time, he shook my hand and told me to make the right decision for Rob Howley. Thankfully, Derrick is not one to hold a grudge and he advised me to concentrate on my own future rather than worry myself about anything else.

I knew what people would think about me for leaving Bridgend for a second time and it did play on my mind. However, I told myself that while it would create a lot of ill-feeling, I was no different from a dynamic local businessman being head-hunted by a rival company. The fact that I was a Wales rugby international and often made the headlines in *The Western Mail* could not affect my choice. I told Derrick of my intention and left with our friendship intact.

We agreed that the decision would remain a secret until I returned from Australia or until I asked for his official permission to move. Then, obviously, it would become common knowledge. I trusted Derrick implicitly and when I left for Australia I knew that my secret was safe.

Derrick asked me to do one favour in return. He asked me not to go shouting it from the rooftops, as he was concerned that any adverse publicity for the club would scupper the growing interest from possible investors. If they saw the club captain jumping ship, they might be somewhat reluctant to invest. I didn't want to be responsible for that.

It was difficult to keep quiet because I wanted to make myself accessible to other clubs. Thankfully, in the end, I had no worries. Secret negotiations opened with Bath and Cardiff and nobody, not even the inquisitive members of the local press, knew anything about it.

At that stage, I convinced myself that if Bath wanted me I would sign straight away. I was envious of the players at the club and was desperate to pull on a Bath jersey and play alongside the likes of Jeremy Guscott, Phil de Glanville, Mike Catt and Nigel Redman, amongst others. I imagined a team sheet containing those names and that of R. Howley. Unfortunately, what I hoped would be a short and painless exercise in transferring from one club to another became a long, drawn-out saga.

The game was less than a year into this brave new era but the WRU had already moved quickly to begin contracting the top players in a bid to reward them for representing their country. However, there was a catch. The £30,000-a-year contracts were dependent upon players remaining with Welsh clubs. Stay, and you would do very nicely; leave, and there was no such available retainer. Considering most of us by that time had given up the day job, it was a significant deterrent.

I understood where the WRU was coming from and couldn't blame them. An injection of cash into the top English clubs meant they were looking far and wide to cream off the top talent. The WRU recognised the challenge and moved quickly to provide an alternative. They were desperate to make sure that at least some of the top players stayed at home.

By the time I had been made aware of the situation, I had already spoken with Bath's team manager John Hall at Leigh Delamare services on the M4. I explained my position but confirmed that I was keen on a move to Bath. At that stage, I didn't think I would take too much persuading.

That first meeting over a coffee on the side of one of Britain's busiest motorways concluded with us agreeing a ballpark figure of between £40,000 and £45,000 for a season. John seemed quite comfortable with that and said we would speak again soon.

For me, however, the confirmation from Terry Cobner that I would have to stay in Wales to obtain a lucrative contract with the governing body altered my situation overnight. While I still wanted to go, I was aware that signing for Bath was tantamount to throwing £30,000 a season down the drain. Later that week, my accountant and I met with John and several members of the Bath committee to discuss the move further. I told them straight that while I still wanted to sign, there was a financial consideration to make. Realising that I was going around the houses in a bid to soften the blow, my accountant interrupted me and came out with the deal. Due to the WRU's stance on players playing in exile, I would need at least another £25,000 a year, in the first year, to make it worth my while.

It was a critical time in the negotiations and I would have understood Bath if they had said 'Thanks, but no thanks'. When they agreed to continue talking, I realised that they wanted me as much as I wanted them. Obviously, they would have to report back to the club, but in principle they agreed. They would go away, discuss the proposal and contact me while I was in Australia.

When you are just about to embark on a tour of such magnitude, contractual issues, new jobs, new clubs and a new direction in life are the last things you want. But it got worse. Once Cardiff, through Jonathan Davies, joined the race, my mind became scrambled once again. I was certainly flattered to be a wanted man but there was so much going on in my head that I found it increasingly difficult to put matters in order of priority.

JD asked whether I was interested in joining Cardiff and when I said yes, chairman Peter Thomas was straight on the phone arranging a meeting over lunch at a hotel in Bridgend. He told me what he had in mind and revealed that he was lining up the likes of Gwyn Jones, Justin Thomas, Steve Williams and Leigh Davies to move to Cardiff. I didn't let on about Bath but he knew that I was in demand. Peter is a very successful businessman and he sold the club to me in less than an hour, over a bite to eat and a soft drink. He also said that Cardiff believed me to be an integral part of their long-term plans for European success. Regardless of the previous move to Cardiff, Peter insisted that I would be made very welcome should I decide to give the club a second shot.

The club had identified the best players in Kevin Bowring's Wales side and they had made available the necessary funds to bring them, *en bloc*, to the Arms Park. For me, it was something else to think about. Moving to Cardiff meant a decent club contract *and* a WRU deal to boot. It would settle everything. The money was right, £50,000 a year plus benefits, but I had to be sure in my own mind that I was moving for the right reason and that in the long term it would be beneficial to my career, not just my pocket. After all, it was only two years since I had left the club under a real cloud of controversy.

In the end, I was glad to go to Australia, although the night before we left there was one more unexpected twist. I had a telephone call from Huw Ceredig, the ex-chairman of Bridgend and a soap star on S4C's *Pobwl y Cwm*. He asked me whether I had made any decision about the following season and said that should I want to stay at Bridgend, a package of £150,000 a year would be made available. Once again, I was flattered, but when I put the receiver down in my hotel room at Heathrow, I lay back and wondered whether this so-called deal would ever materialise. It didn't, and anyway, it would have taken much more than that to have kept me at the Brewery Field for another season.

The flight from London to Perth gave me a chance to relax, consider my options and talk to Leigh Davies who, like me, had spent the previous few weeks in talks with the same two clubs. Ironically, when we arrived in Australia, the two of us were rooming together. We talked in detail about the respective offers and agreed that while Bath was a great club, a move to Cardiff made more sense.

Having spoken with Peter Thomas, I was happy that Cardiff was the right club for me and my family, regardless of any past experience. I was, however, very conscious of what had gone on during that first spell and how it had affected my family. My mum was a little sceptical when I eventually signed, but she was relieved that I had not stooped so low – those were her words, not mine – as to join Bath, 'an English club'!

However, it has to be said that if the WRU had not been so bloody-minded with their decision over exiled players, there might have been a different outcome. I later found out that Bath's financial guys had agreed to a £70,000-a-year salary. I am not saying that I made the wrong decision, nor do I regret joining Cardiff. Far from it, the club has been exceptionally congenial to me and I am very grateful. My only regret is the way I treated Bath at the time. It was pretty shabby. I actually shook hands with John Hall, assuring him that my signature was as good as theirs, yet a few months later I had reneged on that. I felt that I had let him down and I was far from proud of my actions. But, once again, I had to think of myself first.

No sooner had I stepped into my room in Perth than the telephone rang. Leigh was sleeping, so I answered and immediately recognised the dulcet tones of John Hall. I gathered from the call that Bath were becoming increasingly frantic about the situation and were keen to sign and seal the transfer as quickly as possible. John even told me that he was willing to fax the contract to me in Perth so that I could sign it straight away.

While I still had a few pangs of guilt, I felt that John was applying undue pressure by ringing me in the room while I was on tour with my country. Whether he thought I was more vulnerable without my accountant or agent with me, I don't know. But that was the last contact I had with John and Bath, because Leigh and I decided that Cardiff would be our next destination. My agent at the time, Julie Longden, sorted out the remaining phone calls from back home and at last I was able to settle down and concentrate on the real reason why I had travelled half-way around the world – to play rugby for Wales and hopefully cement my place in the national side.

The victory over France at the end of the championship had convinced the players that we could meet the Wallabies with a certain amount of confidence. But, as is so often the case, the itinerary was particularly tough. Two Test matches plus games against Australia A, New South Wales and Australian Capital Territory would have been a considerable challenge for any one of the northern hemisphere nations. For a Wales side that was hardly at its peak, it represented a bridge far too far.

The first warm-up game against Western Australia was quite refreshing, although Andy Moore played and I was on the bench. Andy is a top player and although he had been my understudy during the championship, I knew that he would push me for the position throughout the tour. We won the game 62–20 at a canter and I was not required.

The training at that time was very physical and the boys were feeling it. I think Kevin and Dave Clark, our fitness adviser, saw the opportunity to get in some tough early sessions. Once we were into the harder games, the time for training sessions like that would be at a premium. Nobody said anything, but we felt that everything was squashed into that first week. Llanelli wing Wayne Proctor was the only casualty – he broke his nose and was unable to take any further part in the tour. It was a blow to us, but these are the problems you encounter on tour. While it is difficult for players to accept – as I found out to my cost on the Lions tour 12 months later – it is part and parcel of touring.

Our first acid test came the following week when we came face to face with Australia's up-and-coming provincial new boys, Australian Capital Territory. New South Wales and Queensland were well established in the Super 12 but ACT were beginning to make their mark, and we understood that while we were the national side, they would start as slight favourites. They had been together for around 12 weeks and were as fit as they would be at any time of the year.

Their side was studded with talent. George Gregan, David Knox, Stephen Larkham and Joe Roff were all playing at the top of their games and they would relish meeting us on their soil. Kevin selected a near-Test team and we started well. In fact, at half-time we trailed only 24–23. Their angles of running were acute, though, and although we were hanging on to their coat tails, I was concerned about the second half and how their greater fitness might stretch us.

The legislative changes had come into force earlier that year, although because of the different seasons this was our first experience of them. Now it might seem strange but the law change that caught us cold, in more ways than one, was the International Board's decision to allow the teams to spend a ten-minute break in the dressing-rooms between halves. For the last ten years we had spent the mandatory two or three minutes sucking oranges in the middle of the pitch, listening to an irate coach or a happy captain call the tune. On this occasion, when we got to the dressing-room, we didn't know what to do. Here we were, back inside, eating our bananas and munching on a bit of cake in preparation for the second half. When we came out on to the pitch again, the boys were as flat as we had been all season and ACT took us to the cleaners. We ended up losing 69–30. We were humiliated. But why? It was simple: they had coped better at half-time because they had the experience of knowing how to use the time to best effect.

I spoke to George Gregan after the game and I quizzed him on what they had done differently from us at the interval. He said they had lain on the floor with their legs on the bench, sipping water while the coach talked to them. They were very relaxed when they came out, while we were clearly on edge. The difference in approach might appear subtle, but for us the result was devastating.

There are obvious differences in approach between the two hemispheres and all players would admit that southern hemisphere rugby is currently better developed than northern hemisphere rugby. However, it was a real eye-opener when later that night George informed me of how the Australian squad would warm up for the forthcoming Test. Having given away our secret – practice, practice and a bit more of the same – George laughed and told me how they would spend most of their time in the swimming pool, messing around and doing a few lengths. Their hard work had been done and it was now time to wind down before winding it up on the field. We were soon to find out that too much practice doesn't always lead to perfection.

George is a top bloke and I have to admit that I have learned a great deal about the game from just talking to guys like him. Unfortunately, it has not always been the Welsh way. I am naturally a fairly gregarious person but there have been fingers pointed at Welsh touring sides in the past. It was not uncommon for a Welsh team to spend the entire tour wrapped up in their own little group, never mixing, never talking and listening and, ultimately, never learning. I would like to think that I have enemies on the field and friends off it. I certainly like to talk and listen.

After the ACT game, the next port of call was Sydney, where we met New South Wales. It was the Wednesday prior to the first Test and it was the last opportunity for the fringe players to throw their hats into the ring. I think the management team had settled on 12 or 13 players, but there is always the chance that a good game might just earn you a place in the side.

Sadly, there was only one player who came off the pitch on that occasion with his hat still in the ring and a question mark, rather than a cross, next to his name. He was awesome from start to finish and was thoroughly deserving of a place in the Test team. For Steve Williams, however, the Australia tour saw him peak for Wales and the next three years have been something of a disappointment. There is no doubting his quality but he has never been able to reproduce that form. I know that injuries have hindered his progress but, to be honest, I really did think he would go on to become a regular in the Wales side. Nowadays he can't even make the A team and that is very sad.

We ended up losing the game 27–20 and going into the Test without a significant win under our belts. But we did feel as though we had taken a step in the right direction. Personally, I felt that we could actually win it. It was strange for me because, as I have said before, I am not the most optimistic person in the world. I wasn't over-confident because I knew the Wallabies were a world-class Test team and that on their day, as ACT had shown the previous week, they were capable of exposing any weakness in the opposition's armour.

We travelled to Brisbane and met our first real problem with regard to the itinerary. To be quite frank about it, the problem was one of boredom, both with training and with the lack of off-field activities. We found ourselves travelling for four or five hours before arriving in Brisbane in the late afternoon. Having got off the coach, we were ready to sit back and have a welcome rest. We certainly didn't want to train. As Kevin told us to kit out, I remembered what George had said to me about too much training so close to the game. However, Kevin announced the team and we then had a really tough session. We were exhausted.

From a personal point of view, it was my first real taste of southern hemisphere rugby, and, although I was a bit tired, I was excited by the thought of getting another crack at George and playing in a Test against the Wallabies. But Saturday arrived and once again we were left kicking our heels. Thanks to Aussie TV, the kick-off was not until eight o'clock in the evening, and there we were with the best part of a day to kill.

As my friends will confirm, I am a competitive individual, whether it's betting on two flies on the wall or playing for my country in a Test match. Sadly, being competitive and keen to win was not enough to put one over on Neil Jenkins on the snooker table. We were desperate to escape from the hotel if only for an hour or two, so the pair of us got a bus into Brisbane to find a snooker hall. What a shocking decision! Jenks wiped the floor with me – it was embarrassing. And, what's more, he has never let me forget it.

Having said that, it was nice to relax and to break up the boredom. By that time, a few of the senior players had become sick and tired with the number of meetings called by the management team. I felt then and have often felt since that there is too much talking done about the game and not enough action. Of course you have to watch videos and discuss how and where we are going to attack and defend, but it does get terribly tedious at times.

Unfortunately, we were unable to turn our talking into victory. While I still had this confident air about me, my hopes were never to be realised. We played some great rugby in short spells and scored a couple of top tries. But once again we were unable to keep our fingers in the dyke and our paper-thin defence let us down. We were shocking. The fact that we only lost 56–25 was remarkable.

For me, there was another lesson to be learned from George. It was half-way through the second half and I was close to George as he shouted, 'Seq one, seq two, seq three!' I asked him later what he had meant by this and he said that the side was planning its next sequence of drives. I was gobsmacked – they actually had the confidence to be planning two and three phases ahead. At that stage I don't think we actually knew what we were doing from one second to the next, never mind two or three drives downfield!

Three years on and we have finally adopted the same approach under Graham Henry. However, what has happened in those three years? The Aussies and the other major southern hemisphere nations have moved on to bigger and better things. That we are now competing on level terms with them is another remarkable feat accomplished by Graham Henry.

I was down in the dumps when we got back to the hotel and by the time I arrived in the foyer, the rest of the boys, with the exception of Ieuan Evans, had gone for a night out in Brisbane. After a quick glass of Coke, I turned to Ieuan and said, 'What the hell, let's go and join them.' We had a decent night but I was still not up to having a party. I don't drink a lot and I don't believe in drowning your sorrows. I am also a great believer in turning up to training as fresh as a daisy. There is nothing worse than seeing boys sweating the beer out from the night before.

On the Wednesday we were taught another lesson by Australia A, losing 51–41. Once again we were shown up. We were simply not up to it and again Welsh rugby's lack of strength in depth was clearly evident.

Some of the boys wanted to go home there and then. The players were absolutely devastated, and picking them up for the remainder of the tour was going to be a tough task. Fortunately, and despite a few heads having already gone down, we regained a bit of respect by winning 49–3 against New South Wales Country in Moree. It was one of the worst pitches I have played on, and the conditions were some of the worst I have ever experienced.

But at least we had time to relax a little on the plane as we travelled up country. We chartered two small planes and the squad was split between the two. It was quite hairy because the planes were not that big, but at least Kingsley Jones brought a bit of light relief to the journey.

At that stage, Gwyn Jones was the number one openside flanker, with Kingsley desperate to oust him in time to play in the second Test. As we came in to land, Kingsley stood up and claimed to have received a bit of information down his headset. He said, 'Boys, we have some good news and we have some bad news. The bad news is that the other plane has fallen out of the sky after a mechanical fault and there are no survivors. The good news is that Gwyn is on board and I am going to take his place against Australia.' After the roasting we had just been given by Australia's second string, we were glad to have a comedian on board to lighten the atmosphere.

Playing at a venue like Moree was an education. I was on the bench, having picked up a slight calf strain in the Test, and to be honest I was quite glad. While the team completed their preparation in the dressing-room, the replacements asked where we could go to shelter from the torrential rain. We were a little surprised when a local match commissioner ushered us into the corporate hospitality tent, where we stood like lemons amongst all these guys sipping wine and eating vol-au-vents. The sight of us standing there must have been hilarious. I understand that you have to take the game out of the main cities, but this was a joke. The facilities that day were not even up to a first division game back home in Wales.

Thankfully we won and then beat Victoria 42–9 to put ourselves in a better frame of mind going into the second Test in Sydney. But once again our dream turned into a nightmare. We held on for 40 minutes and were level 0–0 at the interval. We could scarcely believe it. But then it all went wrong and we lost 42–3. It was time to go home, and in the end I was glad to get out of there.

By the time we flew home I had agreed to join Cardiff and the story had come out in the *News of the World*. I was a bit miffed at the way the story read but glad that it was all out in the open.

Sadly, there was one issue remaining – the matter of my WRU contract. It was the Thursday before the second Test when matters came to a head. At that stage I had not signed and Terry Cobner had a word with me at the airport, trying to find out what was going on. When I told him that I was still undecided, he brought Vernon Pugh into the equation. Vernon was chairman of the WRU at the time and had made it quite clear that if I didn't sign my contract, the WRU would shop around for another scrum-half who was prepared to sign. I didn't want to be pressurised but I found myself in an impossible situation. I actually signed there and then in the airport lounge.

It was a disappointing conclusion but it was my first indication of the power of certain individuals within Welsh rugby. I quickly realised that if the WRU wanted something, they would invariably get it. In my case, they certainly did, and that meant bye-bye Bath, hello Cardiff.

6. 'WEAR THESE OR KISS GOODBYE TO WALES'

Contractual Problems

In the four years since the game turned professional I have had my fair share of scrapes with officialdom. Contractual problems, wearing the wrong kit and speaking my mind have all landed me in hot water.

But, as I have said before, if you carry on through life telling lies and sucking up to the powers that be, you get nowhere. I certainly don't regard myself as a controversial figure, far from it. I keep myself to myself and look after my own well-being. However, if I feel that something needs to be said, or if I am asked to speak on a specific topic, I am not one to say 'No comment'. I have never seen any point in that.

Fortunately, my punishment has been relatively minor – the odd fine here and the odd smack on the wrists there. There have also been a few moments where I could have been forced to eat humble pie. Thankfully I have never stooped that low and hope I never will.

I am not sure how the general public perceive the modern-day rugby player or whether they fully understand the contractual obligations and subsequent problems we have been faced with since the game was declared open in the late summer of 1995. Let me say this: while the sums of money on offer to players were and still are way beyond the earning capacity of most people in Wales, the problems that come with the contracts we have to sign are at times beyond belief.

Personally, there were no real second thoughts about turning professional. I enjoyed my job as a sports development officer at Ogwr Borough Council but a salary of £12,000 a year could not compete with what I knew I could earn as a professional player. As a semi-professional at Bridgend, I was earning £50 for a win, while a consortium led by chairman Huw Ceredig was paying me another £100 a week in cash just to play for the club. Not knowing any different, or at least not having been told what others were earning, I was quite happy with the remuneration. Unfortunately, I was not exactly happy with the position at the club and the lack of ambition which I felt would only serve to hold me back. When Cardiff offered me a salary of £50,000 a year, I didn't have to think too long. Yes, my first move to the club had been a wrong one, but Alex Evans had gone and I was sure that lightning wouldn't strike twice. It just goes to prove how wrong you can be!

Professionalism had arrived far too quickly, and while these vast sums of money were being offered and subsequently accepted by players who could hardly believe their good fortune, the transition from shamateurism to professionalism has at times been particularly painful and distasteful. The players were soon to have two masters. On the one hand, the club was paying us a healthy salary in return for 100 per cent commitment, while on the other hand, the following year, the WRU devised its own contract which, as I will explain later in the book, placed hefty demands on us too. Obviously there would be a massive conflict of interests. And that was where the fun started.

In this chapter, I have highlighted three instances which I got caught up in. It was neither rewarding nor comfortable, but it was an invaluable experience to have gone through such difficult times.

'A CONFLICT OF INTERESTS'

We signed our WRU contracts in Australia in the summer of 1996 and although we understood that our commitments would change, we didn't fully understand the implications of what the contracts meant. You might have thought we would have been told or advised, but no. We were left to fend for ourselves – and in my case pay the consequence.

When we signed with the WRU, some players already had contracts with boot manufacturers. Neil Jenkins was with Adidas and Ieuan Evans and I were with Mizuno. However, the Union's deal was with Reebok. Obviously Ieuan, who was at that time one of the biggest names in world rugby, found himself in a strong position when it came to negotiating deals. For me it was a bit different. As far as international rugby was concerned, I was a relative newcomer and could hardly go around shouting the odds. Luckily, I had signed a deal with Mizuno and for that I was very grateful. They sorted me out with plenty of kit and were always willing to help. In return, I felt a genuine loyalty to the company and the reps I dealt with. What's more, their boots are top quality.

On signing our contracts in Australia, we made it quite clear that we already had contracts with other companies. I remember asking for clarification on certain matters, one of those being boots. What would we have to wear and when would we have to wear them? We were told there would be no problem as long as we wore Reebok boots in international games.

The players were quite happy with that, at least until push came to shove in October 1996, just before the national side was due to leave for Dubai to participate in the World Cup Sevens' qualifiers. There had been a number of meetings between the players and the WRU specifically with regard to contracts and I remember one particular meeting, on 31 October, when all the national squad players had met with the WRU secretary Richard Jasinski, national coach Kevin Bowring and Dave Clark. I was convinced that Kevin and Dave were just there to give the WRU support, because it was quite obvious that the moves were being made by Mr Jasinski.

Basically, we were told that there was a problem with our personal contracts. If we had signed a WRU contract back in the summer, as I had, then we *had* to wear Reebok boots for club games too. That had not been made apparent in the summer. In fact, the contract said anything but. In a normal contract there is a heading 'Kit Supplier', next to which is the name of the supplier whose kit you are obliged to wear. After being told by Mr Jasinski that I had to wear Reebok boots, I looked back at my contract to check what it said. The space next to the words 'Kit Supplier' was blank. The Union argued that when they had given us the contracts to sign, the kit supplier was not known. Well, fair enough, but that was no defence.

I don't know whether Reebok applied any pressure at the time, but I was very anxious about it because my Mizuno boots were so comfortable that I didn't want to swap. As a scrum-half, I felt that my boots were an important part of my game.

A compromise, or at least the offer of a compromise, was made when WRU chairman Vernon Pugh said that they were willing to fly Neil and me to the Reebok factory in Italy to have boots specially made. It was a great idea and I felt very privileged. I talked to Jenks about it and we were looking forward to having made-to-measure boots. Unfortunately, three years on we are still waiting for the plane tickets!

The upshot was that I contacted my accountant, John Squire, and my solicitor, Chris Jones, to see where I stood on the matter. I was adamant that I should wear my own boots. However, certain comments almost convinced me that I was being a bit precious about the whole thing. I remember Terry Cobner, the Union's director of rugby, claiming that it didn't matter what we wore on our feet as long as they had studs. Well, that might have been the case in the 1970s, but boots are far more sophisticated now and one pair is far from being the same as the next.

The week after that, Ceri and I got engaged in Paris and I thought everything had blown over. Once again I was wrong. Cardiff had reached the European Cup quarter-final against Bath at the Arms Park and the game was scheduled for the day before the Welsh team was to leave for Dubai. It was going to be a busy time. On the Wednesday prior to the game, I was summoned by Mr Jasinski. Terry Cobner and our squad's liaison manager Trevor James were present, on behalf of the WRU, as was Peter Owens, the assistant secretary. I was uncomfortable about the whole thing and asked if I could take my solicitor and accountant into the meeting.

When I walked into the meeting, I was told by Terry that if I refused to wear Reebok boots in the Bath game on Saturday I faced the probability of a £10,000 fine for being in breach of my contract. Considering I was three days away from one of the most important games in my career, I felt it was pretty insensitive. Other players like Jon Humphreys, David Young and Steve Williams, who were in a similar contractual position, were not being subjected to the same treatment, so why was I? Whether they saw me as the troublemaker in the group, I don't know. However, I was the only one to be summoned.

It got progressively worse as the week wore on. On the Friday morning, Trevor rang me at home to ask if I had made up my mind about what boots I was going to wear. I told him that I still hadn't decided, although I was edging towards my own Mizuno boots. I did say that the pressure was difficult to accept and I know that Trevor felt in an awkward position.

I spent that Friday evening relaxing at home, trying to concentrate on the challenge of Bath in the European Cup. Then the phone rang. It was Trevor. He told me that if I wore Mizuno boots against Bath my contract would be terminated and I would not be going to Dubai on the Sunday. I found that quite unbelievable. The night before the biggest club game of my career and here I was being threatened with my position in the Welsh team and, furthermore, my contract. In the end I gave in, reluctantly, and wore the Reebok boots. I had been forced into a corner and I was seething about the whole thing.

Maybe if we had stuck together as players in the weeks between August and the end of October, I might not have been singled out. Unfortunately, there had been a massive split in the squad because some players were on contracts and others were not. It was a difficult position because I can understand what those players without personal contracts were saying at the time. They were willing to sign a WRU contract whatever it said. To some, it was £30,000 a year and that was the end of the story. I am sure most of them would have agreed to wear slippers for that kind of cash!

In the end, John Rowlands came into the Cardiff dressing-room with some boots that had been blacked out and he had the Reebok sign painted on to them. Humph, however, went one step further. He had Nike boots at the time and he went to Dr Roger Evans and said that he was experiencing difficulties with his feet whenever he wore the Reebok boots. As a result, he was allowed to blacken his own boots and have the Reebok logo painted on the sides.

Fortunately, we beat Bath and the following day I flew out to Dubai with the rest of the squad. However, the whole episode left a sour taste in my mouth.

'THANKS FOR NOTHING, GREGOR'

Thanks to an innocuous tackle in training, I was struggling to be fit for the Five Nations game against Ireland in early 1997. My shoulder was really sore and although I felt I would be okay, Kevin Bowring told me to rest up, take it easy and sit out of training until the day before the game.

On the Wednesday, the squad trained at Sophia Gardens and Kevin decided to concentrate on back-row moves. Being a scrum-half, it was vitally important that I was there to see what was going on, but it was equally important that I didn't aggravate the shoulder and rule myself out of the game on the Saturday. Because of that I pitched up as a spectator, kitted out in a Pringle Scottish tracksuit top that I had swapped with Gregor Townsend after the game in Edinburgh two weeks earlier.

I was having a chat with a few of the press boys on the touch-line when Kevin came over and said that he would like me to feed a few balls into the scrum so that I could get a feel of what would be happening on Saturday. Thinking nothing of it, I obliged, and as far as I was concerned that was that. I suppose I should have known that I was heading straight into another problem. The following morning, *The Western Mail* carried a picture of me alongside the headline 'Howley fit to face Ireland'. It still didn't click, but when I looked again later that morning I saw the logo on the top I was wearing. I knew I had messed up and just waited for the phone call from the WRU.

Nothing happened, and for the first time in a long time I thought the WRU had seen it and decided to turn a blind eye. Perhaps Kevin had explained to them that I was only there as a spectator and that it had been his decision to call me into the session. I thought nothing more about it.

We played against Ireland and lost by a point in a game we should have won. The boys were devastated. Once again we had failed to build on a victory in Scotland and we felt we were back to square one.

As is normal in Cardiff, we went back to the hotel to get washed and changed and to have a drink before the post-match dinner. I wasn't in the best of moods, obviously, and at the time I just wanted to get the pleasantries over and done with and either have a few drinks or go straight to bed.

I walked into the bar and was immediately summoned by Terry Cobner. He took me into a corner and told me that the general committee had come down heavy on him with regard to me wearing *that* Pringle top, and that I was facing a £2,000 fine for being in breach of my Reebok contract.

It was not the best thing to hear, especially having just lost an international. Once again the timing couldn't have been worse. There is a time and a place for everything and this was neither the time nor the place. But, as I found out to my cost later that year, the WRU is not always sympathetic when it comes to handing out a rollicking.

I asked Terry whose responsibility it was to fine me; I was keen to establish who makes such decisions. He said, 'I do.' Considering the circumstances, I asked if on this occasion he could turn a blind eye. He said no and elaborated on the fine. I was to be fined £2,000 over the year with a small sum being deducted from my wages every two weeks.

The following Tuesday I was called in to see Terry and he told me of a letter from Vernon Pugh to Richard Jasinski confirming my fine. I asked if I could appeal, realising it wouldn't do the slightest bit of good. In the end I reluctantly paid the fine and made a note in my diary.

I am not saying I didn't mean to wear that particular top, but if Kevin had not asked me to participate in the session nothing would have been said. What people also didn't know at the time was that I only had one official wet-suit top and I had worn it to watch the sessions on the Monday and Tuesday. By the time it came to Wednesday it was still damp from the previous two sessions.

The WRU didn't want to know about that, as you can imagine. What Terry did say, however, was that at no time should I even contemplate going to the press to inform them of my side of the story. I said 'Okay' and went home, obviously smarting. When I woke up the next day and picked up *The Western Mail*, I was somewhat taken aback by the headlines that stated 'Howley fined by WRU'.

I couldn't understand where the story had come from, although I wondered whether the WRU had got their retaliation in first. That was later confirmed to me. On the one hand they were preaching to me about whinging to the press, yet here they were doing the same thing. At times you have to laugh and put it down to experience, although at the time it bugged me. I rang Trevor James to ask him if he knew anything about it. I trusted Trevor to tell me the truth. He just said, 'Nobody from the WRU would do that, Rob.'

Okay, so how could I prove it? I couldn't. But I never forgot the incident and never will. It taught me another important lesson and made me realise that I should look in the mirror before I even leave the house these days. It's sad, but that's professional rugby for you.

'COME AND JOIN US'

For the first time in the history of the Commonwealth and Empire Games, rugby union, albeit at sevens level, had been included. And, as you might expect, Wales decided to send their own side.

I had just come back from my honeymoon in the United States and I was struggling with fitness, having suffered a hamstring injury during the summer tour to South Africa. We had a new coach in Graham Henry and I was anxious to make a good impression while not jeopardising my chances of playing for Cardiff and Wales. I had been selected as captain of the Wales side for the Games, yet I felt that for the good of both club and country it would be better if I stayed at home and continued my programme of training towards regaining full fitness. After all, in the longer term that would be far more beneficial for everyone concerned.

It seemed quite straightforward. I would withdraw from the squad, train and play with Cardiff in our friendly games against the Allied Dunbar sides and then declare myself fit enough to team up with the full Wales squad for the November internationals against South Africa and Argentina. However, the WRU decided that any player who dropped out of the Commonwealth Games was not able to play until 15 September, when the event actually finished. Well, when you consider we were still in August, that was a long time for me to sit around doing nothing. I needed to play. Graham Henry understood where I was coming from and told me that he was of the same opinion. He didn't envisage a problem but said that he would fight my corner if there was any opposition.

I left it at that, withdrew from the squad and told Cardiff that I was keen to get fit and play whenever I could. I had a call from Gareth Davies, Cardiff's chief executive, and I told him that I wanted to play in the pre-season game against Sale. I wanted Cardiff to take the decision out of my hands by selecting me for the game. However, Gareth said that I had to make myself available and come clean with the WRU. I had to tell the Union that I would be playing in the game and going against their decision.

I had a chat with Graham before the trial game at Bridgend and he told me that he had already had his wrists smacked for allowing me to do what I wanted. Still, he said that it was the right decision I was making and confirmed that he would continue to support me. Terry Cobner was there too and he pulled me to one side. He asked me whether I understood why the ruling had been set in motion. I did, but I let him tell me. He said that it was to prevent players from dropping out of the Commonwealth Games for no reason.

That was the start of a difficult couple of weeks. Gareth and Terry Holmes eventually told me that I had been chosen to sit on the bench for the Sale game and instantly I knew that I would be in hot water. The decision Cardiff made to pick me had been made easier because Colin Charvis of Swansea, who had also pulled out of the Games with injury, had been named in the starting line-up for Swansea's game on the Saturday.

I travelled with the boys to Sale but fortunately didn't have to go on during the game. That was a godsend. Knowing my history with the WRU, I was sure that they would have come down hard on me if I had played.

The following Saturday was our first unofficial friendly against Bedford at Goldington Road. Although Colin had played for Swansea and there was talk about Paul John also playing for Pontypridd, I was still anxious about featuring in the Cardiff side. Cardiff, however, took the stance that I was playing and I had no choice. After all, they paid my wages. There was a lot of press in the week building up to the game saying that I was dumping on my WRU contract. What they didn't say, however, was that I also had a four-year contract with Cardiff. From my own point of view, I didn't want to miss out on what would be an historic day for the club and a vital game for me in terms of regaining my fitness.

The WRU made a lot of noise about me playing, and with the Union and Cardiff locked in their own battle over these unofficial games, I felt that I was being used as a pawn by both sides. Thankfully, and I am sure that Graham had a great deal to do with it, the whole episode was closed shortly after and my latest scrape with officialdom had passed without too much concern.

Unfortunately, it was only a week before I landed myself in it again. The issue of these unofficial games involving Cardiff and Swansea had dominated Welsh rugby over the summer and our first home fixture was against Saracens. As Dai Young was injured, I led the side that day and we won comfortably against a very strong Saracens side. It was everything I had hoped for. Regardless of what a few cynical pressmen said, and whatever the WRU thought, it was a game played at full tilt and with no little passion and commitment.

After the game, I was asked to go to the media room to attend a press conference with Gareth Davies, our chief executive, team manager Peter Manning and coach Terry Holmes. I was ecstatic, yet once again I put my foot in it by telling a few home truths. I later learned from the WRU that I should have condemned the game and the stance Cardiff had taken by saying nothing about what a spectacle this had been. I couldn't say that, however, and when it came to the international against South Africa I felt that those players from Cardiff and Swansea were better prepared than the players who had started their season playing in a series of Premier Division mis-matches in Wales.

I was asked a direct question by David Norrie of the *News of the World* about my initial thoughts about the move and that day's game. Considering I had been reluctant to attend the press conference because of the Commonwealth Games episode, I surprised myself by being so open in my reply. 'I think it is the way ahead for Welsh rugby and, having spoken to the likes of Jenks and Wayne Proctor, I know there is an extreme jealousy at what we and Swansea have done,' I said. If we were ever going to achieve anything at international level, this was the avenue to take. Then I went a bit further. 'What's more, they are quite envious. I am sure they would like to come and join us.'

The headline writers at the Sunday papers had a field day. 'Come and join us' was written all over the back pages and once again I knew I was heading for another roasting. As had been the case so often before, I had a call from Trevor James on the Monday and was asked to go into the Union. When I got there, Trevor had all the press cuttings on his desk and we scanned over them. What the WRU wanted was for me to retract what I had said by contacting a newspaper and redressing the balance. I was gobsmacked. I believed in what I had said and in what Cardiff had done. I couldn't have done what they were asking me to do. Thankfully, the journalist approached by our press officer, Lyn Davies, agreed that it was a ridiculous idea and once again it all blew over.

However, mud sticks, and from that moment I knew my card was marked. It was a case of keeping my head low and my mouth shut. It was a shocking position to find myself in, though I have since learned my lesson.

7. ALEX AND ME

An Experience to Forget

I don't think it was any secret that Alex Evans and I were not the best of friends either on or off the field. Nor do I think it was any secret that during his second spell at the club there was a definite split within the Cardiff squad. There were those who would swear by his every move, his every direction on the training field and his every selection off it. Unfortunately, there were a number of players, like myself, who honestly believe that Alex lost the ability to coach at the highest level when he came to Cardiff for a second time.

I don't dispute that he was the single biggest reason why Cardiff were so successful during his initial spell at the club. Nobody could argue with his achievement; it was first class. However, I was not alone in thinking that Cardiff made a gross error of judgement by inviting him to return. One thing is for sure: if I had known, at the time of signing for a second time, that Alex would be back in charge within a season of my own return, I would never have left Bridgend.

I made it quite clear at the time that I had signed for Cardiff because Terry Holmes had taken over in charge and that I felt the club was ready to make the kind of progress that would bring with it success, both in Wales and in Europe. Of course, my decision was also influenced by the news that Jonathan Davies was coming home, but having a chance to work with Terry on a daily basis was the main reason. Jonathan was just the icing on the cake. He had always been a hero of mine and I longed to play alongside him. In my eyes it was the perfect move. To partner the greatest fly-half of his era and to play for an ambitious coach for whom I had total respect was an opportunity not to be missed.

It was a significant time for Cardiff because they had also signed the likes of Gwyn, Dai Young, Leigh Davies and Justin Thomas. All of a sudden the club that had failed so badly in so many of the previous ten years had made a statement. By the time Terry and chairman Peter Thomas had finished recruiting, I don't think there was one non-international in the team!

But, as is so often the case, it was not long before we started believing our own press. We were pretty ordinary during the first few weeks of the season and nothing seemed to be happening. That can often happen in sport. A collection of international players does not automatically bring instant reward.

We hoped that an early-season visit to Swansea, who were always after our blood, would galvanise the side and prove that Cardiff's investment in us had been justified. It was certainly not the case. Our preparation was poor and injuries to key players meant that we were woefully short of props. Swansea is not the place to go these days with an understrength front row, so when we arrived at St Helens to be told that our bench would include a second-team prop from a local junior side, Gowerton, I suppose we knew what was in store.

Ironically, the afternoon started well. When we arrived at the ground, this guy from Gowerton asked if he could bring his son into the dressing-room to meet the boys and get a few autographs. It put us all at ease and we had a good chuckle. Mind you, by the end of the 80 minutes we could find very little to laugh about. In fact, we were glad to get out of there and back up the M4. Swansea slaughtered us, scoring 40 points without ever breaking sweat. It was an embarrassment and we knew the whole of Welsh rugby would be rejoicing. For want of a better comparison, I suppose Cardiff are the Manchester United of Welsh rugby. Unless you play for or support them, you have to hate them. It's an unwritten law which has survived two world wars and numerous changes of personnel. I quickly found out that Swansea were actually steering the bandwagon!

For those who don't know St Helens, the dressing-rooms are a little archaic, to say the least, and there are one or two windows at the top of the away dressing-room walls. I remember Dai Weatherley, the Swansea full-back, walking past our dressing-room and tapping on the window. He shouted, 'Two million? You're not worth two quid!'

There was a deadly silence in our dressing-room. The new players felt embarrassed while the older players were, I am sure, wondering what all the money had been spent on. Losing by 40 points was not the greatest start to the season. It was certainly not in the script.

It didn't get any better because we lost to Llanelli soon after and found ourselves struggling to compete with the better sides. I started to wonder whether I might have done the wrong thing – again. I could feel the boys in Bridgend laughing their socks off and I was conscious that Cardiff had invested all this money in me in order to help the club enjoy success.

I am sure most people were glad that I was suffering. Then again, that is one of the inherent problems with the game down here and you have to let the criticism wash over you. The game had gone professional and the players, like anyone else in business, were keen to get the best deals on offer. However, trying to get that across to some people is like explaining to a Welsh supporter that England does have the right to win the Five Nations Championship.

It was a difficult time and I was increasingly aware that my move had, once again, caused a great deal of bad feeling. Sadly, the whole matter came to a head a week after the Llanelli game. I had always said that I would never forget my roots and that one day I would like to go back to Bridgend Rugby Club, perhaps as a coach or the team manager, or even as the guy who takes the money on the hot-dog stand, if I couldn't get a job on the playing or coaching side. I had no gripe with the club and I tried to stay in touch with the lads I had played alongside during my time at the Brewery Field. I quickly realised, however, that the feeling I had for the people of Bridgend was in no way mutual.

It was a typical Wednesday night, with nothing on television and nothing else to do. Bridgend were playing South Wales Police at Waterton Cross. The ground is about a mile from my house so I nipped down with my training partner Carl Yardley to have a look. I suppose I was a bit naïve but I never thought my presence would evoke such emotion.

There were the usual moans and groans from local Bridgend supporters when they saw me and there was the usual banter about me being a Judas by taking the Cardiff shilling. I didn't like it, but I smiled and took it on the chin. After all, I didn't want to create a scene and get myself into trouble. As a professional sportsman you can ill afford to strike back. The media would have a field day, as they did with Eric Cantona. Okay, so I wasn't planning any karate kicks, but I certainly felt like putting a few people straight. Unfortunately, as I walked out of the ground, some guy caught me off my guard and, I have to admit, I came close to losing my cool.

He approached me in front of quite a few people, including Carl, and said how despicable it was that I could move to Cardiff for a second time, especially as I had already made the mistake once. I suppose he had a point, and he had every right to air his opinion. But it was the way he said it. I honestly wanted to punch his lights out. I had given Bridgend four years' service and I had given them my all during that time. Now I was trying to better myself as a player by moving to a bigger club who, I felt, could win something. I tried to explain, but Carl, who could see I was getting pretty wound up, dragged me away and we left without any further trouble.

I have the greatest respect for those supporters who pay their money and support their club, but I treat with contempt the idiots who feel they have to take it that one step further. But that's Welsh rugby for you. It obviously hurt the people of Bridgend that I had left, but it only hurt them because I had chosen Cardiff. Had I turned left on the M4 and signed for Swansea, that guy would probably have bought me a pint and wished me all the best. There is a genuine hatred for everything involved with the Cardiff club and I was beginning to feel it. I was only glad that the people who mattered were a little more understanding. Derrick King hadn't wanted me to leave, but he understood fully my decision. Unfortunately, he couldn't convince the supporters or even some of the management committee at the time. They were having none of it. I was definitely public enemy number one.

So, having been subjected to that nonsense, I knew what was in store for me when I eventually had the privilege of returning to play against Bridgend for my new club. It was late on in the season and we had just won the Swalec Cup. The boys had partied well on the Saturday and Sunday and the last thing we wanted was a midweek game against Bridgend. Not only did they hate us but the grapevine told me they fancied their chances of taking a pop at us.

We went to the Brewery Field with a fairly weakened side but were confident that we had enough talent to beat them. I was actually selected on the bench and at the time I was quite glad. It was just as I had thought. By the time the referee brought the fight to an end, there were more stitches than points and more blood than anyone could ever have imagined possible. I sat on the bench until just after half-time and I couldn't believe what I was seeing and hearing. The stamping was obscene and there were punches coming from everywhere. Our boys are no angels but one or two were disgusted by the behaviour of some very good Bridgend players. Then came the dreaded moment when Alex Evans said to me, 'Rob, I want you to go on.' I knew I couldn't say no, as much as I wanted to. I was being well paid to do this job, so I peeled off my kit and started to warm up.

From the moment the supporters saw me stretching on the touch-line, they pelted me with verbal insults. I thought it would be a bit safer if I went on, so at the next stoppage I raced on to the field to join the rest of the boys. It was certainly not any easier. Every time I got the ball I was either kicked or punched and there were moments when I would have preferred to have been anywhere else in the world. It was a sad day for Welsh rugby and I feel sorry for the players and supporters who felt they had to resort to that kind of behaviour.

But, as I found out, the game was only the beginning of the unpleasantness. Then we had to get off the pitch. I went over to a few supporters to sign some autographs as I normally do after a game. I think you have that responsibility to the fans who come to watch you. The next thing I knew, Dai Young put his hand on my shoulder and said, 'What are you doing? Just get off the pitch.' I think he was worried that a supporter was going to come at me and have a pop. But what happened next was unbelievable. We got to the touch-line and as I turned towards the dressing-room one of the Bridgend committeemen jumped out and starting abusing me. Once again, Dai intervened. He leant forward, grabbed the guy's tie and told him to 'f***off'.

I was glad to get back to the dressing-room but disappointed that it had come to this. I have always lived in Bridgend and don't have any plans to move. But to get this sort of welcome was beyond belief. I left via the back door to avoid the supporters' bar before going into the sponsors' room to seek out some friendly faces.

The reception in there was a little more welcoming but, not wishing to push my luck, I eventually said my farewells and walked out to the car park. Derrick followed me and asked if I wanted a lift home. I said yes. It was only about a mile to my house, yet the journey home took us about two and a half hours. We just kept stopping and talking. I knew I had made the right decision to leave Bridgend but here I was trying to convince myself. I certainly didn't have to convince Derrick and he kept telling me as much.

It made me feel a bit better, but the scenes that night lived with me for a long time. That is the sad side of Welsh rugby and I hope I never find myself in that position again. Welsh rugby can be very fickle and this was the perfect example of people running with hares and hunting with the hounds. On the one hand the supporters were calling me every name under the sun, yet on the other the club, or so I was told later that week, was still trying to get me back. Derrick even contacted Peter Thomas to ask how much he would have to pay to sign me.

Now Peter and Derrick get on really well, but Peter is a shrewd and very successful businessman and is certainly not slow in telling people exactly what he thinks. There was no malice, but he said to Derrick, 'Don't bother, it would cost you about £1 million and Bridgend doesn't have that kind of money.' Derrick told me what Peter had said and I felt sorry that he had been shot down like that. All he wanted to do was help me and help the club.

The relationship I had with Derrick was certainly different from the one I had, or didn't have, with Alex Evans. As I mentioned before, we had not had a great start to the season. However, I was quite happy with Terry in charge and felt that in time we would prove a few people wrong. Unfortunately, the position worsened for Terry and a few of us became aware that certain senior players like Mike Hall, Jonathan Humphreys, Emyr Lewis and Derwyn Jones were trying to get the club to contact Alex to offer him a chance to come back to Wales.

While I understood their feelings towards Alex, I thought it was hugely unfair that Terry should be treated like that. He was our coach, yet certain players felt they had the right to go to people like Peter Thomas to try to convince him that Alex had to come back. It was tantamount to blaming Terry for everything that had gone wrong. That is the easy way out for a player. Furthermore, it showed total disregard for Terry.

It obviously worked, though, because the next thing we knew, Alex was coming back to head up the coaching team. It was my worst nightmare. It was worse than leaving Bridgend, worse than getting injured and worse than having had to swallow my pride by going back to Bridgend in the first place. To be honest, I couldn't see where my future lay.

Alex had made a statement during the Five Nations saying that he felt he had treated me badly during my first spell at the club, and the comment surfaced with a few journalists when it was announced he was coming back. I felt he was trying to sweet-talk me and forget the past. No chance: I was cemented in the Cardiff side and the Wales team and there was no way he was going to ruin my career by coming back and meddling in my progression.

His first game in charge was the semi-final of the Swalec Cup at St Helens against Llanelli. I had a good game and I was on a crest of a wave having been selected for the British Lions. Alex tried to discuss various parts of the game with me but I didn't really care. I was hell bent on remaining loyal to Terry. After all, it was Terry who had made me feel so comfortable in a Cardiff jersey, not Alex Evans.

The game went okay and we followed it up by beating Swansea in the final. But that night, having had a great afternoon at the National Stadium, I once again saw a side to Alex that I didn't like.

Dai Young, Leigh Davies and I went into Cardiff for a few beers to celebrate and we arranged to meet the girls back at the club at around 9.30 p.m. When we got back, Dai, Dai's wife April, Ceri and I went for a meal with Alex and his wife and our fitness adviser Gwyn Griffiths and his partner. I was quite reluctant to go but I didn't want to upset the apple-cart after such a wonderful day. Sadly, the night confirmed everything I thought about Alex.

He seemed to take control of the situation as soon as we hit the restaurant. He organised the seating arrangements, making sure he was placed right next to me. He was glued to me all night, ignoring the rest of the group, including his wife, for much of the time. It was obvious he wanted us to have a private conversation. Whether he was trying to play mind games or whether he was trying to convince me that he had changed as a person, I do not know. But still I felt very uncomfortable and I was not about to let him win me over after all that had gone on. Even Ceri said how awkward it had been.

My relationship with Alex never improved. In fact, it wasn't long before I saw the old Alex Evans in all his glory. Having come home early from the Lions tour, I required surgery on my shoulder. From the moment I arrived back in Bridgend, obviously distraught, the phone never stopped ringing. Players, supporters, coaches and friends from all over Wales rang to wish me a speedy recovery and to commiserate with me. The Lions were still playing and I was obviously feeling very vulnerable.

You would have thought that your immediate boss would have been the first on the phone or the first at your front door to see how things were going. Not Alex. Not only did he not ring me in those first few difficult days, but he never once came to hospital to visit me. That hurt. Eventually he rang to apologise about the delay and to tell me that George Gregan had rung to send on his best wishes. I still think, to this day, that that was a massive smoke screen. He was probably so embarrassed about having not rung that he deflected it away from himself.

However, he wasn't so slow in trying to rush me back into action. The surgeon who undertook my operation, Geoff Graham, did a marvellous job and he gave me a comeback date of the end of October. But once I got back to the club, I found myself under increasing pressure to come back a lot earlier. 'You've got to play, mate,' Alex would say. 'We need you.' Strange, really, when you consider what he used to think of me! He had told me when I first signed that I would have to fight for my place, yet now, when he wanted me, I was indispensable.

In the end you start believing that you *are* fit and you *are* that important. I spoke to Kevin Bowring and he said that he didn't want me to play but that he would leave the decision up to me and Geoff. That week Geoff came down to Cardiff training and said that if I was happy to play then I should play. At first, he started talking to me in front of Alex, but he soon turned to Alex and said, 'Do you mind if we talk alone?'

I think Alex wanted to be there to make sure the decision was a positive

one. I desperately wanted to play as Cardiff had not played that well in
Europe. But at the same time I didn't want to jeopardise my long-term
chances, especially with the Five Nations in mind. But I made the decision
that I was fit and I played in Munster the following week. Yes, I came
through, albeit with a few bumps and bruises, but it was a real gamble. It
was a gamble I should not have taken. All of a sudden my shoulder was
forgotten and nobody said anything about it.

After that I could have done with a bit of a gentle introduction to full
training, but to be honest it was shocking. We just spent week after week
battering hell out of each other. I felt there were areas in Alex's coaching that
were outdated. That is only my opinion and there were others, as I said at
the outset, who swore by his methods. But I saw players becoming
disillusioned and very stale.

We played Newport in early December and we escaped with a narrow
victory courtesy of a last-minute penalty from Lee Jarvis. That night, Alex
had a real go. He had this thing about the international players not fronting
up to their club duties. Wales had just played New Zealand and a few of us
had found the following week very difficult. But Alex seemed to take great
pleasure in telling us how disappointed he was in us. I was told that a few
of the non-internationals had also gone running to him claiming that we
were not pulling our weight. That was the type of split we had in the squad
and it didn't make for a good spirit.

Dai, Gwyn and I bore the brunt of it and we thought it was well out of
order. I don't think he understood how much international rugby meant to
us and how much it took out of us. It was crazy. One school of thought was
that Alex was trying to deflect the blame on to the players. Things were not
going that well and supporters were starting to ask questions. I think there
might have been one or two questions raised at board level about our poor
run of performances.

So things were not great. Terry Holmes rang me because he knew things
were deteriorating and he was finding it increasingly difficult. I drove into
Cardiff and met him in a café for a chat. Basically, I said that I felt Alex had
lost it as a coach and that a change was needed. Don't get me wrong – Alex
was a very good one-on-one coach. He was superb. But as a team leader I
felt his skills left a great deal to be desired. At that time, I was actually the
team's vice-captain, yet I was never asked to give my opinion. Occasionally
Humph might consult me and then go off to speak to Alex, but Alex would
never come to me. I don't think he ever rang me at home to discuss things.

Humph quickly identified a problem, but it was not until the weekend of Gwyn's appalling injury that others realised the extent. Gwyn was injured and lying in hospital and Garin Jenkins's father had suffered a heart attack in the crowd. But there we were, the next morning, in two inches of snow, running around a local rugby pitch. Alex hadn't thought about giving us the day off while we recovered from the events of the previous day.

It was a real problem for me. I am a great believer in training if you get something from it, but we were never likely to get anything from that morning. Our minds were a million miles away. He should have turned around to us and told us to have a week off. We would have been much better served staying at home and having a short session on the following Friday to run through a few moves before the game the following day. With respect, we were only playing Abercarn in the Swalec Cup, after all. That was the final straw for me and I couldn't wait for someone to give the players a chance to air our views. Thankfully that opportunity was not long in coming.

Every year, the board, the coaches and the club's chief executive meet to discuss the club's position and how we had done in the first half of the season. We thought that something would have to come up about Alex. I was obviously going to ask a question with regard to him and I think most of us were very wound up about the situation.

Humph, Emyr, Derwyn and Mike Hall were still of the opinion that Alex was the Messiah. I couldn't blame them because Alex had turned their careers around a few seasons earlier. But then there were those players like me, who had seen the split in the party. We couldn't understand how they could stand by and watch the team suffer just to protect Alex.

We all sat down and Peter Thomas was the first to speak. Basically, he said that Alex was an outstanding coach and that any problems being experienced at the club were the fault of others, not the coaching director. I looked at Dai and we shook our heads in disbelief. I think Peter knew the meeting was set up for other reasons, so he came in and diffused the whole situation. He knew that we wanted to have our say and I don't think he wanted us to go down that avenue. Our chief executive, Gareth Davies, certainly did. I think he wanted us to tell the board what the players thought of Alex. Unfortunately we didn't get the chance. We left feeling quite dejected. Well, at least some of us did. The rest just smiled and celebrated another battle won.

Over the next two or three weeks, the position got worse and Humph called a players' meeting to discuss the situation. Whether Alex knew about the meeting, I don't know and I don't really care. However, I did care that once again this was being done behind Terry Holmes's back. If the truth be told, I am convinced that that was why Humph was not selected as captain the following season when Terry was back in charge. He had gone behind Terry's back and Terry never forgot it.

Humph, however, felt it was necessary to call a meeting and I agreed with him. It was a typical players' meeting. We looked at ourselves first to try and solve the problem and then we looked elsewhere. It was time for me to speak. I stood up and said, 'I think the coach has lost it.'

There was a deathly hush. I felt the knives going into my back as I spoke but I was only saying what others were feeling. I felt that if Cardiff were going to succeed as a club then Alex had to go. I felt my words were justified and I had no regrets.

That was on a Thursday and the following Monday came the phone call from Humph. He was obviously in a panic. 'I can't believe it,' he said. 'What you said in the team meeting last week has got back to Alex.' I was never told who had squealed to the teacher but I have my ideas. Anyway, it was out in the open and as expected I was called in. 'Alex wants to see us both,' said Humph. 'He wants to look at what is wrong with the club.'

I didn't panic but I started to question whether I had done the right thing. The last thing I wanted was to be the Wales captain and involved in some almighty row at my club. The press were bound to get hold of it sooner rather than later and once again the name of Rob Howley would be blasted across the back pages for all the wrong reasons.

I walked into the club around 9.30 a.m. and made my way into one of the suites upstairs. In the room were Alex, Terry Holmes and Charlie Faulkner. I just chuckled to myself. I felt he had lost the battle straight away. He couldn't talk to me one on one. It was three against two or four against one, depending on Humph. I thought to myself, 'How spineless can you get?'

Alex never broached the real subject of why I was there, he just skirted around it. Then he started going off at tangents, about the problems at fly-half. He blamed everyone but himself. I left with a knowing smile and that was the last real contact I had with him.

A few weeks after that, I phoned the club to speak to Gareth Davies about a contractual matter. I was told that he had flown to Australia with Peter Thomas. Alex had gone back by then, for a holiday, so I knew what was going on. Obviously Alex had decided not to come back and Gareth and Peter were out there trying to sort out an amicable agreement. That was where the pay-off came and Alex was gone for good. I was one player who was glad to see the back of him.

8. A SHOULDER TO CRY ON

Not So Perfect for Peter Perfect

Those who have spent a morning or afternoon in the house with Ceri or me will know only too well that the day is often ruined by the constant ringing of the telephone. Thank goodness for the invention of the answer machine!

However, the shrill tones often bring good news. A phone call from the Wales coach or my agent is always welcome. A short chat with Ceri to see what's for tea is acceptable too! I never imagined, though, that a phone call from a production assistant at Sky Sports would, at least for a short time, change my life. I only wish that the call I had to make from my hotel room in South Africa six weeks later could have been as joyous.

It had been a decent Five Nations season, I suppose, and on a personal front I was relatively content with the improvement in my own perform-ance. I was carrying a minor shoulder injury and at times I felt that I would have been better served resting for a game at least. But, as every player will tell you, when the adrenaline pumps, the pain often disappears. The Wales physio, Mark Davies, was happy for me to carry on throughout the championship, so I did, finishing the season with a consolation try against England at Cardiff Arms Park.

With the construction work at the new Millennium Stadium soon to get under way, it proved to be the last international try scored on the hallowed turf of the National Stadium. I will forever cherish that moment. However, more important was the individual nature of the try. I think that was the act which finally secured my place on the British Lions tour to South Africa.

Fran Cotton, the Lions team manager, had spoken to me after the game in Paris two weeks earlier, saying that he had been impressed with my contribution throughout the season. I am sure he wanted me to finish on the losing side when it came to the England game but his words of support were like pennies from heaven. I knew from his comments that I must have been close. Unfortunately I couldn't ask him how close.

England beat us comfortably and I spent the next few days waiting anxiously for confirmation that Martin Johnson, Ieuan Evans, Neil Jenkins and Keith Wood would have a new colleague in Robert Howley. It dominated my life during that short period between the end of the championship and the actual announcement and Ceri and I found ourselves talking about nothing else. We wrote down the names of the scrum-halfs in contention and talked about their relative merits. I suppose I felt confident, but at no stage did I count my chickens. Then came the call.

Ceri and I were sitting in the lounge watching television when the phone went. Knowing that I had only six rings before the answer machine cut in, I quickly made my way to the study and answered. The side was not due to be announced until the following day but I hoped it might be a journalist who had been given the nod. Believe it or not, there are times when the writers get to know things before we do. I don't condone that but on this occasion I certainly wouldn't have minded.

'Hello, is that Rob?' said an unfamiliar voice at the other end of the line. I confirmed my name, then almost fell off my chair as the same voice said, 'We would like you to come to the Sky studios in the morning for the announcement of the British Lions squad.'

Now I am not one to take anything for granted. On the contrary, I would have to say that I am one of life's born pessimists. However, when somebody lines you up like that – well, what would you think?

He went on to say that my selection was unofficial and that nobody else should be made aware of the telephone call. Surely it wasn't a wind-up? Surely nobody would do that to me? The conversation ended with the guy telling me I would receive official confirmation by letter the following morning. I rushed back in to tell Ceri and although we were both inwardly elated, neither wanted to pop the cork, just in case.

I didn't sleep all night, not because I was nervous about the selection or what lay ahead in South Africa but because I am not the best at getting up in the morning. This was one morning when I couldn't afford to sleep in. Imagine sleeping through the alarm and missing the announcement in London! That would be the end of me and the name of Robert Howley would never surface again. (See what I mean about being a born pessimist?)

Thankfully, my fears were unfounded and I was up, washed and on the road by six o'clock. I had instructed Ceri to wait by our letter box and to open the mail as soon as it hit the mat. By eight o'clock I had reached Reading services, so I pulled in to ring Ceri for confirmation. Yes, the letter had arrived. It was a wonderful feeling and I immediately phoned my parents to give them the news. I left Reading pretty sharpish and made my way to the studios, arriving about 45 minutes early.

When I introduced myself at reception, I was advised to make myself comfortable in the restaurant upstairs. I think the receptionist must have had a private chuckle. It was obvious that I was in a state of panic. I tried to relax but my mind was working overtime. How would I play, would I get in the Test side, would I be good enough, would my shoulder be okay? They were all questions that neither I nor the receptionist could answer, so I made my way upstairs, hoping that one of the other boys, maybe Ieuan, would be there.

There was one guy up there but it wasn't a player. Jim Telfer was the assistant to Lions coach Ian McGeechan and as I walked into the canteen area to get a cuppa I walked straight into him. Now, Jim cuts an imposing figure, and although he seemed quite comfortable with the fact that it was just him and me, I was a little nervous, to say the least. I couldn't talk about selection and I was worried about becoming too familiar with him.

Thankfully, within a matter of minutes Jason Leonard and Keith Wood, whom I knew quite well from having played against them, joined us and the atmosphere was a whole lot easier.

We were eventually called into the studio and Ray Williams, who was chairman of the Home Unions and who lives about two minutes from me in Bridgend, announced the party. It was a very proud moment. We had a satellite link-up to South Africa, so the South African Gary Teichmann could talk to us and to a few of the English boys who were in a studio in Leicester.

It was a chance for Sky to promote the tour and when we started talking to Gary it really hit home. A Lions tour is the pinnacle of any player's career and I was already feeling a bit special. I knew from what Ieuan had told me that it doesn't get any better. Unfortunately for me, it got considerably worse!

When the formalities were over, Jason, Keith and I went into Richmond to have a few beers to celebrate. I was driving back that afternoon so I took it easy, said my farewells and set about answering the messages on my mobile. Kevin Bowring had rung, along with a few other guys from the WRU and Cardiff, but to be honest I just wanted to get home so I could wind down after a few rather difficult days.

Ceri was obviously delighted and after we discussed how she would come out in time for the first Test, I rang the lads and we went into Cardiff for a proper drink. The championship had dominated the previous couple of months and this was an opportunity to let my hair down. I am not a big drinker, far from it, but we sank a few beers that night and then made our way back to Bridgend.

The next few days were spent fielding good-luck messages from friends and supporters. I also took time to collect my own thoughts and prepare for what would be an arduous couple of months.

Eventually the squad was called together in Weybridge for a week of team-building. A number of previously planned training sessions had been cancelled because of the congested fixture list at the end of the season and time was running out. In fact, according to Ieuan and Scott Gibbs, the preparation for this tour was by no means as intense as it had been in previous years.

The week in Weybridge, however, was fantastic, if a little strange. As a player I was used to meeting up for Wales training sessions with the same guys whom I had either played with or against in recent weeks. This was very different. All of a sudden I was rubbing shoulders and sharing rooms with players from other countries, players who had spent the previous two months trying to make sure Wales finished at the bottom of the championship pile.

That is the aspect of Lions rugby that makes it so very special. In Wales we are often accused of being parochial and I suppose that is not far from reality. We like to keep ourselves to ourselves and we like to hate the opposition.

So when I arrived I made it my business to get to know the likes of Jeremy Guscott and Lawrence Dallaglio. I was determined not to show any parochialism by spending every waking minute with Ieuan, Jenks, Scott Gibbs, Scott Quinnell or Barry Williams. Obviously they were part of the squad and I was glad that so many Welsh players had been selected. But this was not about individuals or about Wales, England, Ireland or Scotland as individual entities. This was the British Lions. These were the guys I would eat with, travel with and depend upon for the next two months.

Intending to do something and actually going through with it, however, are two totally different things and to begin with, I have to admit, it was difficult to mix with the English players. The hatred that exists between the two countries will, unfortunately, remain forever. Ask any Welshman whom he would most like to stuff and he will say England every time.

Thankfully, though, I struck up an instant rapport with the English players and found myself spending more and more time with the likes of Martin Johnson, Dallaglio and Jerry. Jerry was a star and certainly made me feel at ease. He divided his time between teaching me the rudimentary facts of touring with the British Lions and trying to get me to join Bath. I got to know him very well and we struck up a good relationship. Having said that,

I think I might have tested his patience when, later in the tour, I defaced his blazer. Jerry took it quite well, although from then on he kept suggesting that Bristol, not Bath, might be the club for me.

Joking apart, he was a great help to me. I was far from happy with my playing situation back in Wales and my contractual position with the club and the WRU was causing me a great deal of concern. He sat me down on a number of occasions and we discussed my options. There was never any pressure to join Bath but he made everything clear. I sometimes wish that all rugby people were as clear and decisive as Jerry. Not only is he a great player, he also has a great understanding of the game and how it should be run.

Gradually the squad began to grow together and by the end of the week numerous important relationships had been forged. The management team had accelerated the team-building by introducing a training development group called Impact. They were a great help to us and to the management, who took part as well. It was no good us having a great spirit and the team management being at each other's throats. They joined in too and that at times gave us great satisfaction and no little reason to smile. To see the likes of Fran paddling down the Thames was a sight to behold.

Every single area was covered. We had a seminar with John Taylor and David Norrie, two journalists who taught us how to handle the press, and we worked hard on our communication skills. For a week I thought of nothing but rugby and the British Lions and I was very comfortable with the position. Comfortable, that is, until it came to the small matter of saying goodbye to our loved ones. We enjoyed the send-off dinner on the Wednesday night and had a few beers on the Thursday before it came to crunch time.

I am not and never have been the best of tourists because I do miss the home comforts. Ceri came up with Diane, Barry Williams's wife, and we all said our farewells. Ceri knew that I had been in tears and to be honest I spent most of that day in a similar frame of mind. After the girls left, Barry and I spent a few hours walking around the parks of Weybridge, sobbing our hearts out. To think that a couple of lads in their mid-twenties were in this state is quite odd, I suppose. But that was how we felt. Ceri meant so much to me and I had never previously been away from her for so long.

Many people believed that the task ahead was insurmountable and that the Springboks would run riot in the Test matches. After all, they were the world champions and we were the underdogs. On arriving in Johannesburg we received a memorable welcome from the local media. It was memorable because we had never experienced anything like it. However, by the time we cleared customs, we realised that the 1997 British Lions were about to embark on a very special tour. Not only was it the first professional Lions tour but it was a tour which pitched us against one of the great sides in the history of the game. What's more, we were on their patch.

As we emerged through the Arrivals gate we were exposed to the biggest press entourage I have ever seen. Thankfully, it was Martin Johnson as captain who had the job of sitting on the top table, fielding the questions from the world's press. I just sat at the back pinching myself. I couldn't quite comprehend that I was part of a Lions tour that meant so much to South Africa. It was the first time the Lions had gone to South Africa since 1970 and I knew that for the next eight weeks that fact would be constantly rammed down our throats. It was certainly not going to be a tour for the faint-hearted.

From that moment, the Lions dominated the headlines and our every move was monitored. It was my first real experience of how someone like Gazza must feel on a daily basis.

The first of those moves took us to Durban for a week's preparation ahead of the opening game against Eastern Province. It was quite an intense time for the players because we were all desperate to make our mark. It was every man for himself. Nobody wanted to miss out, so you had to be on top of your game at every session. You couldn't afford to show any weakness. For me it was a personal battle with Austin Healey and Matt Dawson and I was determined to make sure I was the one in pole position when it came to selection for the first Test.

I had shared with Austin when we first arrived in Weybridge and he is quite a cheeky sort of person who some might say is in love with himself. Well, I did experience that at times, but he is a decent guy and he is a very competitive player. In fact, one of the first things he said to me was about how he and I would spend the next few weeks ripping each other's throats out in pursuit of that sacred shirt. I get on great with Austin now and would like to think that he feels the same way about me. However, for eight weeks I knew that circumstances would dictate the relationship.

We flew into East London on the Friday before the game and the side was announced by Fran Cotton later that day. I was quite relieved to be picked. I desperately wanted the first chance to prove myself. I had obviously been in similar situations before, with Wales. In fact, my first cap and team-talk with Wales had been very special indeed. However, nothing will ever compare with the announcement from Fran and the subsequent speech delivered by Ian McGeechan. That will live with me forever. Whether he had prepared it on a cold night back at Franklins Gardens or whether it was spoken straight from the heart, I don't know. What I do know is that he spoke as a former Lion and as a current Lions coach. We hung on his every word.

I am an emotional person and I take great care in my own preparation for games, but this was something beyond explanation. You could have heard a pin drop. There were 40 guys in that room and each one was in danger of losing emotional control. Sometimes rugby players are perceived as the heavies with no hearts. That's a misconception. We are no different from anyone else. We all have feelings and we all have emotions and this was stretching us to the limit. Ian gave us a great insight into what was expected of us and I left the room feeling ten foot tall.

Gregor Townsend was my fly-half in that opening game and I was pleased with that. We had played together for the Barbarians and we each understood how the other wanted to play the game. I suppose the real critics would say we struggled a bit in the first half against Eastern Province, but after clearing the cobwebs we played well and ran away with it, winning 39–11. It was a wonderful feeling to have worn the Lions jersey for the first time and it was an equally wonderful feeling to come off the field with a consummate victory under our belts.

I was delighted to have featured in that game and to have made my mark so early in the tour. However, the management were quick to knock us down a peg or two by making it abundantly clear that, despite what we might have thought about selection, there would be no definite Saturday and Wednesday teams. Everyone would be considered for every game and I suppose that kept us all firmly on our toes. Everyone had to earn their stripes; there were no definites or definite maybes. It would be down to form.

I have my own views about touring and I certainly don't subscribe to the view that a weekend side and a midweek side should be established early in the tour. To do that is tantamount to drawing a line down the centre of the squad and saying 'you are the best players and you are here as cover'. There was none of that on this occasion.

We moved on to Border, and although conditions were horrendous, we managed to scrape an 18–14 win thanks to a last-minute try from Rob Wainwright. I was fortunate to miss out on that game but I was back for the Saturday match against Western Province. It was the first really important game. Once again, Gregor and I were selected at half-back, with

Lawrence, Richard Hill and Jenks all making the side. Although we would never question Fran or Geech, we talked between ourselves and those in that side could see the shape of the first Test team.

Western Province are a Super 12 side of substance and we were made aware of that during another heart-to-heart with Geech. However, from my point of view it could not have gone better. I put Jerry in for a try and then made a break to send Ieuan over in the corner. We won 38–21 with Bentos, John Bentley, scoring twice and Tim Stimpson kicking 17 points. As you can imagine, we partied well that night, although for those who are wondering, no, I didn't see any drugs passed around!

We were now two weeks into the tour and quite a few Lions supporters had turned up. A few of them were in the same restaurant that night. That was the night I decided to deface Jerry's blazer by signing my autograph on the back. As I said before, he smiled and took it quite well. However, he never mentioned Bath again and I never asked.

Once the celebrations were over we moved on to play and subsequently beat Mpumalanga 64–14 to keep the bandwagon rolling. Once again I was rested and, to be fair, Matt played really well. In contrast, Austin had not been as impressive against Border and from that juncture it was clear that my main opposition for a place in the Test team would come from Matt Dawson.

That being the case, I knew that I had to play well on the Saturday against Northern Transvaal. The pack comprised mainly English players and we spent all afternoon going backwards. That was the turning point of the tour. While it was somewhat surprising to see this so-called wonder English pack going backwards at a rate of knots, it certainly answered a few questions. It proved to the management that the likes of Tom Smith, Dai Young and Paul Wallace would have to be seriously considered for the first Test. In a perverse kind of way, I was pleased that we had suffered so badly. Although we lost the game 35–30, it proved there would have to be a rethink.

We hit back on the Wednesday by beating Gauteng Lions 20–14 at Ellis Park, although I was confined to the grandstand, having suffered a slight twinge in my knee. I had got a cyst at the back of my left knee and the daily training sessions on the hard grounds had aggravated it. I went to see Geech and he advised me to rest during the week and to play at the weekends. I quickly realised that he wanted me for the Test and although I didn't want to duck out of training I felt good about what he had told me. The not knowing had bugged me throughout the tour. But, if that was the good news, the bad news was not far away.

Natal were next up and I knew that if I stayed clear of injury and had a decent game I would get my chance in the first Test and realise a dream that had begun so many weeks earlier. What's more, by that time the whole of South Africa had started to take notice of what we had achieved. The tour was really beginning to take shape and I was so proud to be part of it.

It was vital that we continued in the same vein by beating Natal. The side was named and although the press made out that this was likely to be the Test team, Fran called us together and advised us not to read anything into the selection. He told us that places were still up for grabs. Fortunately, we did play well as a team. Unfortunately, I was left to curse my own bad luck.

I had looked forward to this game for the best part of a week and was desperate to make an impression. Everyone was talking about the forthcoming Test and the battle between Rob Howley and Joost van der Westhuizen. I was beginning to warm to the idea of pitting myself against a player whom many people rated as the best in the world.

The opening minutes were frantic and the pace was electric. Then, in the 13th minute, my hopes were shattered. I have learned to accept what happened but I must admit that, at times, it is difficult to talk about it. Everything had gone so well and my parents, Ceri and her parents were due to fly into South Africa the following day in time for the first Test. Naturally, I was excited at the prospect of seeing everyone again and obviously very proud to think that I was going to bring them so much pleasure.

The forwards started with a bang and as they drove on, deep into Natal territory, I spotted my first opportunity to make a break. I picked up from a ruck inside their twenty-two on the right-hand side off slow ball. There was nothing on out wide, so instead of passing to Gregor I went myself and ran into Ollie le Roux, a player who tips the scales at around 20 stone. It was not the best choice I have ever made. He was the irresistible force and the immovable object.

It was an innocuous tackle and I would never lay any blame at his door. There was certainly no malice. However, I felt a sharp pain in my shoulder, and although I didn't want to believe I had dislocated the joint, I certainly feared the worst. I had experienced problems during the Five Nations Championship and had not done any weights prior to the Lions tour. I saw Roger Evans, the WRU doctor, before the tour and it was just a matter of getting through these two months and then having an operation when I came back.

I had a bit of treatment on the pitch and carried on. Within a minute or so, I had the chance to pass off my right hand and it felt fine. But then came the moment when I knew I was in serious trouble. The play moved on to the left-hand side and I needed to pass off my other hand. There was nothing there. I think the ball bobbled along the floor and I knew straight away.

Mark Davies, the physio, came on and helped me off. I kept asking Mark if I would be okay for the first Test. I had spent so much time thinking and wondering about the game, yet here I was in real danger of missing my dream opportunity. In my own mind I just couldn't rule myself out of the tour. I suppose my subconscious was saying, 'It'll be okay. Rest for a week and you will be back.'

I was taken to the medical room and James Robson, the Scottish physio, and the South African RFU doctor came in to assess the situation. I couldn't lift my arm so they cut my jersey away. You could see straight away the extent of the problem. James was very diplomatic. He never once said that my tour was over, although we all knew that was the case. The SARFU doctor, however, had no such tact. He just came straight out with it: 'Your tour is over.'

I couldn't believe it. What a dreadful thing to say to a player who is obviously in shock! It angered James and he asked the guy to leave the room. I spent the next five minutes just crying on James's shoulder. The tears I had cried in Weybridge three weeks earlier had been tears of sadness that I was not going to see Ceri for the best part of a month. These were tears of devastation. I don't think there is any better word to describe my feelings at that point. I was in agony and my tour was over. Everything flashed through my head. How do I ring home? What will they think? It was a cruel blow, but that is the way rugby goes.

Thankfully, the side won easily, though it did little to soften the crushing blow. I wanted them to win so badly, yet from that moment I realised that I was just not part of it. The boys were ecstatic when they came in to the dressing-room, having won 42–12. But when they saw me sitting there with my shoulder in a sling, I think they realised the elation they were feeling was in no way as deep as the pain I was suffering.

For me it was an important time. I am not one who chases sympathy, far from it. However, I was feeling very vulnerable at that point and if the boys had carried on celebrating regardless of me, I would have been quite hurt. It was the first time that the real solidarity of this wonderful party had been tested. I need not have worried.

I was the first back to the hotel and Stan Bagshaw, the appropriately named baggage-master, took me up to the room to have a cup of tea. The players came back and from the moment they stepped into the hotel there was a procession outside my door. Ieuan, who knew a thing or two about dislocated shoulders and the subsequent disappointment, was first in and I think he could have wept with me.

I decided to make the phone calls home to cancel everything. The Lions management had not made Sky Sports aware that my tour was over because they didn't want Ceri and my family to hear it on the television before I had had a chance to tell them myself. I thought I would be brave but as soon as I heard Ceri's voice I burst into tears. I suppose I felt more sorry for them than I did for myself. I put the phone down and Ronnie – England hooker Mark Regan – came up to ask if there was anything he could do. He was like a father to me. Anything I wanted was there within a second. It was great to see players like Ronnie and Tim Rodber willing to put their own celebrations on hold to give me some much-needed support.

It was comforting to see the players, although I was a bit anxious about how I would deal with seeing Matt. He knew that his own performances would now be enough to earn him the Test jersey, yet here he was faced with coming in to wave me goodbye. I was not sure how I would feel but when he pushed open the door I realised that he was certainly not revelling in any glory. He gave me the Natal scrum-half Kevin Putt's jersey, socks and shorts from that afternoon and we never spoke about what lay ahead. I had spent ten days with Matt earlier in the tour and we had enjoyed each other's company. He really cared about what had happened and I could see it in his eyes. I wished him all the best and from that moment I just wanted to get out of there and go home.

But there was one last ceremony for me before I made the lonely trek back to Wales. The boys had organised a kangaroo court in one of the rooms at the hotel and in hindsight that was the best way for me to celebrate what was effectively my last supper. I couldn't hide the pain but the boys did their bit to lift my gloom.

They had spent most of the week buying props for the evening and there was plenty of booze flying about. I was on tablets and I had had an injection for the pain, so I couldn't drink. Not that the boys didn't try to persuade me. In the end it was left to James Robson to step in and stop them from holding my nose and pouring a gallon or two down my throat.

I sat on a table at the back and enjoyed a wonderful evening. Keith Wood was judge, Rob Wainwright appeared for the prosecution and then there were the court bailiffs: 'Butch' David Young, 'Randy' Tom Smith and

'Bruce' Simon Shaw. They all dressed up as drag queens; it was a great laugh. Imagine Simon Shaw in a dress! The lad stands at six foot ten inches and is not the prettiest sight in the world. Mind you, there were a few boys who took a bit of a shine to him that night!

I was all ready for a quiet evening when my name was called out. My sentence was first. I couldn't imagine what I had done wrong because my nickname all tour had been Peter Perfect – because, allegedly, I never did anything wrong. Apart from the Jerry blazer incident, that was probably the case.

But then came the charge. Earlier in the tour I had been put in charge of supplying some motivational tapes for the boys and I had delved into my own collection for a few examples. Obviously they had taken a dislike to a few of them and they wanted to punish me by filling my stomach with beer. I couldn't drink because of the tablets, though, so I sat down and tried to enjoy the rest of the night.

The Sunday was an altogether different story. The boys were ready to fly off for the next leg of the tour and I was put on a plane to come home. I was worried about my family and Ceri and her family because of the money they had wasted on booking flights and accommodation. They had taken the decision not to come and I wondered what would happen. Thankfully, Fran knew the tour operators and he had a word with the director and it was all sorted.

As for the rest of my time in South Africa, well, there was a connecting flight to Johannesburg and then a long-haul flight, on my own, back to Heathrow, where I was met by Ceri. The rest is history, but I must say that watching the ensuing Lions games on television was probably the hardest thing I have ever had to do. I was glad they won and delighted for Jenks and Ieuan. But not being there was even more painful than the injury itself.

It had been a miserable few days and I knew that I had a long rehabilitation in front of me. They were difficult times and I will never forget those missed opportunities. I only hope that I get a second chance.

9. THE WORST DAY OF MY LIFE

A Shattering Blow

I am very fortunate to have such a supportive family. Even though we do not always see eye to eye, they have always been there to congratulate me, offer their sympathy or lend an ear.

The injury I suffered in South Africa had been a shattering blow for all of us. It was the worst-case scenario, and although a great deal of hard work and commitment meant a sooner than expected comeback, mentally I was not right for some time. There is no doubt that until I get another chance to play for the Lions there will always be a piece of the jigsaw missing.

Having returned early and undergone surgery, I was obviously keen to get back playing as soon as possible, if only to satisfy myself. The Alex Evans saga at Cardiff had been especially distasteful and the memories of what could and should have been the best summer of my life were bitter, to say the least. Thankfully, the operation was successful and I was soon able to consider a return to action with Cardiff and hopefully, in the longer term, Wales.

Missing the late-August international against Romania at Wrexham in which Pontypridd's Paul John played exceptionally well made me realise that there are times when previous performances count for nothing. The side won at a canter and because of the way they played, Kevin Bowring came under increasing pressure to stick by Paul for the game against Tonga at Swansea. I understood the sentiment but felt that if I played well in the European games for Cardiff, Kevin might go for me. It didn't work out like that. I think Kevin felt obliged to stick with Paul and, to be honest, if I had been in Paul's shoes I would have been pretty aggrieved to find myself back on the bench.

The final confirmation that I was not playing came about two weeks before the game. Kevin rang me and asked if I could drive into Cardiff and meet him in his office at the WRU Directorate in Cyncoed. It was the Monday after Cardiff had beaten Llanelli 24–20 in the quarter-final play-off for the European Cup and I was in a decent mood.

Unfortunately, when I walked into Kevin's room, his face said it all. To be honest, it was only what I expected, although the reality was a bitter pill to swallow. Having known Kevin for some time, I still wasn't convinced that he was sure in his own mind that he was making the right decision. Although he had already told Paul that he was playing, I was sure that he wanted to say, 'Sorry, Rob, I want you to play but . . .'

It was a difficult time for me, as it would have been for anyone in my position. However many caps you have won or however hard you try to understand the reasoning behind such decisions, rejection hurts. I am no different from anybody else when it comes to selection and I was naturally feeling a little vulnerable as Kevin explained why Paul deserved to retain his place and why there was no reason to drop him back to bench duty.

In a strange way I was pleased for Paul because he had spent the previous 18 months sitting on the bench collecting splinters. When you are in such a specialised position as scrum-half or hooker, your chances are clearly limited. It is not like being a wing or centre where you can cover two positions or even three or four if you have a boot and are good under the high ball. Before my injury in South Africa it was quite straightforward: unless I played badly or suffered an injury, Paul was unlikely to start an international.

On this occasion the boot was on the other foot, and I am sure Paul must have looked at me and said, 'Well, how do you like it?' Although we get on really well, there has always been that competitiveness between us, and long may it continue. It's a healthy relationship built on mutual respect, I hope. But at that particular time I was hell bent on regaining my place, regardless of any feelings of respect that we might have shared.

Although I was quite close to Kevin and agreed with the way he had coached the side since taking over, I was desperate to prove him wrong. Perhaps I let it affect me too much, but in my mind Kevin had made the wrong decision. I didn't stamp my feet or change my attitude towards him in any way, but I was so determined to regain my shirt that I am sure Kevin must have noticed a subtle change in my behaviour.

My chance to make that point clear came a week later when Cardiff played Bath in the European Cup quarter-final at the Recreation Ground. While I knew that nothing could alter Kevin's selection, I had built myself up all week realising that a sound performance would obviously get back to him. We didn't play well and lost to a Bath side who went on to win the trophy by beating Brive in Bordeaux later in the season. However, I played really well and was satisfied that by the time the Wales squad next met, Kevin would have been told that I was back and firing on all cylinders.

Whether Kevin was feeling any pangs of guilt, I didn't know, but the build-up to the Tongan game became increasingly difficult for me. It was the first time I had been on the bench since my first cap and I didn't like it.

I was definitely on the outside looking in, just like Paul had been and Andy Moore before him. It was hard to accept, although whenever my chance came to run through the moves, I gave it that extra 10 per cent.

The game itself was played in atrocious conditions at St Helens and for the first 40 minutes we found the Tongans particularly difficult to break down. They lived offside and we lacked ingenuity. As hard as we tried, there was no way through. We were never in any danger of losing the game but never threatened to break free.

With an hour gone, Kevin asked Jonathan Humphreys and me to warm up. The rush was something I will never forget. It was like warming up for my first cap, knowing that I had something to prove. That is what playing for Wales is like for me; that is what being the best is all about. I didn't want to play second fiddle to anyone; I had 20 minutes to prove myself and to make sure that when it came to selection for the New Zealand game a couple of weeks later, Kevin would have no second thoughts about restoring me to the side. In that final quarter, we stepped up a gear and scored three tries. Both Humph and I played our part and I was happy that we had made a significant point.

It was ten days or so before Kevin announced the side to face the All Blacks but, thankfully, when he did, I was back in and Paul was once again relegated to the bench. Just as Kevin had informed me in person of his decision to play Paul against Tonga, he contacted me to say that I was back in for our first game at Wembley. That was a side of Kevin that we all appreciated. He was consistent and honest.

Whether I had shown myself to be a bad loser, I do not know, but there was a real spring in my step as we prepared to meet John Hart's side at our new adopted venue. Construction work on the Millennium Stadium had begun and as a result the national side had been banished to the home of English soccer.

It was nearly 19 months before we returned to our home in Cardiff and, whatever people say, it was a real Achilles' heel for us. Like the rest of the boys, I was very appreciative of the support we attracted to Wembley, especially for the final game against England, but it couldn't mask the reality of the situation. We were playing all of our home games at a neutral venue and it was hugely unfair. It is hard enough to win in the championship at the best of times. However, when you give up home advantage, I think you lose at least four or five points.

To me it spoke volumes about the lack of depth within Welsh sport. With the exception of one stadium, the facilities in Wales are appalling, totally inappropriate and inadequate for international sport. The soccer team has to play at Anfield or in front of just a few thousand at Cardiff City or Wrexham, the rugby league team has been pushed down the M4 to Swansea City, and we had to put up with playing internationals against top-quality opposition at grounds like St Helens or Stradey Park. As club grounds they are adequate but to ask internationals to play Test-match rugby there is a nonsense.

How the supporters kept finding the money to travel to London as well as Paris, Dublin, Treviso and Edinburgh, I don't honestly know. They deserved far more than we gave them during that time, and when we eventually beat England at Wembley in April 1999, our lap of honour was a collective thank you.

Our base before the All Blacks game was a hotel near Slough called Burnham Beeches. It was where the England soccer team had stayed during Euro 96, about an hour's drive from Wembley. For a home game in Cardiff we leave the Copthorne Hotel at about 1 p.m. and arrive at the ground for quarter past. There is no time to get bored or uncomfortable and little time for the nerves to escalate. I wish I could say the same about the journey to Wembley. It's a nightmare at the best of times, but on match day it was like driving through a carnival procession. On those first few occasions the boys became very frustrated with the whole thing and we realised just how much we missed the National Stadium.

So, having spent the past three days locked away in this country retreat with only a pack of cards and a few videos to watch, we were glad to get there and into the dressing-rooms. What happened next was an education. It was a day I will never forget.

The first 20 minutes were the fastest I have ever experienced. They certainly ranked alongside the French game in the 1999 championship in Paris, although on that occasion at least we saw the ball. We were stretched to the limit and had it not been for a few dropped passes in the All Black midfield and a touch of over-elaboration, we could have been 50 points down by half-time. What made it worse was that Scott Gibbs went off after a clash of heads with Frank Bunce and with his departure went one of our main weapons.

By half-time we were 29–0 down and the All Blacks were in total command. It's a long walk from the pitch to the dressing-rooms at Wembley and we couldn't get off quickly enough. However, expecting a bit of a roasting from Kevin, we were pleasantly surprised. He realised that New Zealand had played wonderfully well for those 40 minutes and there had been very little we could do, such was the gulf between the two nations. Kevin just told us that we had nothing to lose and that we should go out in the second half and express ourselves. Whether we had been in awe of the All Blacks in the first half, I am not sure. However, the second half was a different story altogether and although Justin Marshall improved their lead with a try between the posts, we were their equal for much of the second 40 minutes.

That is where Gwyn Jones came into the equation. I spoke earlier in the book about his influence on me as a captain and the lessons I had learned from him during his short reign as captain. Here was lesson number one. As we lined up behind the posts for the conversion of Marshall's try, I said to Gwyn, 'We'd better pull our socks up or we'll find ourselves being blasted in the *Wales on Sunday*.'

Gwyn looked at me and smiled. He called the boys together and told us to look around at the 75,000 people who had paid good money to see us perform. 'We have two choices. Either we give up now and face the most humiliating afternoon of our lives, or we buck up and give them our best shot,' was Gwyn's short response to New Zealand's try.

When Gwyn was injured two weeks later, the boys who had been behind the posts with him at Wembley spoke of that moment with great feeling. Gwyn respected us as his team-mates and we respected him as our captain and inspirational leader. I know plenty of captains whose words would have been lost on that set of players. Not Gwyn's. What's more, those few words did the trick, because Nigel Walker went on to cap a fine individual performance with a try and we finished with a bang. I shook Gwyn's hand at the end and realised how important his contribution had been. Little did we know what tragedy lay in store.

We were obviously disappointed to have lost by such a margin but in a strange way we felt that a barrier had been negotiated in containing the All Blacks in the second half. Our thoughts were soon to be reinforced when John Hart made a personal appearance in our dressing-room to congratulate us on our second-half display. There was sincerity in his voice and at least that helped to cushion the blow. The opposing coach or captain is usually the last person you want to see when you have just finished comfortably second best. However, John is different from most of the coaches I have ever come across. His words meant a lot to us.

I spent the next week, as I usually do in the wake of a Wales defeat, keeping my head below the parapet and avoiding contact with too many people. I suppose I was a bit too sensitive at that time, but I hate post-mortems. However, with such a significant game just two weeks away, Swansea at home in the league, the Cardiff boys were soon back in training and concentrating their attentions on what turned out to be the worst day of my rugby life.

It is always difficult to raise yourself for a club game after an international and it never surprises me when I read in the papers that certain internationals are missing for the next club game. While I am not suggesting that players deliberately pull the wool over anyone's eyes, there are times when you make the most of any slight knock. A Test match can leave you mentally and physically exhausted for some time afterwards, especially if you have just been beaten as heavily as we had by the All Blacks.

Thankfully I was not required until the Swansea game, having been left on the bench for the away game at Newport the following week. We were hugely disappointing that night and it took a last-minute penalty from Lee Jarvis to provide us with a victory we hardly deserved. However, what happened next will live with me, Ceri and every Cardiff player for the rest of our lives.

A Cardiff–Swansea derby invariably produces something special. Reputations go on the line and there is more at stake than a couple of points or one or two places in the league table. It was 13 December and for a change the Arms Park was just about full. Everyone had come to see whether Cardiff could put one over on the All Whites or whether the roles would be reversed.

We went 7–0 down very early on and I suppose from that moment the writing was on the wall. It was not going to be our day. But although Swansea went on to win comfortably, it was a result that not too many people remember. The match was marred by the injury which would ultimately cost Gwyn Jones a career at the highest level.

I remember one of our locks winning a decent line-out around half-way and when the ball found its way into my arms, I took it up and sucked in a few stray Swansea forwards. Stuart Davies tackled me and as I tried to lay the ball back, I was conscious that Gwyn was there to pick up the pieces. Somehow he clawed the ball back and I peeled myself off the floor and supported the attack as we progressed into the Swansea twenty-two.

Referee David Davies blew his whistle for an infringement and suddenly it hit me. Gwyn was nowhere to be seen. He was normally the first on my shoulder to give an encouraging tap or an appreciative 'Well done'. I looked back downfield and saw him lying face down near the half-way line. Doctors Roger Evans, John Fairclough and John Williams and our physiotherapist Jane James were crowding around showing obvious concern.

I was later to learn that not only was it 13 December, but Gwyn's accident had occurred in the 13th minute. Furthermore, Gwyn later admitted that he had followed Leigh Davies, our number 13, on to the field and that his car had been broken into the previous night.

It took until the 20th minute to stabilise his body in preparation to stretcher him from the field and on to hospital. By that time we were all in a state of shock and rugby, Swansea, victory and league points were of no interest to anyone in a blue-and-black jersey. Humph, Gwyn and I had been close friends for a couple of years and at that moment both of us wanted to get off the field. There was no point; there was certainly nothing to play for. At times like that you realise that rugby union, soccer or any sport for that matter is of no consequence. We kept asking the subs to find out what was wrong but the only message that came back to us was that Gwyn had suffered a serious neck injury and was on his way to the Cardiff Royal Infirmary.

It got even worse. About 20 minutes later Garin Jenkins, the Swansea hooker, jumped into the crowd after he had been told by a fan that his father had collapsed. We could see his mother and she was inconsolable. She was just standing there being hugged by Garin as he tried to give his support. Why the game wasn't called to a halt then, I will never know, but somehow it continued and not surprisingly we were hammered. Nobody cared. In fact, some of the Cardiff boys had to ask later that night what the score had been.

After the game the dressing-room was a particularly sombre place, and as we showered and changed in complete silence, the news filtered through that Gwyn had taken a massive blow to his spinal cord and that he was unable to move his arms or legs. They were the words we all feared, the words any player fears when he starts playing the game. Gwyn had seven or eight years of playing top-class rugby ahead of him, yet there he was somewhere in a Cardiff hospital contemplating life in a wheelchair. That may sound cruel to say, but it was reality. I am convinced that the only reason why Gwyn is now back on his feet is because of his unbelievable strength and his ability to tackle situations head on.

Those were my first words to Ceri when I got home that night. We discussed the severity of a compression of the spinal cord and we came to the conclusion that while it was a terrible injury, Gwyn would not give in. He would never admit defeat in what would be an arduous journey over the next few years.

In the early days, I went to see Gwyn at least once or twice a week. Obviously he was inundated with visitors and was not always up to the task of speaking to those who cared so much about his well-being. He lay in the intensive-care ward for what seemed like an eternity before he was finally transferred to his own room where we could spend a little more time talking and reassuring him that everything would be fine.

I am sure that in his quiet moments Gwyn contemplated his future and I know that he would have been very down. But whenever I opened the door to visit, I would be greeted by a smiling face and the inevitable question, 'Any news?' That is typically Gwyn. As a medical student he understood what was happening but he would never allow you to see the pain of suffering; he didn't want anyone to feel sorry for him. The letters that flooded in from all over the world and from every profession were a marvellous support and further confirmation of his standing within the game. He may not have imposed himself on others but he would forever hold a place in their thoughts.

They say there is never a good time to be ill or injured, but Christmas-time has to be the worst. While everyone else was enjoying their turkey and trimmings, Gwyn was being fed a few bits and pieces and trying to keep his spirits up. I made sure I went to see him on Christmas Day to try and share a few jokes with him. I wanted to show him that for us, too, Christmas was far from normal. I think the players wanted to cry, just to show the depth of their feeling, but Gwyn didn't want any of that nonsense. He would probably have buzzed the nurse and asked her to show us the way out.

Eventually I was handed the Wales captaincy and, as I mentioned earlier in the book, that was a difficult time. But it was a difficult time made very easy by Gwyn's attitude; he just told me to get on with it and do the job.

Throughout 1998 Gwyn showed a marked improvement. He was transferred to Rookwood rehabilitation hospital and the constant stream of visitors continued. And, to cap everything, he made an appearance at my wedding in August. He might have been a bit unsteady on his feet and far from fighting fit, but he was there. Gwyn would not have missed that day for anything.

He is now back at home and his battle continues. Life is not the same as it was when he was playing, but he has plenty of friends and is due to go back to his medical studies in the not too distant future. He is even writing newspaper columns and commentating on television. He speaks and writes with the same authority with which he played.

Over the last two years, Gwyn has been through some of the darkest days and it is only through his unparalleled courage that he has arrived at the position he is in today. I am proud to say that he is a friend and that I played under and alongside him, at both club and country level.

But as far as 13 December 1997 is concerned, I will never forget it.

10. A NATIONAL DISASTER

Shooting Ourselves in the Foot

The story of the 1998 Five Nations Championship falls into three separate chapters. First and foremost, there was the humiliation of Twickenham and the lie that I told Kevin Bowring. Secondly, there was the battening down of the hatches and our success in restoring some pride with victories over Scotland and Ireland. Thirdly, there was France, 51 points and the beginning of the end for Kevin as national coach. There is no doubting the fact that the penultimate Five Nations Championship was an emotional roller-coaster ride from start to finish.

Not only did we suffer that record defeat at the hands of England, we also conceded 145 points in four games and in losing to the French at Wembley failed to register a single point for only the sixth time in 42 years of Five Nations rugby. I was distraught. It was a national disaster. And to think that two months earlier I had been celebrating my selection as Wales captain with a victory over the Italians at Stradey Park. How times can change.

Kevin's decision to appoint me as Gwyn's successor meant that this, my second Championship campaign, would be far more important than the first in terms of responsibility. As a player you concentrate on yourself and your role in the side. As a captain you have a responsibility to the entire squad.

Still, I was relishing the trip to Twickenham and the opportunity to play against the guys I had played alongside in the British Lions team the previous summer. Although injury had meant an earlier than planned return, the experience had also convinced me that English rugby was perhaps not as strong as many made out. Yes, they were still a cocky, confident side with big men in key positions. However, the decision by Ian McGeechan and Jim Telfer to ditch the likes of Mark Regan, Graham Rowntree and Jason Leonard for the first Test gave me realistic hope.

In contrast, I felt that we were emerging as a decent side. Players like Barry Williams had matured with the Lions, while Jenks, Gibbsy and Allan Bateman were hailed as three of the best backs in the world when they finally came home after having beaten the Springboks. Furthermore, the performance against Italy was just what the doctor ordered. We had beaten Tonga and played well against New Zealand, yet in almost wasting the chance of securing a rare win bonus we had given ourselves a warning. If we were to have any realistic hope of winning the Five Nations Championship or at least finishing in credit, we would have to become far more consistent.

Whether it suited us to play England first, I am not sure. However, the media were not complaining and they immediately set about increasing the pressure on Kevin, me and the rest of the squad.

As anyone who has ever played in an England–Wales game will tell you, the rivalry and intensity is unparalleled. It certainly doesn't need the players or the pressmen to throw fuel on the fire. Unfortunately, that was exactly what happened in the two weeks leading up to the game. It was also the reason why Lawrence Dallaglio walked past our dressing-room after the match shouting 'You've been dicked!' as loud as he could.

For some unforgivable reason, the players were made far too accessible to the press in those two weeks prior to the match. It was inevitable that in the end somebody would speak out of turn or, even worse, incense the England side by sledging one of their players. After all, when you get thrust in front of the cameras, sometimes twice a day, there is only so much you can say. By the end of the first week, we didn't have anything left to report. But still the press boys pushed and probed for that inflammatory answer.

Unfortunately, it was Barry who opened his mouth at the wrong time and said the wrong thing. I had spent a great deal of time with Barry on the Lions tour and would say that he is almost always considered and thoughtful when he speaks about the game and the various levels of opposition. On this occasion, however, he dropped his guard and paid the ultimate price. The quote about England hooker Richard Cockerill seemed quite innocuous in the greater scheme of things but the English camp reacted angrily to the suggestion that their number one hooker had 'a big mouth'.

It was an isolated incident but the consequences were inevitable. I thought long and hard about how I would have felt and realised that England would be desperate to prove that Richard had something to be big-mouthed about. It was a classic case of shooting yourself in the foot.

We did our best to stay quiet in the final few days before the game and I still felt that we had a decent chance of achieving that first victory at Twickenham since Adrian Hadley scored a couple of tries in the 11–3 success in 1988. On paper, we had 15 players as good as if not better than England, as well as genuine match-winners in Neil Jenkins and Allan

Bateman. Our set-piece had improved and our loose forwards would certainly not be found wanting if England were to take it wide and play us at our own game.

If there was a concern, however, it was about Jenks. Although he had been impeccable at full-back for the Lions, it was clear that he didn't want to play there for Wales. But Kevin was in a difficult position. He saw Jenks and Arwel Thomas as two of his best players and wanted both of them in the side. It was just unfortunate that we had two very good fly-halfs and only one shirt. As Arwel had never played international rugby at full-back, it was Jenks who drew the short straw. If anything, his success with the Lions had cost him his place at fly-half for Wales.

I don't think too many people outside the squad realised how badly Jenks was dealing with the situation. As everyone has seen from the ice-cool way in which he plays the game, nothing much ruffles him. He is not one to show too much emotion. At the time I was closer than anyone to Neil and it was clear that he was keeping a lot inside. We have become very good friends over the years and at that particular time he told me how much he hated seeing Arwel wearing his jersey. It was nothing against Arwel; he just wanted to be there himself.

There was never any question about him dropping out of the side, regardless of what some might have thought or said. Kevin spoke to Neil about the situation on a number of occasions and once again the press made a big thing out of it. That really got to Kevin and I dare say Arwel wasn't best pleased either.

Nothing was going to change Kevin's mind once he had cut his cloth and, anyway, after 26 minutes of the game, that issue and numerous others had been forgotten as we dominated every facet of play and took the lead thanks to a couple of wonderful tries. England were a shambles and we had them exactly where we wanted them.

I remember talking to Paul Grayson, the England fly-half, at the dinner after the game. While he was obviously pleased to have won so handsomely, he did admit that his own shocking performance in those opening 26 minutes might have been the reason behind our eventual downfall. He had missed three or four kickable penalties in the first quarter so when Lawrence asked him to have a go at goal from the ten-metre line, he refused and said, 'I can't do it, my head's gone. Let me kick for touch.' His kick was inch perfect and from the ensuing line-out they drove over. Had he kicked at goal, well, you never know what might have happened.

It was a crucial time to score and a crucial time for us. In the remaining

On holiday at Middleton Towers, Morecambe, with Mum, Dad and sister Karen, when I was seven

RIGHT: Sitting at home with Dad, proudly wearing my Bridgend and District Under-11 shirt

BELOW: Taking time out with my nephew Lloyd Thomas in 1992

Accepting the man-of-the-match trophy from Wilf Wooller after the inaugural East Wales v. West Wales match at the National Stadium in December 1992

(© *The Western Mail and Echo*)

Arch rivals: battling with Robert Jones for Bridgend against
Swansea in March 1993

(© *The Western Mail and Echo*)

Cutting the cake after tying the knot with Ceri on 1 August 1998

Arch rivals: battling with Robert Jones for Bridgend against
Swansea in March 1993
(© *The Western Mail and Echo*)

LEFT: My first big game at the National Stadium. I came on as a replacement for Gary Armstrong in the Barbarians' game against New Zealand in December 1993
(© *The Western Mail and Echo*)

BELOW: Quarter-finals of the Hong Kong Sevens in 1996
(© Huw Evans)

Smile for the camera: members of the Welsh squad having
an afternoon off while on tour in Australia in 1996.
Doc Roger Evans is leading from the front
(© Huw Evans)

Celebrating our Swalec Cup final victory over Swansea in May 1997
(© *The Western Mail and Echo*)

Cutting the cake after tying the knot with Ceri on 1 August 1998

Smile for the camera: members of the Welsh squad having
an afternoon off while on tour in Australia in 1996.
Doc Roger Evans is leading from the front
(© Huw Evans)

Celebrating our Swalec Cup final victory over Swansea in May 1997
(© *The Western Mail and Echo*)

Having a quiet chat with Gregor Townsend before the real
action began on the 1997 British Lions tour to South Africa
(© Colorsport)

My first appearance in a Lions jersey against Eastern Province in 1997
(© Colorsport)

Wales v. Ireland in the 1998 Five Nations Championship. Kevin Morgan
and I help Neil Jenkins celebrate his second-half try

(© Huw Evans)

Cutting the cake after tying the knot with Ceri on 1 August 1998

minutes before half-time, we touched the ball on two or maybe three occasions. In contrast, England had six or seven penalties and scored virtually at will. It was heartbreaking. They absolutely destroyed us.

There were one or two comments flying about as we walked off at half-time, although nothing to compare with after the game. I tried to collect a few thoughts and to remain calm but it was very difficult. Not only were we staring down the barrel of a record defeat by England but I also felt that one or two of the guys had let me down. I looked around the dressing-room for some inspiration and didn't get anything back. I was honestly concerned that certain players had thrown in the towel.

The second half was just as bad, if not worse. We simply fell apart as England ran in try after try. It was total humiliation. I would have given anything to be back at home locked in my room.

Considering what had been said prior to the game, I could understand a few of the passing comments as we trudged off at the final whistle, having lost 60–26. But it did surprise me when Lawrence shouted, 'You've been dicked!' He was right, but it wasn't really Lawrence's style. I suppose it was his retaliation for Barry's comment before the game.

The dressing-room was like a morgue. Kevin, Terry Cobner and Keith Lyons, our analyst, just sat there. We were all stunned; it had been the worst afternoon of our lives. Not wishing to cause any further pain, I called for the players' attention and just said a few words. My theme was that while we would obviously take some time to get over this defeat, we had to make sure it never happened again. I didn't know how I would cope with another defeat of this magnitude. Unfortunately, I didn't have to wait too long to find out.

Still a little angry at the contribution of certain individuals, I asked the boys to look at themselves first before looking elsewhere for the reasons why we had been so bad. Ten minutes after the final whistle is never a good time to make rash comments or to hold a post-mortem, but I did feel as though there were three or four players who had not given me their all. That was disappointing.

There have been times in the past when players have got away with playing badly but the modern game is so technical that only a 15-man performance will suffice. Anything less is tantamount to playing on one leg. For 14 minutes of the first half and for 40 minutes after half-time, we played like a side without any legs. It was shapeless, painful and humiliating. And, what's more, we still had the bloody dinner to come.

I struggled through the press conference and made my way back to the team hotel with the rest of the boys. The bus journey gave me time to think about what lay ahead. All I could think of was the increased responsibility of being captain and how I would face my mother and father, Ceri and the boys back home.

Unfortunately, the weekend went from bad to worse and by the time Monday came I realised that if I was going to continue as captain of Wales, I would have to learn from the mistakes I had just made. I would also have to show greater maturity.

That weekend coincided with Cardiff Rugby Club's annual weekend away. Every year Peter Thomas invites the staff and their partners to spend a weekend in a really plush hotel, all expenses paid. On this occasion, the club went to a hotel in Windsor.

Although Andrew Lewis, Dai Young, Humph and I had not been able to travel up with the Cardiff team, Peter invited all four of us back to the hotel on the Saturday night to have a drink. Ceri and April Young had gone up to Windsor with them on the Friday, so we decided that we would eventually get there late on the Saturday night or early Sunday morning before going back to the hotel in time for the bus leaving in the morning.

I left the dinner in Park Lane having had a good chat with Lawrence and I made my way back to the team hotel. I had said to Ceri before the game that, whatever happened, my duty that weekend was to Kevin and the Welsh team. I couldn't be seen to be leaving early, just to go and have a few beers with my club colleagues. Well, they were my feelings before we conceded 60 points.

Having got back to the hotel, I made up my mind that I just wanted to get out of there. Call me a coward and a deserter, but my head was gone and I didn't want to be there a moment longer. All I could think about was waking up in the team hotel the next morning and having the papers shoved under the door. I packed my bags and got a taxi over to Windsor with the other three lads. The rest of the night was spent drowning our sorrows and discussing the future.

I woke up on Sunday morning with a huge feeling of guilt. I knew I should have stayed at the team hotel and come home on the team bus with the rest of the players and the management team. I had bottled out. I could imagine what the reception would be like back at the Copthorne Hotel. The press would be waiting there like vultures and as captain I would be thrust in front of them, expected to answer the million-dollar questions.

So I took the easy option and decided to go back on the Cardiff team bus, although I spent the entire journey home planning my excuses. When we arrived back in Cardiff, our hooker Paul Young gave me a lift to the Copthorne, where I had left my car on Thursday night. I didn't wait for the Welsh team bus, I just drove home and locked the doors. It was a shocking decision on my part and I half expected to pick up the papers the next morning to read how Wales captain Rob Howley had deserted the side in its hour of need. Fortunately, no one picked up on it – no one except for Kevin, that is.

We pitched up on the Monday at the Copthorne for a chat about the game and Kevin pulled me to one side and made specific reference to my absence on Sunday morning. My respect for Kevin was enormous and, considering what he had just experienced that weekend too, I felt awful about the whole situation. I knew I couldn't tell Kevin that I had gone back to the Cardiff team hotel on the Saturday night while the rest of the Welsh boys were back in London. So I told him a lie. I said that because I had been in such a state after the dinner, I had gone back to the hotel early and had travelled back on the WRU committee bus an hour and a half before the team's departure on Sunday morning.

It was a big mistake, yet I couldn't see another way round it. When I got home that evening, I tried to come to terms with what I had done. But I couldn't escape the facts. I had told my coach a barefaced lie and that was that. I suppose this is a cowardly way of apologising to Kevin, but I have never forgiven myself for what I did. I am sure that Kevin knew the real score all along, although he never said anything to me.

My state of mind was pretty bad at the time and on the Wednesday I made another big mistake. I couldn't contemplate training with Cardiff so I complained of a knee problem and requested a scan. That was granted.

Later in the day Kevin, Terry Cobner, Dave Clark, Trevor James and I had a meeting to discuss the Twickenham débâcle and to look ahead at the games against Scotland and Ireland. It was the first time that I had been asked my views on selection and I must admit to feeling a bit uneasy. Okay, if we had won by 60 points I might have enjoyed it, but all Kevin and Terry wanted to know was who I felt had let me down.

There was no doubt in my mind that a number of players had done so but I found it difficult to come out and name names. In the end I did, but that will forever remain secret. However, I will say that despite a great deal of criticism from other corners, I never once blamed Neil or Martyn Williams, one of the players who was subsequently dropped. If anything, I defended them.

Kevin and Terry said that they wanted to make six or seven changes and although I didn't really agree I let them get on with it. At the end of the meeting, Kevin and Terry put a side down on paper and we then went into another room at Sophia Gardens to meet with the Wales A coaches Lynn Howells and Geraint John and the team manager David Pickering.

With the A team having beaten England at Leicester on the Friday night, there was an obvious temptation to introduce half a dozen members of that side for the game against Scotland at Wembley. I was quite surprised that although Lynn was enthusiastic about his side's performance, the panel felt that there were precious few real candidates for places in the senior side. Chris Anthony was one of the names mentioned, along with Garin Jenkins and Andy Moore. All three had been in the Swansea side that would go on to win the league and it was felt that collectively they might add a bit of steel to the front five.

Then came the bombshell. Lynn, like Kevin and Terry, had pencilled in his side for the Scotland game and at scrum-half was Paul John. I was gobsmacked. I couldn't comprehend that after two games as captain, the Wales A coach was suggesting not only that I should be relieved of the captaincy but also that I should be relegated to the bench. I didn't agree with Lynn but what annoyed me more was the fact that I was actually in the room and part of this discussion. I quickly made my excuses to Kevin, saying that I had another pressing meeting to attend and that I would have to go. I made eye contact with him as I left and he knew exactly why I was leaving. It was certainly not to go to another meeting.

Fortunately, Kevin and Terry felt that I was the right man for the job, and although there were changes made, I kept my place as a player and as captain. The players to be axed were Martyn Williams, Scott Quinnell, Barry Williams, Gareth Llewellyn and Arwel Thomas, while Nigel Walker was ruled out through injury. It turned out that Nigel had played his last game for Wales. Rob Appleyard came in at blindside, with Colin Charvis taking over at number eight from Scott. Kingsley Jones replaced Martyn on the openside. Jenks moved to fly-half, Kevin Morgan came in at full-back, Andy Moore replaced Gareth Llewellyn and Garin Jenkins started at hooker.

The build-up to the Scotland game was quite intense and the message from everyone involved was that we had to win, regardless of method. This was about regaining some respect, not about pretty rugby. I don't think any margin of victory would have made up for the England defeat but it was imperative that we got our season back on course. The press's access to the squad was limited and although the horse had bolted, the players felt a lot more comfortable with the position.

It didn't matter that the game was awful and that we should have lost. We won and that was that. However, had it not been for an injury to Derrick Lee, the Scottish full-back, I think we would have lost. Rowan Shepherd came on for Lee and we immediately played on him. Having been out of the game for so long, he had a bit of a nightmare and we managed to get the upper hand for long enough to scramble a 19–13 victory.

The relief was apparent, although when we sat down to look at the video we cringed at the performance. Now it was up to us to build on that by beating Ireland for the first time since 1994. We would then return to Wembley to play the French with a realistic chance of finishing second in the championship.

In between the Scottish and Irish matches, I went to see Gwyn a few times to ask him what he thought. Gwyn once again hit the nail on the head with his analysis, and as usual I took his thoughts away with me and digested them before I next met up with the squad.

Stuart Davies, the Swansea number eight, had been in outstanding form for the All Whites, and although his previous cap had been way back in 1995, Kevin felt that he could do a job in Dublin. Anyone who has ever played in Ireland or has seen a game at Lansdowne Road will know that it's not a place for the faint-hearted. Stuart was one of the game's hard men and I was very disappointed to see him later forced to retire because of a neck problem. On this occasion, however, Kevin included him as one of the replacements.

It was a typically difficult game but we played our best rugby of the season and once again pulled it out of the fire. One player who was chuffed about that was Doc Stuart Roy. He had been on the bench against Scotland and consequently picked up his win bonus, and then once again in Dublin he was a replacement but didn't play. We had a joke with him that weekend because it must have been the easiest pay-packet he has ever earned. He did actually get on the pitch just after the half-time break, but before the referee blew for the start of the second half Andy Moore was back on the pitch having had a spot of treatment.

Anyway, we won 30–16 thanks to an excellent second-half performance that included a top try from Jenks near the end. Stuart Davies, who had come on as a replacement, gave Jenks the scoring pass and in my mind he had done more than enough to earn a place in the starting line-up for the French game.

The dressing-room was a good place to be that day, as was the post-match dinner. I said a few words and felt that after the calamity of Twickenham we had finally regained some respect. Ireland are one of the most difficult sides to play against in world rugby. What's more, at Lansdowne Road they come at you like a bunch of screaming banshees. Thankfully, we had fought fire with fire that day, and to win in Dublin by 14 points proved that we were not that bad a side. Arriving home from Dublin was certainly a great deal easier than it had been arriving back from Twickenham.

With Kevin unlikely to make too many unenforced changes, the players were anxious to stay fit in the build-up to the French game. I had been suffering with a slight groin injury for most of the championship and was quite keen to have a break. Unfortunately, Cardiff had reached the final of the Challenge Trophy, against Pontypridd at Sardis Road, and Terry Holmes expected us to play. I understood where he was coming from but I am a great believer in players being given time to rest between Test matches.

The Challenge Trophy meant nothing to any of us. There was no place in Europe at the end of it and no great kudos in winning this meaningless piece of silverware that remained unsponsored. I had a strange feeling that someone would get injured, maybe Jenks or Leigh Davies. I never thought it would be me. I had suffered enough misfortune over the previous 12 months so I didn't want to find myself missing out on another opportunity.

The game was about 35 minutes old when I was tackled into touch on the far side of the pitch. As I rolled into touch I slammed into the advertising hoardings and took a whack on the ankle and head. I was more concerned with my head than my ankle, and although neither was anything to worry about, I decided not to train with Wales until the Wednesday before the French game. It was far from perfect but I was glad to give myself that extra 48 hours' break.

Kevin kept most of the side together but we were still without Scott Gibbs, who had missed the Ireland game through injury. Furthermore, by the time the game came around we had lost Allan Bateman too. Allan had been in sparkling form all season but on the Tuesday before the game his daughter had been taken into hospital having lost her sight. She is fine now, thankfully, but at the time Allan was obviously very concerned and in no shape to play rugby at all, let alone in an international. Kevin released him from the party and announced a side with Leigh Davies and Neil Boobyer in the centre.

Losing two players of Scott and Allan's quality was a disaster for us, especially as we had already lost Nigel at the start of the England game.

Kevin must have seen the writing on the wall from that moment. He rated Neil and Leigh very highly but it was a rookie midfield partnership and one that was up against a French side particularly strong in that area.

To their credit, our forwards gave the French pack as hard a game as they had had throughout the championship. They never gave an inch. But behind the scrum we were appalling, as they tore us to pieces and scored virtually at will. It was a dreadful experience to see them rattling up point after point while a big orange zero shone out after our name from the Wembley scoreboard.

We let the forwards down that day. I thought back to the meeting a few weeks earlier when Kevin and Terry had asked me whether I felt that anyone had let me down. On this occasion, I felt that I was one of those letting Kevin and Terry down. Nothing went right: our tackling was poor, our defensive alignment was all to cock and, to be honest, on another day it could have been 70, 80 or even 90 points. That was the gulf between the sides on that occasion and 51–0 was perhaps not what the French deserved on the overall balance of play. Having regained some respect by defeating Scotland and Ireland in successive games, we had suddenly gone backwards at a rate of knots. It was difficult to see where we could go from there and I think that was the final nail in the coffin for Kevin.

I spoke to Thomas Castaignède after the game just as I spoke to Gary Teichmann after the 96–13 defeat in Pretoria later that year. Neither player gloated or took any great satisfaction in seeing us grovel. Welsh rugby is respected around the world and the great players have a special feeling for us. Seeing a Welsh side on its knees was far from satisfying for Thomas and in the end he shook my hand and wished me luck for the future.

On the evidence of this performance, I wondered whether Lynn Howells might have been right. I also wondered whether the inevitable departure of Kevin might also bring with it the eventual disappearance of Rob Howley and one or two others.

11. AU REVOIR KEVIN BOWRING

A Coach Who Paid the Ultimate Price

The humiliations of Twickenham and Wembley had left the guillotine poised precariously over Kevin Bowring's head. In hindsight, I suppose it was the inevitable consequence. However, the players who had been given their chance by Kevin watched his slow and very painful demise with a great deal of regret. There was no doubt that we had let Kevin down against England and France, yet here was the coach copping the flak.

Unfortunately, in sport the facts are not always that important to the executioner. That was very much the case on this occasion. There is no doubt in my mind that Kevin was not solely responsible for the record defeats against England and France – so why were the knives out?

After all, he refused to take the plaudits for the victories over Scotland and Ireland, so why should he shoulder the responsibility for two inept performances by his players? What's more, he wasn't exactly well blessed with good fortune in the build-up to the French game. In my eyes, it was simple: our shameful demise was the result of many years of neglect and the subsequent absence of any real strength at international level. The upshot of having such a mediocre domestic system was that when first-choice players became injured, their replacements were often not up to it. That was certainly the case against France. Neil Boobyer has become a very good player but at the time he was simply not prepared.

Kevin highlighted these problems throughout his final year in charge and wanted the WRU to address the situation sooner rather than later. However, there appeared to be a reluctance to do so and by the time we lost to France it was apparent that Kevin's course had been run. The blade had been sharpened and was poised to fall.

As the dust settled on the championship season, I don't believe the players had the slightest inkling of what the next few weeks would bring. However, there was a definite feeling that the WRU were looking at Kevin's position. From my point of view, I thought it was imperative that the players and the WRU should look at themselves first before taking what seemed to be the easy option.

Sadly, achieving domestic stability takes time, something the WRU felt that it did not have. A British league was never likely to materialise for the coming season, and the improvement in playing strength would only come about when such a competition was up and running or when the national coach was allowed to go outside to hand-pick his own Welsh-qualified players. Kevin wanted to do that but the French farce came at the wrong time.

Within hours of the final whistle at Wembley and with the players keen to forget what had been a public humiliation, I was confronted by a member of the WRU committee. He asked me whether I believed that Kevin had a future as national coach. Great timing, I thought. I wouldn't have answered it anyway, but with my towel still wet in the bag I was unlikely to make any rash comments about the future of a man for whom I had the utmost respect. However, I realised by the tone of the committee-man's voice that Kevin's position must have been discussed and that his time at the crease was all but up.

Kevin was obviously hurting, for himself and his family. For me, that hurt too. I felt that Kevin had been solely responsible for my elevation to the status of international player. Without his continual prompting and words of encouragement, I would not have won a single cap, let alone gone on to captain my country. I would probably still be a member of the bitter and twisted club, living off what might have been rather than what had actually happened.

Kevin put his trust in my ability and enabled me to realise that boyhood ambition of playing for and leading my country. As we sat in the press conference after the French game, I thought he was probably as close to tears as he had ever been in rugby union. He was hurting so much that it pained him just to answer the searching questions from an audience of journalists who probably had the power to force the WRU's hand.

Although we had enjoyed victories over Scotland and Ireland in our two previous games, it was the manner in which we capitulated against the French – and England, for that matter – that would serve as the lasting memory of this appalling penultimate season of Five Nations rugby. Kevin would be judged on those failures, not on the hard-fought victories over the Scots at Wembley and the Irish in Dublin, nor by the distance we had travelled since the shallow performances at the 1995 World Cup.

For me, the agony of sitting at Wembley and being asked the same difficult questions that I had been asked at Twickenham earlier in the season was the last straw. I am sure Kevin felt the same way. If the truth be known, he had been living on borrowed time since the England defeat. He never said as much, but it was obvious.

The press attack after the game at Twickenham had obviously taken its toll but I think what hurt more was the fact that for the first time he had received some really disturbing mail. Once again, the punters were criticising Kevin instead of the players. The letters hurt Kevin because they got to his family. In the end, I believe he finally realised that his family was far more important than rugby union. The way he was treated was appalling.

As a player who spent the best part of three years playing at the highest level for Kevin, I can honestly say that his eventual departure had nothing to do with his quality as a coach or a person. I would counter any suggestion otherwise by claiming to have been in a far better position to make a judgement than some of the jokers who took their pound of flesh in the wake of the French game. I remember reading what a bad coach he was and how Welsh rugby would be better off without him. With Graham Henry having done such a good job, those same critics would now claim to have been right.

Hindsight is a wonderful thing, but if you had asked the players at that time whether a new face would suddenly change the fortunes of the side, the answer would have been 'no'. We were an average side who failed to perform on two separate occasions. It was as simple as that. Kevin was a top coach, a top person and he had principles. In the end, he walked away and maintained his dignity. To Kevin, that mattered more than anything else.

What was disappointing for me, however, was that in the final six months of his reign I felt that he changed as a person. At times, he lost his sense of humour. He found it increasingly difficult to laugh at things. He knew that the knives were out and he struggled to come to terms with that. So did I – after all, we went back a long way.

Kevin and I first ran into each other when he was coaching the Wales Under-20 team. I was at university at the time and Kevin picked me to play for and captain the side against Breconshire Under-23s at Builth Wells. For those who don't know, the distance between the ground and the clubhouse at Builth Wells is about a quarter of a mile, so we decided to complete our warm-up on the bus as we made our way to the pitch. My team-talk was shocking, we went on to lose a poor match and everything I did was a disaster. Kevin could see that I was totally lost and he told me in no uncertain terms that not only had I played badly but I had also not performed as a captain should. He said that if I was going to become an international captain in the future, I had to work on certain areas of my game. Preparation and team-talks were two of them. I can't remember the other 56!

I felt a bit cheesed off because I am sure that any captain faced with those circumstances would have struggled. Coach journeys are for playing cards and having a laugh, not for giving a team-talk before an important representative game. But that was my first real contact with Kevin and it couldn't have been any worse.

I also played for Wales Under-21s under Kevin and then at A level. The early years with him in charge were great because I understood his way of thinking. The way Kevin wanted to play the game was the right way, or so I thought. It is just a pity that others were blind to that when he got to the senior job. While I understand that results count for everything, you must never forget the supporters who pay good money to watch rugby. I know for a fact that many of them enjoyed Kevin's style and approach.

Kevin always kept in touch with my career, even when I found myself out in the cold between January 1994 and the beginning of 1996. He never came rushing up to me asking after my welfare and telling me that one day I would win that elusive cap. However, he did keep in touch with Geoff Davies, one of my coaches at Bridgend. Kevin had assured Geoff that I would eventually go on to make it at the top level with Wales and that if I was patient it would happen sooner rather than later. Geoff would pull me to one side after I had played or trained well and throw that into the conversation. Whether I actually believed him at the time, I can't remember, but in the end Kevin once again proved true to his word.

You can imagine my delight when Kevin finally got the job. Alex Evans and Mike Ruddock had taken Wales to the World Cup after the departure of Alan Davies, but when it came to appointing Welsh rugby's first full-time, paid coach, it was Kevin Bowring who got the vote. Whilst I knew that Kevin would not simply call me up and say, 'Rob, you're in because I like you,' I did think that it was my best chance yet.

I was picked on the bench for Wales A against Fiji shortly before Kevin's appointment, and I remember talking to Allan Lewis, the Llanelli backs coach. It was around the time of my second move from Bridgend and he told me to keep at it because things would work out okay in the end. Whether he knew then what was about to happen, I don't know, but within a month Kevin had been appointed with Allan as his number two.

Straight away, I was named on the bench for the Test against Fiji and it became quite apparent that after the débâcle of the World Cup Kevin and

107

Allan wanted some fresh faces. Kevin was prepared to stick his neck out in a bid to stabilise the national side and hopefully rejuvenate the game at its highest level. Unfortunately, at the end of his reign, I felt that Kevin lost that individuality. Maybe I am wrong in my assumption but I felt that he ended up listening to too many people. I suppose in the end some of those people were responsible for his departure.

I had always hoped that the players would not be responsible for his downfall if he was to go the same way as so many others before him. We didn't need to be told that we would play a part in his future because as players we understood the necessity for us to win and to keep things as they were. However, Terry Cobner didn't think we understood because after the Twickenham affair he told us all that our performances in the coming games would ultimately keep Kevin in or cost him his job.

The players could not believe that Terry could come out with such a statement while Kevin was present in the room. We were desperately trying to get over the defeat by England, yet here was our director of rugby heaping even greater pressure on us by stating that Kevin's future was effectively dependent upon the results of the next three games.

It was like having ten bags of sand thrown on your back. I know Kevin must have been squirming. He didn't want any more pressure put on us, nor did he want us to feel sorry for him. We were in this together and we didn't need to be told that his career was dependent on us. As far as we knew, Kevin had signed a contract until the end of the following year and would therefore take us through to the World Cup. If I had been in Kevin's position, I would have quit there and then. I might have understood Terry telling us in a quiet room and on an individual basis, but that wasn't the case. It was embarrassing if nothing else.

When the news finally came through that Kevin had gone, I was gutted for him. He wrote to all the players individually and that once again proved that his relationship with the players remained intact until the final moment. The respect had been mutual and I hope it still is. He felt for the players. Okay, sometimes we felt that he worked us a bit hard at the wrong times, but you will always get that, especially if one or two lazy players creep into the squad.

Kevin wrote to me to tell me what he felt about me as a player and captain and his words made me feel sad. Having worked so closely with an individual who had paved the way for my entry into international rugby, it was disappointing to see him depart.

When he took on the job, he was certainly no Messiah but his vision was spot-on and I think he did a decent job in putting the national side back on the right track. Kevin sat in front of the technical committee and said that if he was going to continue, changes would have to be made. Deep down, I think he knew that those requirements would not be met.

Kevin wanted a commitment from the WRU to the 1999 World Cup, he wanted an assistant coach and he wanted to contract 25 players for the duration of the 1999 Five Nations. He felt that it was necessary to contract core players up to the 1999 World Cup and to create a more competitive club structure with an Anglo-Welsh league and four regional teams in Europe. Finally, he wanted the resources to support the national-team requirements and to have a proactive and positive public strategy as well as a financial consultant to negotiate player contracts.

Kevin might have been surplus to requirements in the WRU's eyes, yet his vision and foresight made the path much easier for Welsh rugby in the 18 months following his departure. He was a clever man with a great deal to offer Welsh rugby and I think his departure was both unfortunate and unnecessary. I only wish that he still had some part to play.

12. 'ON THE BUS PLEASE, GENTLEMEN'

A Tour Too Far

Touring used to be fun, or so the story goes. It was always regarded as a privilege, an end-of-season opportunity to sample the delights of southern hemisphere hospitality.

However, the game has changed dramatically in recent seasons and the pleasures of travelling around the world are not what they used to be, especially when your season has been as calamitous as it had been for us in the early months of 1998. We had suffered the humiliation of record Five Nations defeats against England and France and the upshot was that our national coach had left the post some 15 months before his contract was officially due to expire.

Surely nothing else could go drastically wrong? Well, it's not that straightforward. Although we could have done with a summer on a beach in the Caribbean, the national team was faced with the unenviable task of a five-match tour to Zimbabwe and South Africa, culminating in a one-off Test against the Springboks in Pretoria. The itinerary was exceptionally challenging and was made all the more difficult by the fact that most of the championship squad had made themselves unavailable, either through injury or through having played too much rugby during the second half of the season at home. By the time we left for Harare, the squad was looking more like an Under-21 party than a senior squad faced with a tour which included games against the Emerging Springboks, Natal and, finally, the world champions.

As people know by now, I have never been one to keep my views to the dressing-room, even if they are likely to land me in hot water. On the contrary, I would much rather be honest with people and tell it as it is. You don't get anywhere in life by cheating and lying to people. Although I am obviously aware that my opinions are not always shared by those in officialdom, I sometimes feel that they are better out than in. That's life, and it doesn't unduly concern me what others say.

In my opinion there are too many players in Wales scared to speak their minds through fear of retribution. They would rather toe the party line and whinge in private than stand up for themselves in a bid to improve the game. If things are going to change then certain senior individuals have to have the courage of their own convictions, on and off the field. And if others don't like it, well, so be it. At that time, I felt that it made no sense whatsoever for us to be embarking on a summer tour of such intensity, so I said as much in an article in the *Wales on Sunday*.

It was no secret that the success of the British Lions tour to South Africa 12 months earlier had come at a considerable cost to Welsh rugby. Players like Scott Gibbs, Ieuan, Neil Jenkins and me suffered with injury, either on the tour or in the ensuing months. By the time the championship season was finished and the domestic season had been wound up with Llanelli beating Ebbw Vale in the Swalec Cup final, we were desperate to have a break. The following season would be the last before the World Cup and players would have to be at their peak to start pushing themselves into contention for places in the squad. There was no benefit to be gained by taking players to South Africa and then finding them washed out by the time the 1999 Five Nations came around. What would that achieve?

I felt that it was the perfect opportunity for the WRU to say to their counterparts in South Africa that, due to an unprecedented injury list, there was no point in going ahead with the tour. Perhaps that was a bit naïve, but by the time Wales had returned home after the humiliation in Pretoria, the South Africans were making the same noises. There had been a great deal of media interest with regard to the English and Scottish tours down under because, due to injury and unavailability, both nations were sending virtual second-string squads on their respective tours to Australia, New Zealand and, in England's case, finally to South Africa.

I aired my views in the article with Paul Rees of the *Wales on Sunday* and as usual there was no shortage of criticism flying in my direction once the paper hit the streets. Instead of agreeing with me and realising that perhaps I knew a bit more than they did, the usual short-sighted critics brought into question my role as captain. If I was blasting the tour so much, how could I go out with the squad, let alone lead them with any vim or vigour? It was a fair point, I suppose, but those who know me will have laughed at such a suggestion. Okay, so I didn't agree with what was going on, but I am not one to turn my back on responsibility.

What would have been the point of me telling the papers a pack of lies about how terrific it was to be travelling to South Africa without most of our first-choice team? Can you imagine how that would have been thrown back in my face? You can see the headlines – 'Howley nonsense'.

Yes, it was still a privilege to represent my country on foreign soil, but I was simply stating a fact. I was trying to safeguard the young players who were about to be exposed to the toughest examination some of them would ever encounter. By the time we conceded our 96th point in Pretoria less than two months later, I believe the same critics understood what I meant. I honestly believe that the tour spelt the beginning of the end for one or two decent players.

But for all my reasoning, and with no shortage of political problems, the tour was eventually given the go-ahead. After that, there was a mad rush to see who would take charge in terms of coaching and to see who was fit enough to crawl on to the plane after such a miserable season.

The former Swansea coach Mike Ruddock's name had been linked with the position of national coach and it looked an odds-on certainty that the man who had left Wales to take over as coaching director in Leinster would get the opportunity to make a quicker than expected return. It was not to be, however, regardless of him allegedly being offered the job on a full-time basis some weeks prior to the tour. Eventually the Pontypridd coach Dennis John was asked to assume the role of caretaker coach, with his Pontypridd assistant Lynn Howells appointed as his right-hand man. I rate both men very highly but I knew they had very different ideas from Kevin. Because of that I immediately raised the question of whether I would get the job of captain.

I said at the time that if Dennis did not feel I was the right man for the job, or if he wanted another member of the party to assume the role, then I would have to abide by his decision and accept it as yet another kick in the teeth. But I also said that, having led the Wales team throughout the previous season, I wanted an opportunity to sit down and discuss the position with him. I wanted to hear his opinion about me as a captain before he made any decisions. Furthermore, I wanted to discuss a mode of attack for what promised to be an arduous trek across Africa.

From the outset it was clear that Dennis was going to do it his way. He had his own ideas and was not about to share the problem that lay ahead. I am sure that some of his selections were based on club form and not what he thought the players could achieve at national level. It was very similar to what Alex Evans had done before the 1995 World Cup. Of course, it's nice to know that when the chips are down you have players you can rely upon. But international rugby is more than that. Unless players were good enough to be out there, no level of honesty would make up for an inadequacy in terms of class. My main concern was that there were certain players who would struggle to transfer their form from the soft grounds and relative mediocrity of the Welsh league to the hard grounds and mental toughness of South African rugby.

The party was named and although I was included in the squad, there was no indication that I would captain the side. It started to get to me. I enjoyed that side of my game and felt I had done a decent job for Kevin, despite one or two dreadful results. But things had changed and I slowly convinced myself that Dennis wanted anyone but Rob Howley as his captain.

I don't know whether he was eventually told to pick me as captain, but when the phone call finally came I was still very sceptical about the whole affair. I felt I was a reluctant choice and that Dennis would have been more comfortable with Paul, his son, as captain. I have the greatest of respect for Paul as a player and he and Helen are very good friends of mine and Ceri's. But I have really felt sorry for him over the past four or five years. It must be very difficult to have your father as coach. I know I wouldn't like it.

Dennis left a message for me to ring him back when I had the time. The message tailed off with Dennis saying, 'It's good news.' I rang him straight away and he congratulated me on being his captain for the tour. But that was it. It was a very short phone call and he didn't expand on anything else. Having struck up such a wonderful player-coach relationship with Kevin, I felt a little ostracised. Time and time again Kevin would call me up to talk about the game and the players in the squad. He always had an open mind and would always bounce things off me. It was a mutual trust. But here I was being shut off from everything. I was told that Garin Jenkins would be my vice-captain and that both of us would sit on the selection panel with Dennis and Lynn. That was as far as it went. Then the fun started.

We were three years into the new era of professionalism and players understood that selection for the Wales squad meant the possibility of a cap and the probability of a decent financial reward. Okay, so the money side of it should be the last consideration, but it's not and it never will be. When it's your living, you have to make sure that things are right.

Unfortunately, the financial package for the players on this tour was paltry, to say the least. We were going to get a flat rate of £1,500 per man, with no match fee. However, there was a bonus of £500 if we beat Zimbabwe, Emerging Springboks, Natal and Border. If we pulled off the unthinkable, a first Welsh victory over the Springboks, we would earn another £1,000.

I felt at the time that it was my duty to defend those players who had actually made themselves available. It was only fair that we were given a decent incentive. It was not that I questioned any one of those players who had made themselves unavailable. Far from it. I agreed that players needed a rest, whether they were injured or not. However, the package that was put together for us was simply not acceptable. A few senior players sat down with Dennis and Lynn and we expressed our views. We then told Dennis Jones, the team manager and a member of the WRU's general committee, our problem and asked him to take our thoughts back to the finance sub-committee along with a request for a better deal.

I wanted to see more of an incentive for the players. There was nothing wrong with the tour fee, but I felt the WRU had to reward the players for success. When you consider that the likes of England would earn at least £12,000 per man for their tour down under, whereas we were likely to earn about £4,000 per man if we were lucky, it was easy to see that this was a derisory offer.

Not surprisingly, decisions like that take time. The committee structure of the WRU means that one sub-committee's proposal must go before another committee before being ratified. We knew that time was certainly not on our side.

The news came back to us that an answer would not be given for at least three weeks. That was when the pressure increased. As captain, I took control and called the squad together after a training session at Glamorgan Wanderers. I said that we had to stick together, otherwise our bid for improved terms would fall on deaf ears. We all agreed that we wanted a better package and that we should go back to the WRU once again to state our position. The real crunch came when we arrived at the Copthorne Hotel in readiness for our departure. We had a squad meeting in the snooker room downstairs and it was decided that unless changes were made we would refuse to get on the bus.

It was a critical time for the squad, and we needed to stick together. Unfortunately, the solidarity was soon weakened when a number of the more inexperienced players decided that it was too risky to take such steps. I have to say that I understood their view. While I wanted the younger players to see how the others felt, I also realised that for them it was all about winning a first cap. In their eyes money should not come into it.

The split was very noticeable and as we went back upstairs to the foyer, Terry Cobner came into the hotel. Andy Moore, Garin Jenkins, Arwel Thomas and I pulled him to one side to air our views once again. Terry was having none of it and told us in no uncertain terms that a decision could not and would not be made before we left for South Africa. He did say that our proposals would be high on the agenda of the next meeting of the general committee and that a fax would be sent to Zimbabwe to outline what changes, if any, had been made. That was the real acid test for the senior players. We knew that once we got on the bus our position would be significantly weakened.

Furthermore, Terry said to us, more as a parting shot than anything else, that unless we got on the bus we were putting our international careers on the line. Trevor James told us to get on board and we did. But everyone was clearly upset. The previous two weeks had been hard enough without us becoming embroiled in this financial problem. Many people would have said 'forget it', but that's easier said than done. I was livid. Our bargaining position had been lost and we knew that once we left Cardiff there was no chance of the WRU making any acceptable offer. We were confident that a fax would eventually arrive, but what would it say?

By the time the fax arrived, we had already played and beaten Zimbabwe and we were nearly two weeks into the tour. The proposals were ludicrous. The fax talked about motivation and about a win bonus of £4,000 per man if we beat South Africa. How generous! I asked myself one question. How likely were we to beat South Africa with a side missing 17 or 18 players? They might just as well have offered us £25,000 for what it was worth. Several players looked at the guarantee of £1,500 for a difficult tour and thought, rightly or wrongly, what's the point? After that, several players went home with injuries and suddenly our task became even harder.

The victory over Zimbabwe was straightforward, but once we arrived in South Africa the real problems began. I remember sitting in a hotel in London with Garin, Dennis and Lynn just before we left, talking about how we should approach the respective legs of the tour. Although I wasn't consulted, my thoughts were quite simple. While it would be nice to get another cap, I felt that the dirt-trackers should play in the capped international against Zimbabwe, leaving the first-choice side to face the Emerging Springboks – our second game on tour and what we, as senior players, regarded as the first real test.

Dennis, however, looked at it in a different way and felt that the first side must play against Zimbabwe. That was what happened. He felt that by selecting a second team for a Test match, he would be handing out cheap caps. I could understand what he was saying at the time because there have been far too many cheap caps and one-cap wonders in the recent past. However, by the end of the tour Dennis had turned full circle. In the final few minutes of the Test defeat by the Springboks, he gave all his replacements a cap. It was probably done as a thank you, but I didn't agree with his change of heart. I know some players felt that such a decision did nothing but devalue the cap.

So, having beaten Zimbabwe 49–11 with a first team, we moved on to face the Emerging Springboks. It was another calamity from start to finish. The preparation for the game was ridiculous and put us all on edge. We spent three hours on the coach in the early morning and a further four hours sitting around in a hotel before we left for the ground.

It was certainly not an ideal way to prepare players for a game of this importance. Dennis and Lynn were far from happy about the cramped conditions on the bus and just as disenchanted with another three-hour journey back to the hotel after the game. We arrived at about one in the morning and were told we had to pack our bags so we could be up in the morning for a seven o'clock departure.

That is the worst part of touring. If everything is not right off the field it can affect what happens on it. I think we got it wrong on this occasion. The arrangements have to be spot on and they were not. The transportation was poor and the venues for one or two of the games were inadequate.

Thankfully, we did have a few boys on tour who kept our chins up. Garin is a top tourist and he and Kingsley Jones were worth their weight in gold. Sadly, they could do nothing to help us against the Emerging Springboks and we lost.

The concerns I had had before the tour were all coming home to roost. Throughout the Five Nations Championship there had been players to take the lead and others who required a shoulder to lean on. Take Arwel Thomas, for example. I think he found it difficult to take the responsibility at international level. In previous games for Wales he had enjoyed the support of senior players like Scott Gibbs and Allan Bateman. They would ease the burden. But here he was having to take the lead and I am sure that is why Arwel struggled to perform. We all know what great talent he has, but this was particularly tough and I really felt for him. It was not doing his long-term chances any good. However, to his credit he put his head on the line.

In contrast, Arwel's contribution off the field was wonderful. Players like Arwel and Garin are invaluable when you are away from home. I remember after one game a few of the boys went out for a drink. While there is nothing wrong with that, it is always sensible to keep your wits about you. On this particular occasion, the Swansea trio of Darren Morris, Andy

Moore and Arwel missed the bus to the airport the following morning and had to take a taxi. They just made the flight but it didn't go down well. It made us smile but I think all three were fined for their moment of madness.

We moved on to play Border believing we had a chance to get a win under our belts. How wrong we were. We left all our good intentions in the dressing-room and were, to be honest, bloody awful.

The game had given a lot of fringe players a golden chance to stake their claim for a place in the Test team. Most of them blew it there and then. I don't know why, but it was a totally inept performance and once again we were beaten. Although I didn't play, I felt a certain responsibility for the result, and after going through the motions of the after-match function, I went back to the hotel and went to bed. After a while I was thirsty and slipped downstairs to get a drink. Dennis and Lynn were sitting in the hotel foyer having a beer and for the first time on tour I think they realised the magnitude of what lay ahead in the shape of Natal and then South Africa. The training sessions were going very well and both coaches were showing just how good they were in that area. But the players were letting them down by failing to transfer that competence on to the field.

From the moment I sat down for a chat, I felt there was a definite change in Dennis. For the first time, he wanted to share his problems and bring me on board to discuss the difficulties. It was very different from early on in the tour. Suddenly my views counted for something. I was glad about that because having seen what Kevin had gone through on his own in those final few weeks, I didn't want to see another coach suffer in the same way. Two heads are better than one. On this occasion it was three, because Lynn's input was considerable.

The side was picked for the game against Natal and it didn't take a rocket scientist to see that it was the backbone of the side that would subsequently play against South Africa. Unfortunately for me, it was yet another nightmare. After an inauspicious start we played really well and actually came close to winning. For the first time on tour we had successfully taken our training-ground drills on to the playing field. That was pleasing.

Sadly, I had nothing to smile about. I tore my hamstring and that, once again, was the end of my tour. I had medical attention for the next 48 hours but I could not have played against South Africa at anything more than 60 or 70 per cent. Dr Roger Evans pulled me out of the side and I was once again left with nothing more than a stand ticket and plenty of thoughts of what might have been.

It turned out to be every bit as bad sitting in the stand as it would have been if I had played. We were completely outgunned and outclassed, and the fact that South Africa failed to reach three figures was a miracle. Terry Cobner actually missed the game because he was at the airport awaiting a flight to Australia to meet Ian McIntosh, the Natal coach, and Graham Henry with regard to the vacant job of Wales coach. He was in the best place, because the crowd ribbed us and humiliated us as we conceded try after try after try.

I remember seeing Jonathan Davies as I took my place alongside the non-playing members of the squad. I said to him, 'What do you think?' He said, 'I think we will be lucky to keep it down to 70.' I just laughed and said, 'Don't be soft.' I thought we would be competitive for 60 minutes before finding the last 20 minutes too much. That would give South Africa victory, but not by a huge margin. Both of us were wrong, although JD was closer than me.

It was humiliating from start to finish. Dennis had told the players to go out and play rugby against them. We tried and we paid the price. I am not saying we should have kept the ball tight or played too negatively, but we knew we couldn't compete with them by throwing the ball around.

The worst memory for me came about three minutes from the end. There were 40,000 South Africans around me shouting for 100 points and they were really taking the mickey out of us. They were loving every minute of it. It would have happened, too, but for a dropped pass by Naka Drotské, the Springbok forward.

The players were shell-shocked by the score, 96–13, the worst in Welsh rugby history. It took me back to what I had said in the press a couple of weeks before we left. We should never have gone, yet here we were having thrown inadequate players into the lions' den. When those same players walked back into the dressing-room, I looked around at their faces and wondered whether some of them would ever surface again. It was a shocking experience and I wasn't sure how much damage had been done.

The final memory of that tour was speaking to the Springboks captain Gary Teichmann at the buffet dinner after the game. He is a great guy and said how sorry he felt for some of our younger players.

As I turned to leave, I said, 'See you in November. It'll be a different story then!' I didn't really believe in what I was saying but I just hoped that I would never witness anything like that again.

13. AN INTERNATIONAL ARRIVAL

Henry Wings in from Down Under

The nightmare of our much-publicised tour to South Africa was over and Ceri and I were married and on our honeymoon in California. The wedding had been a great day, and to see Gwyn on his feet and helping the day go so well was the icing on the cake. Of course, there was a long road ahead for him, but once we had arrived in Los Angeles and settled into the hotel, Ceri and I toasted our marriage and the fact that one of our very close friends had been there to enjoy the day with us.

Back home, however, it was business as usual for Welsh rugby. Following Kevin's departure and the subsequent appointment of Dennis John as caretaker coach for the ill-fated tour to South Africa, the WRU had finally come to realise the importance of Kevin's successor. If we were to make any headway in the 12 or 13 months before the World Cup then they had to make a significant appointment. Furthermore, they had to make it fast.

Being captain, and having got on so well with Kevin, I was understandably concerned. I was scared that a wrong move by the WRU followed by a bad appointment could bring an end to my career. What's more, I was afraid that it could cost Wales any chance of achieving respectability during the World Cup. After the experiences of the previous 12 months, that would have been the final straw.

Although it cost me a few quid in phone calls, I kept in touch with Dai Young, who was back home monitoring the papers and listening to the radio whenever he could. We both had a view on who should get the job, although neither of us was ever asked our opinion despite the fact that we were two of the more senior players in the squad. Whether that was right or wrong, I still don't know. I suppose the WRU felt the selection of Kevin's successor had nothing to do with the players. Maybe they were right. After all, there are not too many employees who get to choose their own boss!

Having said that, we all cared very much, and considering our recent record, it was obviously imperative that the right choice was made. At the time, I felt that it was the most critical decision the WRU would ever make.

It would be a crucial 18 months in the long-term future of Welsh rugby and another wrong move could be catastrophic.

My only concern for the new man, whoever that might be, was that in offering the position the WRU might not reveal the extent of the problem. You couldn't blame them for adopting such an approach, because after the calamities of Twickenham, Wembley and Pretoria the job must have been as appealing as a night out with the mother-in-law. (Not mine, I hasten to add!)

In the last months of his reign, Kevin felt that there was a serious problem with the domestic game in Wales and that unless the situation was addressed Welsh rugby would find itself flogging a dead horse. In the short time between Kevin's departure and the appointment of Graham Henry, nothing much had changed, if anything at all. I constantly asked myself why anyone would want to take on the poisoned chalice.

The senior players had discussed this during the summer months and we didn't want our new man to be led up a blind alley. He had to know the full story, otherwise it would be a pointless exercise. Glanmor Griffiths said that the WRU would scour the world looking for the best available coach. My opinion at the time was, 'Why bother?' After all, what do they say about silk purses and sows' ears?

Not through any real fault of our own, the structure of the game in Wales had, for some considerable time, left a great deal to be desired. The recent results on the Test stage and the fact that Cardiff and Swansea were about to jump ship to play in a series of friendly games against English opposition merely compounded a very deep-seated problem. For those on the inside, it was a dreadful position. It was almost certainly the reason why not one Welsh-based coach threw his hat into the ring. They had seen it all before and I know for a fact that certain coaches looked at the position, looked at Kevin's demise and immediately set off in the opposite direction.

In the end, it was felt that a new face, probably a southern hemisphere coach, would be the best bet. It made sense; an outside influence was what we needed. He would come in with fresh ideas, without prejudice and with a definite idea of how to produce that silk purse. I felt that a Mike Ruddock or a Gareth Jenkins would struggle to cut through the red tape. They knew too much and I think Mike was glad when he finally turned his back on Wales to concentrate on the job he was doing with Leinster. A new start was needed, and although I had a lot of time for Mike, he would not have been the right choice.

In the months between Kevin's departure and Graham's arrival, I remember reading an interview with our rugby director, Terry Cobner. Terry has always spoken his mind and I have a great deal of respect for people who do that. He said in no uncertain terms that while all was not lost, this appointment was possibly Welsh rugby's last real chance to find a solution to more than a decade of underachievement. He was probably right, although I never thought that one man could achieve that on his own in the current climate.

By the time Dai next called me, Ceri and I were into the second week of our honeymoon and were having a great time. I didn't realise how desperate I was to know what was going on back in Wales. However, when Dai called on the Wednesday of that second week, I kept him on the phone for about 20 minutes. Although his information was based on what he had read in *The Western Mail* and the *South Wales Echo*, it was clear that a New Zealander by the name of Graham Henry and the Natal coach Ian McIntosh were the front-runners for the job. *The Western Mail* even suggested that if Henry won the battle, the WRU would have to splash out in excess of £1 million over five years just to land him. Yes, it would be a great catch, but £1 million over five years is a considerable sum.

Ceri and I found ourselves talking about it over the odd glass of wine on the remaining evenings of the honeymoon and by the end of that week Dai had rung again to say that Graham had been appointed.

In a strange way, I was glad to learn that his appointment brought with it such a large annual salary. Although it was almost certainly close to being five times what Kevin had been earning, which was obviously a bit unfair, I felt that in offering that kind of money the WRU were making a bold statement. If they were going to pay that much to one person, he would be expected to perform a miracle. And if he was to perform this miracle, he would need a free hand.

To a certain extent, Graham has enjoyed that freedom in the 16 months since his arrival, although at times the red tape has threatened to hamper his development of the national side. Thankfully, he is a strong person who speaks his mind. He has a unique ability to find a way around things, and long may it continue.

Dai's final call came a couple of days before we returned home and in the same telephone conversation he told me that Graham had already organised a trial match which would involve around 40 players. That was when I started to panic. Not only had I missed the Test against the Springboks in Pretoria with a hamstring injury but here I was sunning myself on the west coast of the United States, celebrating my marriage with a few glasses of

Californian red and plenty of junk food. I had done very little in the way of preparation for the new season, let alone for a trial match in front of my new boss!

My parents had been checking my mail while I was away and when I phoned to ask if there was anything official, they told me about a letter from the WRU. The players had been given a date on which to report to the Copthorne Hotel and, unfortunately, that date coincided with my last day in California. I was really annoyed. I had informed the Union of my departure and return flight dates, yet they seemed to have ignored that information and sent out the letter regardless. I thought that I might have had a personal copy highlighting the situation and requesting my early return.

Once again, there seemed to have been a breakdown in communication, and when we finally arrived back in London, my mobile phone was overflowing with messages from Trevor James. The final message said that Graham wanted to meet me in person at the hotel before embarking on the trial weekend. It was a dreadful journey back from Heathrow; I couldn't think of anything else but how I might have blotted my copybook. It had been hard enough convincing people that I was good enough to play for Wales in the first place. Now I was faced with the possibility of losing that coveted jersey and the captaincy.

On my return the jet-lag set in and I asked to postpone the meeting for a day or so, which Trevor kindly sorted out. It has to be said that Trevor is a really popular guy with all the lads. He is always there and is invariably prepared to fight your corner. Graham and I finally met at the Copthorne Hotel on the eve of the first trial game. I don't mind admitting that I was quite apprehensive, although I need not have been because Graham was the same on that first day as he is now. He is very easy to get along with, providing you play it straight with him, and I feel very comfortable in his company. However, at the time I knew nothing about him other than his name and pedigree.

My first impression was that Graham knew exactly what he wanted from the job. First and foremost, he wanted to be the master of his own destiny and to change the image of and attitudes within the Welsh game. He was keen to overcome the parochial behaviour that has so often hampered Welsh rugby and to make sure that Welsh rugby improved its own environment. It was obvious that he had done his homework, although at that time I am not sure whether he understood the depth of parochialism that exists. He certainly didn't realise there was so much red tape. In fact, I don't think he realised that until about seven months down the line.

I explained the Cardiff–Swansea situation as best I could and how the players had felt after suffering the biggest hiding in Welsh rugby history. I told Graham that I felt professional rugby was exposing the shallow foundations of the Welsh game and that Kevin's demands had been justified. I don't mind admitting that I thought Graham was crazy to have turned his back on the most successful non-international side of all time in a bid to help Welsh rugby salvage something from yet another year of discontent. Obviously, the salary package was attractive, but apart from that, Welsh rugby had nothing else going for it. It just shows how wrong you can be!

We moved outside and sat on one of the benches at the back of the hotel where I had spent many an hour with players, talking tactics and families and generally putting the world to rights. This conversation, however, was very different. With respect to Graham, it felt like a job interview.

We spent the next couple of hours talking and he left no stone unturned. He wanted to know every precise detail about players, coaches, administrators and who I thought were the best men for the job. At no stage did I honestly believe that my opinions would have any real bearing on Graham's selection, but it was comforting to know that he felt he could confide in me. It was a welcome change from Dennis John, who had shut me out in the weeks leading up to our arrival in South Africa. I am sure that Graham was trying to find out what kind of person I was and whether I had the balls to tell the truth.

I suppose that the early relationship between the two of us was formed after about 20 minutes when Graham took me completely by surprise. While there had never been any question of Kevin dropping me as captain, regardless of results, I was obviously concerned that a new broom might sweep all before him. It took a few moments to sink in but I was very grateful for what was effectively a massive vote of confidence. He told me that I would be his captain. I felt that it was a brave move on Graham's part but a very shrewd one. We had only been introduced about 20 minutes earlier, yet here was the new national coach telling me that I was his first and hopefully his last choice as captain. Graham had won me over and from that moment on I don't think we have had a cross word.

It was a very different feeling from three months earlier when Dennis had taken over. Instead of 20 minutes, it took Dennis about three weeks to tell me that I would lead the squad in South Africa. I have to admit that I resented that. If the coach had to delay such an important announcement for so long, perhaps he might have been better off appointing somebody else.

However, the topic of conversation between Graham and me changed quickly from me as captain to whom I rated as backs and forwards coaches and who I believed would do a decent job as a possible assistant coach. From what he said, I knew straight away that he wanted an assistant coach and a very high-profile team manager. He also made it clear that there would be a selection panel, probably comprising himself, his assistant and one other. It was important for me to discard my blinkers and not just think about who would be the best for Rob Howley. It is always the temptation but that would have been a wrong move. I had to think hard about what was best for the team.

There is no doubt that Graham is a players' man and he proved as much throughout those initial games against South Africa, Argentina and in the Five Nations Championship. He spoke about his rugby relationship with Zinzan Brooke and how he had developed a rapport with the senior players at Auckland. That would be his way of reducing the pressure. He wanted others to take responsibility so as not to expose me to the prying eyes of the media on a daily basis. It was in stark contrast to Kevin, who had been keen to channel every playing matter through his captain.

Under Kevin, I would call the back-row moves, the line-outs and every-thing else involved with the game, on and off the field. But Graham told me early on that he saw players like Scott Quinnell, Colin Charvis and Scott Gibbs as having a significant input.

It can work both ways, although at the time I must admit to being a little sceptical. I didn't have a problem with any of the players Graham mentioned but, as any captain will tell you, making decisions is part and parcel of captaincy. Whether he was exposing a bit of insecurity in me, I am not sure, but I never let on that I was concerned about his views. I was worried that while he wanted me to be captain, he might be grooming someone else just in case.

I think my fears were allayed by the fact that he was obviously a loyal person. That was quite comforting, especially later in the season when the pressure came to land on my shoulders. I will talk about that later in the book. Loyalty counts for a great deal in sport and I know that the other players involved with Graham have seen that loyalty too. One or two, and perhaps Matthew Robinson would make a good example, might think otherwise, but generally he has given people a chance and stuck by them. What he did was to identify very quickly a pool of players who would take Wales into the World Cup and he had no intention of ditching too many of them along the way.

I agreed with that logic. Graham realised that there was very little strength in depth within Wales and that too much chopping and changing would be counterproductive in the long term. His favourite phrase was that in certain positions 'the cupboard was bare'. So why not identify 35 players at the outset and make sure you work on them in the months up to a major tournament?

Under previous coaches, players had often found themselves out on their backsides if they underperformed in any one international. But with so few players to select from, you often found that the same player would surface a couple of years later. It's the same kind of thing that is happening with the England cricket team. I think Graham Hick has had seven careers with the Test team, yet he is probably no different from how he was when he first played. I am not saying that with Graham Henry there is any less of an incentive to work hard or that it becomes harder to get out of the team than it is to get in. However, it was understood that a bad game did not spell an end to your international career. There is a subtle difference.

To bolster the squad, Graham also identified one or two 'adopted' Welshmen along the way, but nobody minded that. It increased the pressure for places but didn't overly concern the players. I think we were glad to have an input from the likes of Shane Howarth and Peter Rogers.

The other major change in policy that Graham introduced was with regard to the younger players. He is a great believer in allowing Under-21 players to develop within their own age group and enjoy that stage of their development. If you look back over the last decade in Wales, that has certainly not been the case before. Neil Jenkins, Scott Gibbs and Leigh Davies were all thrown in at the deep end and it could be said that they missed out on a crucial part of their career.

I found myself agreeing with Graham's every suggestion and that suggested to me, not normally a 'yes' man, that we were on the same wavelength. His knowledge is second to none and when you consider that his success rate with Auckland was something like 85 per cent, it was no wonder that the boys quickly warmed to him. The public did too. I just wondered at that juncture whether he appreciated the enormity of the challenge in front of him. Then again, perhaps that was what drove him on.

Thankfully, and considering I had not trained for the best part of a month, Graham gave me the option of playing in or sitting out of the trial games. I chose not to play, although I was conscious that it was not the best start. However, Graham was very up front about things and said that if I was not sure then I should not play. There was never any pressure. I cast my mind back to the British Lions and how Ian McGeechan had reacted when I informed him of my knee problem. I had a feeling of *déjà vu*. Geech had put the ball in my court and Graham was doing the same.

Like other players, I do get a bit concerned about missing trial games and practice sessions, but I knew that on this occasion I could not do myself justice. There was no point me playing and underperforming, although I am sure that there are several coaches who might have forced my hand.

The trial was actually quite amusing in many ways because while the players were dead keen to make an impression on Graham, the coaches and team managers were also vying for position. It was apparent by then that Graham wanted an assistant and a third selector. The trial games at Pontypridd and then Bridgend were to be used to select a team manager, so I suppose everyone was on trial. Because I was not playing, I could watch the various candidates running around throwing their respective hats into the ring.

Graham had already asked me my opinion on the various individuals in the frame and I must admit that the one name I put forward was Allan Lewis, who was on his way back from Moseley to take over as coaching director at Newport. I am a great admirer of Allan and always have been. He was around at the time when I won my first cap and when I came out of school he was keen to take me to Llanelli, where he was the backs coach. I admired the way that he wanted to play the game and I felt that it was about time Wales appointed a backs coach of substance. The least I wanted was for Allan to have some input, whether it be as a coach, adviser or just a selector.

That was the one thing we never had under Kevin – stability in terms of coaching the back division. In his two-and-a-half-year reign, Kevin must have had four or five people coaching the backs. We had John Schroeffer, John Bevan and then Geraint John as actual backs coaches, while the likes of Clive Griffiths, the Wales rugby league coach, worked with us on a temporary basis after the humiliating defeat at Twickenham in 1998.

I believe that the instability in that area was highlighted in the last game of that championship season when we lost 51–0 to France at Wembley. Our front row was of no concern, our line-out was productive, yet our back play was awful, both in attack and in defence. In my mind, there was no doubt that our failure was the end result of three years of not having a full-time backs coach.

I am not being disrespectful to any one of those aforementioned coaches, because they all had their own skills and attributes. However, their appointments were all made with the short term in mind. As a squad, we were never able to build up any long-term relationship and I have always thought that to be a vital part of any successful side. You need to work with people for long periods of time before you understand how they think.

John Schroeffer was a WRU development officer and a very technical coach. He was also a really top bloke but I think he spent too much time talking rather than actually performing the moves. Geraint's problem was that it all came too early for him. He was still learning his trade when he took over as Welsh backs coach, and while I believe he will eventually be one of the top coaches in Britain, I felt that he lacked the experience to be in charge at the highest level. As for John Bevan, well, I think his contribution was summed up by the performance against England. We lost heavily and the way we defended behind and implemented our system was abominable. I think that John regrets the way we defended and after that he played very little part.

So while Graham, as backs coach, would obviously play a major role in that area as Kevin did with the forwards, he was keen to avoid making a similar mistake in terms of appointing a forwards coach. He wanted a reliable individual who would complement his own inimitable style of play.

Lynn Howells was the obvious candidate and I said as much to Graham over the weekend. The South Africa tour had been the first time I had got to know Lynn and it certainly helped. My only reservation about him was that some people felt he had a chip on his shoulder about Cardiff and Cardiff players. That is another inherent problem with the Welsh game. Swansea hate Llanelli, Newport despise Cardiff, Neath and Aberavon fail to see eye to eye, and Pontypridd would do anything to put one over on us. Lynn was the assistant coach to Dennis John at Ponty, and although I get on famously with him now, I did have a few worries when he was first appointed. Having said that, Lynn was the obvious choice; I suppose it is quite ironic that he has since left Ponty to coach Cardiff. It was clear that Gareth Jenkins did not want the position and that Mike Ruddock, who was the only other name to be mentioned, was never going to accept second best after being so close to landing the main job earlier in the year.

It wasn't until a few of the Swansea boys starting talking that we realised just how close Mike had been to getting Kevin's job on a permanent basis. I had mixed feelings about it because Mike is a very sound coach and a very popular bloke. I am sure Mike felt pretty mixed up too. According to the Swansea lads, he had been offered the job and then told he couldn't have it.

It was very harsh and I would fully understand it if he never accepted a job with Wales again. You can't treat people like that.

The final pieces of the jigsaw were eventually put in place when David Pickering was made team manager and Allan was named as a selector. It was the perfect team to placate the doubting Thomases. There was a New Zealand coach, a Pontypridd assistant and a Newport coach from Llanelli. There was no reason for east to criticise west on this occasion and certainly no reason to claim bias.

Once the trial was out of the way, Graham named his squad for South Africa and we were all very excited. I was fit again after having missed the Commonwealth Games in a bid to regain fitness, and although the Springboks were a formidable side, it was clear that Graham had injected new life into the Welsh game.

His views were very strong and he was extremely forthright in what he did and said in those weeks leading up to the game at Wembley. That was another difference between Graham and Kevin; I think Kevin listened to too many people at the end of his reign. That is not a criticism, because by that time it was clear that the knives were out. He had been just like Graham at the start of his career with Wales, and I suppose only time will tell whether Graham is pushed down the same road.

The strength of Graham's character was confirmed when he and David Pickering chose to ignore the stance taken by other WRU men in staying clear of the rebel games involving Cardiff and Swansea. As players, we were very anxious to see Graham at our games and it was a great relief that he did his own thing at that very delicate stage. I think it sent a message to the public that Graham did not intend to have his strings pulled by anyone. He had been given a job to do and he was not ready to allow anyone to stand in the way of that.

Gradually, the players who had underperformed during the previous season were starting to rediscover their desire for the challenge and I think that was evident in the time leading up to the Springboks game and during the match itself. We had copped a lot of flak for our performances against England, France and South Africa away and nobody gave us a chance against the 'Boks again. But Graham and Steve Black, whom Graham had taken from Newcastle to assist with our mental and physical preparation, insisted that we had nothing to fear. We were all a bit sceptical but in the end they were right.

Blackie, like Graham, has been like a breath of fresh air and his contribution has been immense. We work hard but we enjoy our sessions too.

Leading Wales out at Wembley before the Ireland game in March 1999.
Shane Howarth is the one on my right!

(© Les Loosemore)

On a Reebok photo shoot at stables in
Buenos Aires while on tour to Argentina
(© Fotosport)

Leading Wales out at Wembley before the Ireland game in March 1999. Shane Howarth is the one on my right!

(© Les Loosemore)

Leading Wales out for the second half against
Ireland in 1999. We were trailing 26–9

(© Les Loosemore)

Scott Gibbs goes over for the try which broke English
hearts at Wembley on 11 April 1999

(© Les Loosemore)

The Wembley scoreboard tells the whole story
(© Les Loosemore)

Rebels with a cause: Cardiff v. Wasps at Cardiff in January 1999
(© Les Loosemore)

Down and definitely out: Cardiff v. Llanelli, Swalec Cup semi-final, 1999
(© Les Loosemore)

Celebrating with Neil Boobyer after winning the first Test
against Argentina in Buenos Aires

(© Huw Evans)

On a Reebok photo shoot at stables in
Buenos Aires while on tour to Argentina
(© Fotosport)

The final whistle is blown and at last we have beaten South Africa
(© Les Loosemore)

Giving the Millennium Stadium crowd the victory salute
after beating the Springboks in June 1999
(© Sacha Miller, *Wales News*)

Getting the ball away from a ruck during the victory over South Africa
(© Dave Hollins, *Wales News*)

Ceri and me with Megan when she was just a week old
(© *The Western Mail and Echo*)

Graham leaves him to his own devices and walks away shaking his head. I don't think he can believe what he sees. What Blackie does is unique. I have never seen anything like it, but it works a treat and I know that Graham believes he is one of the major reasons for the upturn in Welsh rugby's international fortunes.

As for Graham, his work was in stark contrast to Kevin's. Under Kevin, we would meet every Wednesday afternoon and train together as a squad. Well, at least we did until the clubs kicked up such a fuss that we had to stop. Under Graham, we met on very few occasions, and before the South Africa game we only trained once on grass. It was an amazing transformation and obviously we all started asking questions. At the time, I felt that we were not doing enough, and although I didn't want to question Graham before his first game, it was spoken about by some of the senior players. The answer, however, came in the shape of our performance. It was exceptional. In fact, had it not been for a few moments of indiscipline, we would have won.

That game was the first step for us as a squad, and although the public were still smarting from the trials and tribulations of the summer tour, I think they too believed that something might be about to happen. It was also a game that provided my first real insight into Graham as a coach. If I had ever doubted his ability to turn this hopeless situation around, then I need worry no longer.

He also showed me that the smiling face can give way to a more serious side. At half-time, I was up on my feet ranting and raging about our defence and how certain moments had cost us 14 points in about four minutes. We had led 14–0 early on following a Gareth Thomas try and three penalties from Jenks. Then we had made two errors and they scored two tries. I was standing there reading the riot act to my team-mates when Graham walked in with David Pickering. He looked at me, told me to shut up and said that I would be better off sitting down and having a drink. He had made his point and I knew from that moment that Graham Henry was the boss.

I didn't make the same mistake again. As for Graham, well, the next twelve months will go down in Welsh rugby history. Graham Henry was here and Welsh rugby was slowly but surely finding its feet.

14. REBELS WITH A CAUSE

Playing in Exile without Permission

The summer of 1998 will go down on record as one of the most turbulent in Welsh rugby history. The national team was humiliated in South Africa, the national coach had departed and the WRU was at loggerheads with two of its biggest and most influential clubs, Cardiff and Swansea.

I have already spoken of my thoughts about Kevin Bowring and how badly I felt about being beaten so heavily on a tour that should never have gone ahead. However, it was the issue of the rebel clubs and the WRU that left the players wondering exactly what, if anything at all, lay in store for Welsh rugby.

The battle between Cardiff and the WRU had raged for the best part of 18 months. The arguments over the building of the Millennium Stadium, access and various other loyalty agreements and golden shares had left the two sides agreeing to disagree on most issues. But the final straw came when the WRU announced that there was no chance of a British league for that season. The players and board members at Cardiff had pinned their hopes on the formation of a high-profile competition, if only to bring an end to the mediocrity of our own domestic structure.

Cardiff and then Swansea felt that there was little point in playing in a domestic league that had no real depth to it. I thought that it had been the reason behind our demise at international level and others agreed. We had to increase the standard of competition and when the British league was mentioned as a possibility, I think we were all genuinely excited. When the WRU met at the Copthorne Hotel and finally announced that there was no chance of such a league being up and running in time for September 1998, I think that a lot of people resigned themselves to playing in the incestuous Premier League in Wales forever.

Thankfully, Cardiff and Swansea stood their ground. After many, many meetings with the leading club owners in England, they adopted their stance and the unofficial friendlies against English opposition were accepted as reality. Everyone involved with the Cardiff club was anxious to support the option that Peter Thomas and the board had chosen and the Swansea players were very supportive too. Obviously there was a certain amount of anxiety but we realised that anything would be better than another season of mediocrity.

Like the board of directors and the management team, the players saw the competition as being far greater and far more intense. With the World Cup a mere 14 months away, it was the perfect opportunity for the top players – most of whom were playing for Cardiff or down at St Helens for Swansea – to take a step in the right direction.

There was a great deal of opposition to Cardiff's stance at the time and the critics wanted to know why Cardiff had not exactly set the league alight in previous seasons if the standard was so poor. The answer to that was simple. We were an average side because of what had been going on in Wales in previous seasons – it was just that our board of directors, and those at Swansea too, were not about to sit around and watch the game fall even deeper into crisis. There were 20 players at the two clubs who had a realistic chance of being selected for the World Cup squad and it was felt that another season in the Premier Division would be counterproductive.

Because of the threats and counterthreats that had compounded our summer problems in South Africa, the saga had dominated *The Western Mail* and was becoming rather nasty. When the confirmation came through that the English clubs were prepared to put their own futures on the line by playing against us in unofficial games, it was as if a massive weight had been taken off our shoulders. When the fixture list was produced, it left us all purring with anticipation.

The WRU and the RFU said from the outset that they were unable to sanction the games or to provide referees or touch judges. But surely people understood why we were not prepared to sign a loyalty agreement for eight years when we didn't even know what would be going on next week, let alone in the year 2006?

The press boys who supported Cardiff also supported the concept of this unofficial season of Anglo-Welsh games. However, the more cynical members, of which there were one or two, were convinced that the gamble would backfire. They said that from the outset the English clubs would field second-string sides and that as a result our exercise would be meaningless and unrewarding.

The players were told that the English clubs had agreed not to field shadow XVs and were told not to worry about the rumours that were circulating in the press. We were a little sceptical because we understood that for the likes of Leicester, Saracens, Wasps and Bath, the Allied Dunbar

Premiership would be their main focus of attention. Our other concern was that, having missed out on the first weekend of the Welsh Premier Division, if anything went wrong with our games in England we would have nowhere to go. It might have been the case that in the final 12 months before the World Cup, some of us had played only a handful of games.

To be honest, it started well. However, by the time Christmas came around and the countdown to the Five Nations Championship was under way, the attitude towards the games had changed. By the time March was upon us, the fixtures were not worth the paper they were written on.

Still, the club was glad to have made its choice and in those early weeks of the season we saw the gulf in class between the best of the top English clubs and the best of the Welsh. With respect to the likes of Aberavon, Caerphilly and so on, they were never going to provide us with anywhere near the competition that Saracens, Wasps, Bath or Leicester could. Furthermore, we would get a chance to play on good pitches at grounds with good facilities. I know that certain clubs like Bridgend and Newport have spent a fortune on improving their pitches and facilities over the past six months, but at that time the standard of club grounds in Wales was generally poor.

Graham Henry raised that point half-way through the season after watching us in action against Aberavon in the quarter-final of the Swalec Cup. We had recently played against Saracens at Vicarage Road on a surface that I can only describe as carpet-like. A week or so later, we were in Aberavon on a bog. Graham said how farcical it was that rugby players should be asked to play in such conditions. He was dead right. The national coach was actively encouraging a handling game played at pace, but we were being expected to play like that on pitches that were hardly conducive to bog-snorkelling, let alone fast-flowing rugby. How do you expect international players to show off their skills and develop as top-class players if you ask them to play on a mud heap? It defeats the whole object of the game.

So, having driven a wedge between ourselves and the Union, we opened our account with a victory against Bedford at Goldington Road. The week leading up to the game had been spent wondering how many people, if any, would support these so-called rebel games and how the press would treat us. To be honest, I was shocked by the interest the game generated. There were reporters around every corner when we arrived and close on 2,000 supporters pitched up to watch. Considering that Bedford's average home crowd during the previous season had been similar, I thought that it made a point.

As expected, there was one final problem before the game kicked off. As we got to the dressing-room, the news filtered through that Bedford had received a fax from the RFU reminding them that if they went through with the fixture they were in breach of the regulations and faced possible expulsion. It was a real test of strength. If Bedford had caved in then, our season would have been over. Fortunately, they had the balls to stick two fingers up to Twickenham and the game went ahead, albeit with 'unofficial' officials. It proved that the club owners were not afraid of the authorities.

Much had been spoken about Bedford's lack of quality but that first game proved to us that the weaker sides in the Allied Dunbar Premiership One were as good as many of our top sides back home. What's more, it was comforting to know that Graham Henry was happy that we were being exposed to that level of competition in the build-up to the autumn internationals against South Africa and Argentina. He would not dare to come out and publicly condone the fixtures, but by the very fact that he broke the alleged agreement that no WRU officials would attend a rebel game, he was agreeing with our stance.

At the time, *The Western Mail* gave us the backing we were after, although one or two other papers were in total disagreement. They felt we should have stayed put. We knew that regardless of how good our games were, we were never likely to receive any plaudits from that direction. Even when Saracens pitched up with a full side and we beat them, one newspaper report claimed that Saracens could not have been trying their hardest. That was nonsense. I was out in the middle that day and if they were firing on only two of their four cylinders, I dread to think what might have happened if they had been firing on all four.

I felt that it was the easy way out for those who disagreed with us. When the quality of opposition did decrease, it was a case of 'I told you so'. We had to take that on the chin just as others should have earlier in the season. We beat Bedford on the opening day and attracted nearly 12,000 supporters for the opening home game against Saracens. We were outstanding on the day and the performance was more than enough to satisfy the players. However, my lasting memory of the afternoon will be when the crowd starting chanting, 'Are you watching, Vernon Pugh?'

Vernon had been at the centre of the negotiations with Cardiff that summer and he felt that we would have been far better served staying put. I suppose that many members of the WRU would have liked to have seen just a few hundred people turn up for that game, if only to say our choice had been the wrong one. Unfortunately for them, the ground was creaking at the rafters and just before the final whistle was blown the chant came up from the main stand. A few players had a chuckle, but it was not about proving anyone wrong, it was about getting on with playing high-quality games against high-quality opposition.

Our biggest problem at the time – and it continued to haunt us throughout the season – was the small matter of not being granted any official referees or linesmen by the WRU or the RFU. Both Unions had refused to sanction the games, which consequently prevented any of their own officials from taking charge. In response to that, the clubs appealed to a number of former referees or lesser officials to cross the divide and come to our aid. About nine or ten took up the offer and, whatever might have been said, we will be forever grateful for that. However, there was a downside to all of this. With respect to some of the referees in question, most were not as experienced as the likes of Derek Bevan and Clayton Thomas and had not refereed consistently at the highest level. Once again the critics had a field day and deep down we knew that sooner or later something would happen.

The problem came to a head when we played Bath in a midweek game at the Arms Park. I wouldn't like to criticise the referees because without them we would not have had any games that season. But it did make me smile when after the Bedford game we were told that all three officials had flown to Bedford in Peter Thomas's plane. It was that kind of relationship; Peter and the club owners in England were indebted to them and made sure they were looked after. But then came the Bath match.

Alun Ware, whom most of us knew, was in charge that night and just before half-time there was an incident involving the Bath and England prop Victor Ubogu. Alun was justified in penalising Victor but unfortunately Victor turned round and told him where to go. Okay, Victor might have thought he had a point, but you can't go round telling referees to f*** off, whoever they might be or whatever standard they are refereeing at. Alun had no choice but to send him off. I have no sympathy with players like that, England international or not.

Victor realised that what he had said had been totally out of order and started walking before Alun had even pointed to the tunnel. It was a very tense situation because the Bath players were suggesting that Alun was favouring us. Not surprisingly, there was a pretty nasty free-for-all straight after Victor's dismissal, and when it came to half-time, Andy Robinson, the Bath coach, threatened to keep his side in the dressing-room.

I couldn't believe it. There were 10,000 people in the ground and it wasn't a bad game. However, here was an ex-international player, who had had quite a bit to say for himself when he was playing, threatening to ruin everything that Cardiff and Swansea had been fighting for. Our chief executive Gareth Davies tried to calm him down during the break and I think Andy realised what the repercussions might be. Bath eventually came out and we went on to win the game. However, the headlines the next day were about Victor's sending-off and the reaction of Andy Robinson. It was the first problem either we or Swansea had experienced but we realised that a precedent had been set. It was a critical moment in our battle with the Unions and the whole issue of rebel games was suddenly put in doubt.

I spoke to a few of the Bath boys after the game and we agreed about the standard of refereeing. On the whole, it wasn't great, but we were only too pleased that we had these rebel refs on board. There is no doubting the quality of Alun's performance that night but I didn't think we were in any position to criticise. Anyway, he awarded me a try when I got nowhere near the ball to ground it, so I wasn't complaining! In the end, the players had a laugh and a joke about Victor's outburst and nothing more was said.

The Cardiff and Swansea players involved in the autumn internationals agreed that they felt better prepared for international rugby having just come off a series of high-quality matches. With several other squad members playing in the official Allied Dunbar Premiership, it transpired that very few had actually been playing their rugby in the Welsh Premier Division.

Unfortunately, after Christmas the games went from being very competitive to being very tedious and meaningless. As feared, the sides selected against us were normally minus all but one or maybe two first-team players. It became a joke. It wasn't too bad for the international players because we had the Five Nations to look forward to, but the other players had nothing to test themselves against.

The WRU agreed to allow us to play in the Swalec Cup, although I knew that the rest of Welsh rugby would be gunning for us and desperate to see us lose. It wasn't so bad for Swansea because the neutrals are quite supportive of the All Whites. Sadly, and I don't put the blame at our door for this, there are thousands who despise the turf that Cardiff play on. As I mentioned before, it's the Manchester United syndrome.

We cruised through the first couple of rounds and then found ourselves drawn away to Aberavon in the last eight. I didn't play in the game but I went down to watch. It was abysmal. Not only was the pitch in a terrible state but you had to be careful where you sat in the stand because the rain was pouring through a hole in the roof. Graham was there that day and judging by what he said at a press conference during the championship he was shocked by the facilities and the state of the pitch. It was a great leveller and, without making too many excuses, it was the reason why we only just scraped through. Much to the disappointment of Welsh rugby, we were now in the last four, just a game away from a possible final against Swansea. Now that would be a bitter pill for the WRU to swallow!

By the time we came to play against Llanelli at the Brewery Field, our rebel games had died a painful death. We were just glad to be featuring in a meaningful match. Well, at least that was the plan. The game against the Scarlets turned out to be a living nightmare. We lost heavily and for coach Terry Holmes it was the beginning of the end. The rumours around the club about Terry and the coaching set-up were rife and everyone knew that a defeat by the Scarlets could signal the end of another short era in the history of the club. Terry, unfairly, was coming under increasing pressure, along with Hemi Taylor and Mark Ring. The suggestion was that if we lost to Llanelli, it could be the end for all three, as well as one or two others on the playing side.

Having been there himself, Terry understood the pressure that the international players were under during the Five Nations campaign and as a result he had never once pressurised us into playing or training if we felt it would not be beneficial. However, you could tell that things were changing because he pushed us very hard indeed that week. He told me to make sure that my head was in gear and to train as hard as I had done at any previous time that season.

On the Thursday before the game, we trained at our Talybont training ground in Cardiff. The pressure was obviously mounting because as we were getting changed Peter Thomas and Gareth Edwards came into the dressing-room to give us a five-minute chat about the importance of the game. Peter said that without doubt it was the biggest game in the club's history and we simply had to win. Having taken the gamble to play in England, we had to prove that we were better for the experience. Once again, losing to Llanelli would offer the other Welsh clubs and the WRU committee members justified reason to criticise us. And who would blame them?

I was a bit surprised at Peter's decision to tell us how important it was to win – we knew that anyway. So why do it? I think it showed the pressure building within the club. Peter and Gareth were desperate for us to win and I think they would have gladly foregone the final, providing it was against Swansea, just to win that one match.

On the day we were stuffed and it went down like a lead balloon with everyone at the club. However, for the rest of Welsh rugby it was the perfect result. We went 7–0 up and looked good until I was sin-binned for deliberately killing possession in front of my own posts. I knew I had done wrong and understood that a yellow card was the least punishment I would get. However, as I walked off to the bench, once again I experienced the other side of Welsh rugby. The reaction from the crowd reminded me of the game in which I had played for Cardiff against Bridgend some two years earlier. The abuse was incredible. Picture the scene: the Wales captain had just led his country to victory in Paris for the first time in 24 years, yet here I was being called everything under the sun by the same supporters, many of whom had spent their hard-earned cash just to cross the Channel to watch us in action. I sometimes don't know why they bother. They would be better off saving their money if that's how they feel.

Derwyn Jones followed me into the sin-bin before half-time and after that we were convincingly beaten in every facet of the game.

The next few weeks were very difficult. Swansea had reached the final yet Cardiff were still going through the motions of playing meaningless friendlies, primarily on Sundays in front of small crowds. The pressure on Terry was mounting and I felt for him. We met up in Cardiff after training one day to discuss the situation and he asked me what my plans were for the next season. There had been plenty of rumours around the club with regard to myself and Terry wanted to know what was happening.

Playing against the Allied Dunbar clubs meant the market had been that much bigger and although I was still on contract with Cardiff there had been a number of tentative enquiries. Leicester, Harlequins and Perpignan had contacted me – indirectly, of course – to say they were interested. Obviously, I was flattered, but I was happy to remain at Cardiff if the club had ambition.

I told Terry that I wanted to see out my contract and nothing has changed. Sadly, Terry won't be there on my expiry date. He announced his resignation before the end of the season and within 24 hours the news filtered through that Lynn Howells, the assistant coach at Pontypridd and Graham Henry's right-hand man with Wales, was taking over. I felt for Terry, as I had done when Alex came back for his second spell at the club. Whatever people might think of him, he was in a very difficult position. There was plenty of dead wood at the club; the playing staff was simply not good enough. Unfortunately, the buck invariably stops with the coach and not with the players.

The appointment of Lynn took a great many people by surprise. After all, it was well known that Lynn was not a great lover of Cardiff during his days at Pontypridd. Thankfully, I had got on well with him since he had teamed up with Graham Henry and I was quite excited about the prospect of working with him at Cardiff. He targeted a number of players, including one or two key names, and as the summer wore on he came up trumps. The signing of Craig Quinnell and Nick Walne was important but to get Neil Jenkins and Martyn Williams was crucial.

Jenks and I go back a long way and we have been through some pretty testing times for Wales together. We were there at Twickenham and Wembley and we spent time together in South Africa when we travelled with the Lions. I feel privileged to have played alongside Neil and he was the one fly-half above any other that I wanted to see at Cardiff.

I spoke to Neil at great length about the move while we were in Argentina. He had spent nine years at Pontypridd and had a great deal of respect for the club and especially for the likes of Bernard and Gerald at Buy as You View, the TV company for whom he works. He certainly didn't want to get anyone's back up, nor did he want it to look as though he was ditching them after so many great years. All he said to me was that he wouldn't mind moving to Cardiff if the chance came about.

Only time will tell whether Cardiff can succeed on the highest stage and whether Lynn can make us great once again. However, the club learned a great deal from its season in exile and is probably all the better for it. We are certainly all the better for having attracted Neil Jenkins, that's for sure.

15. MY HEAD ON THE CHOPPING BLOCK

Double Defeat and an Unnecessary Attack

I am no stranger to criticism. I suppose it comes with the territory. My first spell at Cardiff coincided with some pretty sharp comments, while my performances for Wales have not always been appreciated by the various members of the Welsh media.

Thankfully, I have always kept my cool. Whilst I might have been hurting inside, I have never once lowered my guard and confronted those people who felt it so necessary to take a swipe. However, when somebody puts your head on the chopping block for no apparent reason, it can be quite disturbing and particularly frustrating. The 1999 Five Nations Championship was the perfect example of how the press can adopt that Jekyll and Hyde approach.

The arrival of Graham and the performance against South Africa at Wembley in November provided such a buzz that in the weeks immediately before Christmas the press were talking in terms of us winning the Five Nations. It was quite amazing. After being pilloried in the papers at the end of the South African tour in the summer, suddenly we were being tipped to win the championship. It was madness.

In my eyes nothing much had changed and the talk of Graham having turned things around was very premature. Although he never showed it in public, Graham was already losing his patience with a few journalists. He kept his calm but made sure that in all but a handful of his interviews he talked us down. I echoed those sentiments whenever I could, but still we were unable to convince some of the more short-sighted members of the media that while we had secured the early footings, our foundation was far from complete.

They were having none of it. In their eyes there was little doubt that victories in Scotland and against Ireland at Wembley would set us up for the second half of the championship season during which time we would play France in Paris and England, in the last ever Five Nations game, at Wembley. The belief on their part was that if we could win one of those games we would at least gain a share of the championship. A friendly victory over Italy in Treviso to boot would also provide further evidence of this latest supposed rejuvenation.

In one sense they were right. We did win one of our games in the second half of the season; in fact, we won two. Furthermore, there was a comprehensive success in Italy. But as far as the details were concerned, they could hardly have been further from the reality of events. As for winning the championship, we were not even close.

It was around this time that I started to leave the papers on the front doormat – I was sick and tired of reading about 'Graham Henry the Messiah'. I am sure that Graham was cringing too when he read how in a little less than four months he had transformed the national side from also-rans to supposed front-runners. It was utter nonsense. Yes, Graham had injected new life into the side, but we were far from being transformed. To even suggest that we had closed the gap on the better sides in the world was to show an unbelievable lack of understanding. It's a trait of the Welsh press and one that does annoy the players. When the side is down, the knife goes in, and when the side wins one game, albeit a little fortuitously, as was the case against Argentina at Stradey Park in November, we are the best thing since sliced bread. Okay, talk about the improvement but talk about it in relative terms. After all, whilst we had improved, so had the rest of the nations waiting for us in the forthcoming championship.

By the time Christmas and New Year were out of the way and the championship season was upon us, I felt a little uneasy about the strength of our squad. Although we had enjoyed a decent festive break, there were clear signs that we were out of shape and far from ready to beat Scotland at Murrayfield.

Although Graham had introduced a number of new faces to the squad, players like Darren Morris, Ben Evans and Ian Gough, I was not sure whether they were ready to step on to the Five Nations stage. They were good players in their own right and deserved the recognition Graham had given them. However, international rugby is a different ball-game altogether and I wondered how they would cope.

My other concern was that Graham appeared to be underestimating the championship and what it meant to the Welsh public. Once the season had been put to bed, Graham told the press that he had made certain glaring errors. Primarily, he had misjudged the importance of the Five Nations. He had never experienced such emotion, such a partisan feeling, during his time in New Zealand. Kiwis are incredibly passionate about their rugby but with the Tri-Nations series played in three different countries with a huge distance in between, travelling support is sparse to say the least. That obviously dilutes the atmosphere of any game.

Graham was visibly shocked when we arrived in Edinburgh. He couldn't believe that around 10,000 Welshmen and women were in the Scottish capital some 48 hours before the game had even kicked off. We were used to it and told Graham to watch out for the following on Saturday morning when we took our traditional run-out in the gardens of Princes Street. More than a thousand Welsh supporters, and some Scots too, pitched up at the park to watch us jog up and down and make a few passes.

When we got back to the hotel, you could see that Graham had been taken by surprise. It does not happen in New Zealand or Australia. We are idolised during the championship, even by those supporters who spend the first half of the season slating us. The Cardiff, Swansea, Llanelli and Newport fans come together for a weekend and forget about the petty jealousies that exist between the clubs. It's wonderful to see and Graham, like us, now appreciates that. It just takes a bit of getting used to.

Unfortunately, by the time match day arrived, we had already lost Craig Quinnell and Dai Young to injury, and with Darren Morris, Chris Anthony, Ian Gough and Chris Wyatt in the front five along with Jonathan Humphreys, who had hardly had a comfortable start to the season due to a back problem, I was very apprehensive. If nothing else, Scotland would scrummage us and expose any weakness we had. For a scrum-half that's the nightmare scenario. I talked to Humph in great detail during the build-up to the game, asking how well he thought we would do. Although he respected those players around him, he was unable to convince me that we should be as confident as the press had been before Christmas.

To Graham's credit, we had done a great deal of work prior to the game with regard to our line-out. The only problem was that we were far too one-dimensional. We didn't really have any options. While I have never questioned Graham's approach, I did ask myself what would happen if . . .

Unfortunately, my worst fears were realised. We struggled in the scrum, made far too many mistakes in the loose and found referee Ed Morrison in no mood to tolerate our unique line-out mode. That was a key area of the game for us and we knew that if we failed to gain parity we would concede significant ground and perhaps the game. Graham had once again made an interesting decision in the build-up to the match and one that some people might believe cost us dearly.

On the Friday night before an international, the referee allows the two coaches half an hour of his time to come and have a chat about the game and to bring to his attention any concerns they might have. The respective coaches used to go in separately, have their say and leave it at that. Unfortunately, that has changed and the coaches are now expected to go in together. Graham was not prepared to meet with Jim Telfer, the Scottish coach, and Ed because he had worked hard on his game plan and was not about to reveal the secret of our revolutionary line-out. But when it came to the game it backfired. Ed was unhappy with the way our forwards arrived late at the line-out and kept telling us to stop talking and to get on with it. Maybe he might have understood if Graham had turned up on the Friday and explained what it was all about. But then again why should we pass on our game plan? Telfer is a shrewd enough coach as it is. Giving him the answers to the questions would have been tantamount to committing rugby suicide. We didn't blame Graham for not having spoken up on the Friday, we simply blamed the inconsistency amongst referees. Two weeks later we adopted the same approach and got away with it.

So, with our line-out nullified and our scrum struggling to provide a platform, we were facing an uphill battle. Scotland made the most of our inadequacies and thoroughly deserved to win.

For me, however, it wasn't that easy. From being a captain who had almost led Wales to victory over South Africa earlier in the season and who had celebrated a much-needed victory over Argentina a week later, I was suddenly public enemy number one. Although I had set up our first-half try by tapping a penalty deep in my own half, I was seen to have messed up when another tap ended up in Gregor Townsend's hands. My old Lions pal dashed 50 metres to score a try and knock a conclusive nail in our coffin.

I have replayed the tape a thousand times since then and I still back my judgement. We were in a good position and I felt it was time to up the tempo of the game. I am sure that a try at that stage would have settled the issue in our favour. However, I knew the press wouldn't see it that way. In my eyes, the Scottish flanker Peter Walton had not retreated ten metres so when I collided with him I expected Ed to blow up and give us those important ten metres. Instead, he played on, somehow we lost the ball and Gregor did the rest. Maybe I was just feeling a little vulnerable at the time but I knew the press would have a field day and for that reason I was a reluctant member of the top table at the press conference.

It is only a few yards from the dressing-rooms to the press-conference area at Murrayfield and when I came out of the dressing-room door I would have done anything to have slipped on to the coach and hidden beneath the back seat. However, if you are prepared to sit and smile when you win you have to grin and bear it when you lose. For the few guys who wanted me out of the captain's seat and possibly out of the side, it was obviously an opportunity to seize.

The press conference was a nightmare and although Graham Henry supported me I just didn't want to be there. I wanted to say that Peter Walton was not ten metres, if only to convince people that the defeat was not solely down to Rob Howley's so-called poor decision. But you have to avoid mud-slinging in those situations and hope that, come Sunday morning, the press will have seen the replay and realised that I might have been right.

However, bottling it up inside me did precious little to lighten the load. I sat there faced with around 100 reporters who wanted to know what I had been thinking about when I took the tap instead of kicking for goal. It seemed to last for hours and when it finally came to an end I was glad to escape and get on the bus. A few members of the Welsh press gathered around the coach but I was in no mood to go back out and give any one-to-one interviews. Sadly, the day went from bad to worse and what happened next will live with me for a long time.

Players often take for granted the supporters who pay good money and spend a lot of time travelling the length and breadth of Europe to support them. Through thick and thin, come rain or shine, they are always there, yet at times like this you couldn't give a stuff. Well, at least that is the case for certain players. On this occasion we were taught a real lesson, and I suppose that helped me to come to terms with what had just happened. As we were about to pull away from the Murrayfield car park, a lady with a Welsh scarf and rosette climbed on to the bus and asked if she could have a few autographs before she headed off home. She got a pretty poor reception from the boys, who wanted nothing to do with her. We just wanted to get out of there. But instead of turning around and leaving us to sulk on the journey back to the hotel, she delivered a stinging retort. She was clearly upset by our attitude and said, 'I have paid a lot of money and travelled a long way to watch that rubbish out there. Don't you think I deserve a few autographs to take home to the children?'

Her response hit me very hard and I spent most of the night thinking about those words. It taught me a lesson in manners and respect. That lady had probably spent the best part of £300 travelling and watching us play and we had let her down. Then, to rub salt into her wound, we were telling her to get off the bus because we were not prepared to sign her autograph book. Thankfully the boys all felt the same as me and we did sign the book, regretting that we had acted in such a selfish manner in the first place. After all, had we won I am sure it would have taken a pack of wild dogs to have torn us away from the fans. You can't have it both ways and I hope the players continue to realise as much.

It had been a bad weekend for me, as captain, and I felt the pressure mounting as I got back home. As usual, I kept a low profile over the next few days and was not exactly enamoured with the thought of playing for Cardiff against Bath in one of those now meaningless friendlies against English opposition. I was even less pleased when I picked up a shoulder injury in the first half and had to come off. With only a week to go before the Ireland game, I was suddenly back on the physio's couch and facing a race against time to be fit. It was a game that we had to win, if only to regain some self-respect.

The injury seriously hampered my preparation and because I was unable to train until later on in the week, there was a school of thought, especially amongst the more critical members of the press, which suggested that I should not be risked. But Graham said he wanted me to play and, to be honest, by the time Friday came around I was fine, if a little annoyed that I had missed out on four days of preparation. Unfortunately, the game itself could not have been worse. Although we finally got out of neutral in the second half, we were unable to claw back a significant half-time deficit and again lost to the Irish, 28–20, on home soil. It was a catastrophe and once again I felt very uneasy about what was likely to be said in the press. It was becoming a problem for me, although I desperately tried not to show that I was conscious of what was being said and written.

Our discipline had let us down in the first half and, in my own way, I had told the players as much. I told them that while sticking together and fighting might appear to be the right way of beating Ireland, on this occasion it had lost us the game. Okay, we needed to find an edge after Scotland, but we gave away too many kickable penalties and we were quickly in a difficult position. We never recovered.

I steered clear of the papers on Sunday, but come Monday I was shown a *Western Mail*. I felt I had done my bit and didn't believe my captaincy would come under such close scrutiny. *The Western Mail* obviously saw things differently and suggested that the Swansea second row Andy Moore, a player who was not even in the Wales side, would be a good bet as captain. I think Andy Moore is a top player and for Swansea he is a key forward. But I am sure that he would be the first to admit that his immediate aim at that juncture was to get into the side, not lead it.

Then, the following day, the same newspaper ran a story on its back page quoting some guy from Ebbw Vale who said that Garin Jenkins should be the man to take over as captain from Rob Howley. I was perplexed. Successive defeats are bad enough to cope with, but to get this shoved down my throat as we turned our attentions to the small matter of a championship game in France was too much. I felt like picking up the phone and asking why. But, as some of the other guys told me, while it might be a pile of rubbish, the papers do have the right to say whatever they want. I just felt a little saddened that the captain of Wales no longer enjoyed a relationship with his national newspaper. Like Andy, Garin is a great boy and he has been an integral part of the side over the past 18 months. But why should he be captain? Why, all of a sudden, had I become a bad captain? I chose to dismiss the comments, although they will never be forgotten.

What amazes me about journalism is that one minute you should be booted out of the Welsh squad, while the next the same reporter wants to do a one-on-one interview with you. That sticks in my craw. If I am not rated and should not be in charge of this dreadful Wales side, then why on earth would anyone want to speak to me? Surely my views count for nothing?

Perhaps I might have found it a little easier to understand if the journalist had come up with a few suggestions as to how I could improve as captain and tried to help me through the situation. Instead, in the eyes of his readers, my head was on the chopping block.

Graham Henry was a real rock throughout that period. He supported me 100 per cent and was himself annoyed at the comments. I met him for lunch that week and asked how I could improve as a captain. We had a very good chat. Perhaps I hadn't been thinking things through well enough, but that was his only criticism. With Graham obviously on my side, I thought it might finally hit home. If the man the papers were calling the 'Messiah' thought I was the man for the job, then perhaps I was.

Unfortunately for me, things got worse before they improved. The next press conference was called to announce the team for the French game and I must admit that I was ready for another onslaught. We had lost the two games that everyone believed we would win and we were now preparing ourselves to play the championship holders and the 1999 championship favourites.

Having said that I was ready to cop another load of flak, I was a little surprised at the direction from which the real searching question came. I wanted to get the conference over with because I knew that the question of captaincy would be raised once again. David Parry-Jones, a journalist whom I have known and respected for a long time, popped the question: 'Rob, do you think you are hard enough as a captain?'

As a result of the article in *The Western Mail* the matter had become an issue of national importance, or so it seemed. What he meant, so I believe, was whether I thought I had the strength of character to change things on the pitch if they were going wrong. My attitude towards that part of captaincy is very simple. It's not all about giving someone a public rollicking if things go a little pear-shaped. Players react in different ways and I can get my message across without having to be too demonstrative. You don't have to wave your arms about and start pushing people around. Graham Henry doesn't do that to us, he just tells us straight. I know my players better than David and the other journalists do and I said as much, albeit in a diplomatic way. I never felt like jacking it in as captain, but I admit to feeling a little vulnerable.

I was glad to see the back of that press conference and delighted to be in my car and on my way back home to Ceri. I was also quite pleased with myself that I had not reacted to that question or to a couple of others from journalists who had previously chastised me.

France had faltered despite winning in Ireland and in the eyes of many were beginning to experience the kind of problems that all of us had experienced in recent years. I have the utmost respect for French rugby and having played there on numerous occasions, both for Wales and in the European Cup with Cardiff, I have seen how clinical they can be. They couldn't care a toss that Welsh rugby was, once again, in the mire. In fact, they are the kind of rugby nation that enjoys rubbing your nose in the dirt.

They had blasted 51 points into us at the end of the previous season, and although their performance in edging past Ireland four weeks earlier had been anything but impressive, they were still on home soil and playing a Welsh team that was firmly rooted to the foot of the Five Nations table with nothing to show from two games against Scotland and Ireland.

I was particularly aware that had we gone to Paris and lost by 20 or 30 points, a number of players, maybe myself included, would have been out on their ear. The players felt that pressure during the build-up and the senior members of the squad like Dai Young, Scotty and Garin Jenkins talked a great deal about the importance of the game and our performance. It was shit or bust, and that was the motivation for us.

Changes were made post Ireland, with Ben Evans and Peter Rogers coming into the side to try and shore up the scrum. Garin was already there, because of Humph's back problem, while Neath flanker Brett Sinkinson was given his first senior cap after performing well for the A team. Once again, Martyn Williams was axed, and I felt for him. It was not his fault that we had lost in Edinburgh or at Wembley, although Graham felt it was an area of the game that we had to address. Martyn had been made a scapegoat after the defeat by England 12 months earlier and it was very awkward to see him and speak with him once Graham had named the side. But once again Graham was proved to be right. Whether Martyn would have performed as well as Brett, nobody knows. However, it was a game that would have suited him. It was just a shame that only one of them could play.

In the immediate build-up to our departure, I was particularly concerned about the pack. I was far from convinced that everybody understood what was happening and how much this meant to us, both as a side and as a proud rugby nation. There would be no hiding places after this particular game if we were beaten heavily. It was a watershed and the side was visibly anxious about what lay in store.

What made it even worse was that the French papers were questioning their own side, asking whether coach Jean-Claude Skrela had got the balance right and whether the performance in Dublin was a sign of things to come. As I mentioned before, French rugby is particularly strong and, as has been the case on so many previous occasions, they become even stronger and certainly more determined if their ability is questioned. I knew that as captain I had one chance to get it right and convince those less experienced members of our squad that here was a chance for us to make a name for Welsh rugby. Similarly, it was an opportunity for the French to stick two fingers up to their own press and make us pay for what had gone on at Lansdowne Road.

When we got to Paris, my whole attitude towards the team changed. On arriving at the hotel I dispensed with the normal routine of allowing players a quiet half-hour to unpack and collect their thoughts. Instead, I called a meeting. I didn't even let the boys go upstairs to their rooms. I had so much to say. What's more, I felt that one or two players needed to be told a few home truths. It was not a case of ramming my work ethics down people's throats; it was more about Welsh rugby and the responsibility that lay on our shoulders. I told the players straight that I was not going to walk out of the Stade de France saying 'I only wish . . .' or 'What if . . .'.

I laid it on the line at that meeting and told every player that we were in it together and that when we stepped out on to the pitch the following day we were battling for each other's future. There were reputations on the line and lucrative contracts in the pipeline. However, those deals were based on playing and succeeding. I wanted everyone to know that and to understand that if one player was caught slacking, we would all suffer in the long term.

I cast my mind back to the press conference earlier that week when David Parry-Jones had asked me about my strength of character as captain. I wanted the door to open and the press to walk in and listen to what I had to say. For the first time in my career as captain, I was like the teacher talking to his pupils. I was dictating, telling them what I wanted from them. This time there would be no mistakes, no moments of ill-discipline and no lost opportunities. If we played well, I believed that we could win this game and put our season back on track. If we failed to achieve our best it would be the beginning of the end.

I actually made every player go away and write down every move he was involved in. Some of the boys didn't like it, but I couldn't have cared less about that. It had been a failing in the past – some players believed they were bigger than the team. On this occasion nobody was bigger than Wales and I told them as much. And, thankfully, it did the trick. When the boys came back to the meeting room it was obvious they had done their home-work. For the first time, I was convinced we would win. That gave me a great deal of satisfaction and subsequent confidence for the challenge that lay ahead. For the first time since we had walked off at Wembley having been taught a lesson by Ireland, I really believed we could beat France for the first time in Paris since 1975.

It was no coincidence that the training session at the Stade de France that morning was practically faultless. We were in great shape and everyone was longing for the game. We dropped one ball all morning – Ben Evans was the culprit, and he took some stick. But, as one journalist reminded me on the Sunday morning at the airport, it had been a similar situation 14 months earlier, before the England débâcle at Twickenham. We had had a great session at Sophia Gardens before travelling to London and eventually letting ourselves down. But this time it was different. We talked about it on the bus back to the hotel and I told everyone that the session had proved what we were capable of.

The captain's meeting on the Friday night was very rewarding, although when Scotty Gibbs and I sat down in the hotel before going off to bed we talked frankly about the other side of what might happen. He reiterated what we had said back in Wales the previous week. We were all drinking in the last-chance saloon.

The fear factor was crucial. The press were ready to pounce if we lost, and although I might have been wrong, I felt that a number of journalists had written the script and the post-mortem before they had even arrived in Paris. That spurred me on, although when the final whistle was blown on the Saturday, I certainly had no inclination to do a Paul Thorburn and stick two fingers up to the press box. Sometimes you feel like it, but this was neither the time nor the place. The victory was enough for them to digest – it certainly was for us!

From the first minute of the game we showed that with ball in hand we can be a real force against anyone. The way the players expressed themselves was magnificent and I have never played in a game with so much space. But that is the Graham Henry way. Like the players, Graham was under extreme pressure, having shouldered so much of the blame after Scotland and Ireland. He said that his coaching had not been up to scratch and it hurt him a great deal to have led a 'decent' Welsh side to successive defeats against the sides tipped to finish fourth and fifth in the championship. The fact was that we lost to a good Scottish side, who finished as champions, and failed to perform at all for the first 50 minutes against the Irish. You learn by your mistakes.

Against France, however, it was a different story altogether and the fact that he stuck by his beliefs tells you more about Graham than anything he might have said. The first half was non-stop. Colin Charvis, Dafydd James and Craig Quinnell all scored tries, although France broke us on three separate occasions to leave us with a narrow half-time lead.

However, it was Jenks once again who came up trumps. He wobbled a little with a couple of second-half kicks but managed five penalties and two conversions to see us home. Ironically, Thomas Castaignède, who had murdered us at Wembley 12 months earlier, had a kick to win it for France in injury time. I was sitting on the bench by that time after picking up a knee injury in the closing minutes, and for all the world it looked as though it was going through. But it missed and that was that. We had won 34–33 and for the first time in Paris in 24 years.

My own performance gave me an immense amount of satisfaction and I hoped that for the first time in a long time certain people would look at me as a captain and then as a player. I felt I led the side well and played well before having to come off. I think I was justified in feeling ten foot tall when I walked out of the dressing-room to meet some of those journalists who had questioned me not only as a player but also as a leader.

The elation was unbelievable. None of the boys had ever won in France before and you had to be there to experience it. Fortunately, in between the press conference and making our way back to the hotel, I had a chance to sit down in the dressing-room and reflect on the previous 48 hours. I had put my own head on the line by speaking as directly as I had done on any previous occasion in my international career. But as the rest of the side danced a merry jig around the plush new dressing-room, I realised I had done the right thing by turning up the heat and telling them straight.

Whether Graham would have stripped me of the captaincy had we lost badly, I don't know. I don't think so. However, he might have had good reason to. Nobody but Graham will ever know that.

I learned a lot that weekend, both about myself as a player and about Rob Howley the captain. I learned to go with my gut feeling. If you believe something is right then you have to go with it right to the very end, regardless of what others might think or say. I don't think I was naïve or insecure about the position, but the success of that weekend and the support the players gave me enabled me to move on to another plane. That was important. Sometimes it is easy to go with the flow and do things that people think are right as opposed to saying no and going with your own instincts.

For the first time in a long time, I enjoyed the post-match dinner and decided to let my hair down. But for me the icing on the cake came when I spoke to the likes of Thomas Castaignède and Marc Lievremont. They said how happy they were at the way we had played. That made me very proud.

I ended up on the Champs-Elysées at about 5 a.m. with Peter Thomas, the Cardiff chairman, and a few of the boys who were a little bit the worse for wear. I kept thinking back to that final penalty when Thomas had had the chance to win it for France. I kept thinking of how different the night would have been but for the thickness of a post. It's true what they say – there is a fine line between success and failure.

16. ECSTASY BENEATH THE TWIN TOWERS

Beating the Old Enemy

The history of the Five Nations Championship, and Wales–England games in particular, makes for fascinating reading. The great players, the spectacular tries, the ice-cool kickers and, unfortunately, the record victory that England enjoyed at our expense in 1998 are well documented.

Regardless of what the southern hemisphere nations might say, I have no doubt that a Wales–England game is the most powerful and passionate affair in world rugby. The bitter feeling and intense rivalry that exists between the two nations is very difficult to explain. However, at times it borders on hatred. It may be very short-sighted on their part but there are thousands of Welsh rugby supporters who would swap consecutive victories over Ireland, France and Scotland in any one season just to see the Welsh Dragon slay St George.

It happened in 1989. John Ryan was coach and the side lost its first three championship games. However, in the final game against England at Cardiff, Mike Hall scored a late try in front of the East Terrace and suddenly everything in the garden was rosy. Although Scotland had beaten us 23–7 at Murrayfield, Ireland had won 19–13 in Cardiff and France had wiped the floor with us in Paris, winning 31–12, the reaction at the final whistle was one of unbridled joy. It was as if we had won the championship.

Sadly, while victory had successfully papered over the cracks and ensured a wonderful night in Cardiff, the real problems were still there, as the side found out the next season. They managed to beat Canada 31–29 on the summer tour but the following season they lost all four Five Nations matches and finished with the wooden spoon.

It should have taught us all a lesson. Unfortunately, we can be a stubborn rugby nation at times, and while the performance had been nothing to write home about, the victory certainly was. In the long term, it probably cost John Ryan his job, but the masses wouldn't have worried about that. After all, it was our fourth successive victory over England and in any Welshman's book that was good enough.

Having played in so many passionate games at domestic level, I understand how easy it can be to get carried away with certain fixtures. To be honest, some of the current players are not too different from the supporters. Thankfully, coaches like Graham Henry and Lynn Howells are pretty shrewd, and while victory over England is understandably greeted with unbounded delight, they constantly remind us that success over the Old Enemy brings nothing more in terms of reward.

Still, having said all of that, beating England in the manner in which we did at Wembley in 1999 will go down as one of the greatest moments in my rugby career. And I won't pretend that I didn't enjoy watching Clive Woodward squirm during the television interviews after the game.

There is no escaping the fact that our record against them in recent times has been appalling. In fact, in the ten championship games since the start of the decade, we have won only twice – and never at Twickenham. So, having beaten France in Paris, you can imagine how keen Graham was to unleash the side on Clive Woodward's team in what would be the last ever game in the Five Nations Championship. The fact that we had to play them away from Cardiff was not to our liking but should we win, it would be the perfect way to round off the great five-team championship.

At the beginning of the season, nobody believed we could beat England. Our domestic game was in turmoil and we were not exactly firing on all cylinders after the débâcle of Pretoria. However, having beaten France we were desperate to give it our best shot. The only disappointing fact about the whole episode was that we couldn't play them straight away. Had we been given the choice, I think we would have played the game the following week. We were that buoyant after the victory in Paris that we felt we could finish the season and the millennium with a victory to prove that we were no longer the victims of professional rugby.

But, as is so often the case, we didn't get what we wanted. The introduction of Italy to the Six Nations Championship meant that the last season of the Five Nations would be used as a dry run. Italy would get an opportunity to play the other nations during the championship season, albeit on a friendly basis, and it just so happened that our game was sandwiched between the Paris match and the game against England at Wembley. We were hugely frustrated at the time but, in hindsight, I think it gave us an opportunity to digest and subsequently evaluate the Paris victory and to make slightly better preparations for what would obviously be our most difficult examination of the season.

While we were far from convinced by our own success in Paris, our real concern surrounded England's mediocre form. Although they were heading towards another Grand Slam if they beat the French at Twickenham and us at Wembley, there was a genuine feeling throughout the squad that Woodward's side had underachieved in terms of performance. We were concerned that in the four weeks between our game in Paris and the Wembley showdown they would cement the cracks in their side and come out with all guns blazing.

When they brushed aside the French at Twickenham, our fears were confirmed. Although the English press were still critical of certain aspects of their game, from our point of view it was clearly a more polished performance, with the pack in particular proving themselves as good as any in the championship. Furthermore, they were coming to play Wales with a championship, a Triple Crown and a Grand Slam on the table. Knowing how cocky they can be, and regardless of our so-called upturn in fortunes, I am sure they fancied a repeat of Twickenham.

We had to make sure that we used the four weeks well; we couldn't afford to waste a minute. After all, as we had beaten the French in Paris, the supporters would expect us to finish on a high by winning our next two games, regardless of opposition or venue. Graham Henry, in his own inimitable way, congratulated us on the victory in France when we arrived back in Cardiff on the Sunday afternoon, but then openly criticised us for a second-half performance which bore no resemblance to that of the first. He wanted us to be bold for 80 minutes, not just in the first half. In the second we had failed to live up to his expectations and he told us so in no uncertain terms. He made it very clear – he wanted us to be twice as good in Italy.

To play a friendly while the other four nations were playing each other in championship games back at home was very difficult for us. However, it was a good opportunity to consolidate. Gareth Thomas, who had been ruled out since Christmas with a shoulder problem, came in for Matthew Robinson, who had done an excellent job in the games against Scotland, Ireland and France. I felt sorry for him at the time because he had been arguably our best player in the first two games but seemed to pay the price for fumbling a ball in his own twenty-two which led to one of the French tries. In contrast, Alfie, a second-half substitute in Paris, was desperate to prove to Graham that while Matthew had done well, he was very much the number one on the right wing. Graham was quite keen for Gareth to perform too, I think, after being less than pleased with his performance against Argentina at Stradey Park.

On the coach journey back to the hotel from the Stade de France, there was an awkward moment involving the two of them. The boys were obviously ecstatic after winning in Paris for the first time in 24 years and Alfie was on his seat leading the singing. Graham turned around to him and said, 'Just remember, Gareth, you were only a sub!' Not only did it knock Alfie down a peg or two but it proved that while Graham recognised his enormous potential, he was not about to open the door and lay down the red carpet. He hadn't really said much to Gareth with regard to the various silly penalties he had conceded against Argentina, but he was very annoyed. One of the boys told me that after one of the penalties, Gareth had been caught on camera laughing. It was a bit unfortunate because S4C had a giant screen up at Stradey Park that night and just as the camera focused on Alfie, Graham looked up at the screen and saw him smirking. I am told it went down like a lead balloon. This was obviously Graham's way of telling him who was boss.

Alfie's response was perfect: he scored four tries against the Italians and we won comfortably, producing a performance that once again sent a message to the other championship teams. For Graham, seemingly difficult to please at that time, it was no more than he expected. But as far as Alfie was concerned, nobody could have been more pleased than the coach. He still had no intention of unrolling the red carpet, but then again Graham doesn't need to display his gratitude like that. A firm handshake and a quiet 'well done' was more than enough.

As far as the bigger picture was concerned, Alfie's success was small beer. Although we were pleased to have him back to full fitness, it was the overall performance that left us purring with satisfaction. We felt we had sent a positive message to England as they celebrated a comfortable victory over the French. Even more important, however, was the way in which I felt the side displayed its commitment to Graham. I believe that the attitude that weekend proved to Graham that his decision to spurn the possible oppor-tunity of succeeding All Blacks coach John Hart had been the right one.

He had been a bit sceptical about the overall character and ability of the side in the weeks leading up to the French game and he constantly reminded us that while a victory in Paris was worth celebrating, our lack of consistency throughout the second half was of real concern. Graham and I discussed the matter at length before we left for Treviso and I remember saying to Ceri that it wouldn't surprise me if Graham had a bit of a dig at the players before the game, if only to prevent the vulnerable members of the side from slipping into the comfort zone. He didn't let me down.

Everything had gone well in training on the Thursday and Friday in

Treviso and the boys were keen to get to the ground and get cracking. The hotel was pretty average, right by the main road and the railway line, and we felt a bit frustrated. The A team had been beaten on the Friday night but the Under-21s had won well and we were keen to follow suit.

The ground is quite close to the centre of Treviso and we arrived in plenty of time to have our customary stroll on the pitch with a drink of water and a cake or banana – or a Mars bar and a can of Coke, in Chris Wyatt's case. The players were really upbeat as they came back into the dressing-room at one end of a rather modest international ground and the banter was good. Chris was the centre of attention as usual and we listened to him arguing with Blackie about sunburn. Blackie said that Chris should cover up his chest and back as he walked around outside otherwise he would get sunburnt. Chris looked at Blackie with a straight face and said, 'Blackie, if you are worried about sunburn then shouldn't we stay in the dressing-room and let the Italians play against themselves?' Everyone had a chuckle and we felt very much at ease. It was certainly the calm before the storm.

Graham had been doing his own thing while we got a taste of the atmosphere but when we came back inside he was waiting to strike. I have played under some strong characters in my career; people like Jim Telfer and Ian McGeechan spring to mind straight away. However, Graham can be just as strong and every bit as intimidating.

He reminded us of how well we had done in beating France and of the obvious importance of winning for the first time on French soil since 1975. But then came the bombshell. You could have heard a pin drop in the dressing-room when he told us that while he respected us all as individuals, he did not yet respect us as a team. His address was short and to the point and then he left. It was a masterstroke.

The reaction was mixed. Some of the boys said, 'We'll show him,' while others, like Gibbsy, Jenks, Garin and Shane Howarth, said nothing. We knew what he was up to. It was Graham's way of keeping our feet on the ground and driving us towards perfection. He wanted the side to go out and turn the 40 minutes of quality rugby we had produced in Paris into 80 minutes of quality rugby in Treviso. Nothing less would suffice.

When the boys walked into the team hotel for a drink later that evening, Graham was sitting back in a comfortable armchair smoking a cigarette and wearing a smile that spoke volumes. He didn't have to say a word. His pre-match message had struck a chord with each and every player and if any member of that squad had had any doubts about the ability of Graham Henry, they didn't have any now. To a man we were convinced that the

WRU had spent its £250,000 wisely and we discussed it that night in Venice. Trevor had organised a trip on the waterways and we had a great night. But while we tried to take in the various landmarks, the conversation kept coming back to Graham. I remember asking one of the boys, 'How many other coaches would have the balls to say that 25 minutes before an international – and, what's more, keep the respect of the players?' I think the answer was 'not many'.

As an exercise, the game was perfect. We played well in the first half without ever pulling clear but in the second we mesmerised the Italians with a display of real quality. Knowing what Graham had expected from us, I knew that he would be relatively content with the overall performance and result.

Now we had to regroup and prepare for England. That would be the acid test and Graham wasted no time in telling us that while he had been pleased with certain aspects of the game in Italy, he still wanted a 20 per cent improvement from everyone. So, having worked out that Alfie would have to score five tries and Jenks would have to kick another 30 points, we set about the task in hand.

The previous year's visit to Twickenham had been calamitous and the nature of the defeat still hurts. Not only had we suffered the ignominy of a record championship defeat, but the whole weekend had been a humiliation. The journey back over the Severn Bridge was awful and I, for one, spent the next three days locked indoors. Yet here we were again, preparing ourselves to face an England side of equal strength, if not stronger. However, this time they had more to play for.

Thankfully, the arrival of Graham and the acquisition of players like Howie and Peter Rogers had given us a timely boost ahead of the World Cup. For the first time in two or three years, I felt as if the side had really conquered a significant hurdle. In winning two games in succession, both away from home, we had made a positive statement. Now we had to take it one step further. If that meant a decent performance and defeat, well, so be it. However, if it meant a gritty display and victory, we would take that too.

As professional rugby players, we had learnt a hell of a lot in the 14 months since the Twickenham débâcle. We had learnt to keep our mouths shut in the build-up to the game and to keep our talking until afterwards. Although Graham is never short of a word or the odd wisecrack with the press, on this occasion we were all singing from the same hymn sheet. He had been told of our collective problems 14 months earlier and he was not in any mood to preside over a similar catastrophe. In fact, such was his desire to get it right that he took it one step further. Not only did he give us a gentle verbal warning on the way home from Italy, but he also wrote a letter to the players instructing us to mind our p's and q's and not to speak out of turn to the press. If we were interviewed, we should talk about England's 'obvious strength' and of the 'enormous task' facing a Welsh side that had already lost twice that season, to Scotland and Ireland.

Once again, it was anything but a threat, though we knew that if anybody overstepped the mark they would probably find themselves hung, drawn and quartered. Graham doesn't mince his words and he doesn't suffer fools. We had learnt very quickly that if he said jump, the only response was 'How high?'.

Graham's final attempt to ensure a smooth ride into the game was to meet the Welsh press to ask for their assistance. Once more, he was breaking new ground, but such was his rapport with most of the press boys that the response was excellent. They met in the Marriott Hotel and Graham said his piece. On the whole, the Welsh press boys are good value and Graham was very encouraged by his meeting with them. He explained to us the reason behind his decision and said that while he was not trying to gag anyone, he felt that a quiet word might help us all.

That meeting with the press also saw the start of the mind games between us and England. Clive Woodward had been quoted in one of the papers in Wales as saying he was surprised to have been rung so soon before the actual game. He was trying to say that we in Wales were obviously placing more importance on the game than he was in England. That's nonsense; I know that England thought about nothing else in the two weeks before our meeting. They wanted to win as badly as us.

Unfortunately, the build-up didn't go as smoothly as we had hoped. Jenks, Dai Young and I were invited to a Millennium Stadium press conference on the Tuesday after the Italy game, just for a few pictures – or so we were led to believe. When we got there, we did the shoot and said our goodbyes. However, before we could slip away we were told to go to the Angel Hotel, where the London press boys were waiting to speak to us about the game.

Having been told by Graham about the plan of attack with regard to the media and how we should only attend certain press conferences, I was a bit disappointed. Once again we had not been given the whole story. I was really angry at the time, although in fairness to Rob Cole, who was organising the press conference, he was very supportive and gave us a good steer on what to expect.

Mindful of what Graham had said, all three of us refused to talk about our chances, preferring to concentrate on how good England were. The likes of Peter Jackson of the *Daily Mail* and David Hands of *The Times* were having none of it, however, and Peter questioned why we were adopting such an approach. 'Aren't you just playing mind games here?' he asked. To be honest, we were, although I was not about to give the game away. What's more, you have to remember that we were coming up against one of the great sides in world rugby whom we hadn't beaten for far too long. They were a top side, so I wasn't lying when I said we were the definite underdogs and had no right to be thinking in terms of winning. Maybe I went a bit OTT but who wouldn't have done in my position? I certainly wasn't going to get pushed into saying how we would beat them. We had made that error once before and had it shoved down our throats.

We trained well during the week and by the time we left for London we were feeling quietly confident. We still regarded ourselves as underdogs, but we were comfortable in the knowledge that everything had gone well and that the boys were fit and ready. Graham had been very strong in his leadership for the five days we were together and although he spoke of a lack of respect from England towards us, he never made an issue of it until after the penultimate training session at London Welsh. We had a really good session and when we finished Graham called us in behind the posts, away from everyone else. We sat down and Graham talked about the session and our game plan and about the responsibility we had on our shoulders in three days' time. Then, just as he had done in Treviso, he hit us with another bombshell.

He told us that he had received a fax from a complete stranger that morning. The person who had sent the fax said that he had been on a train the previous day and had sat opposite some of the English management team. He said that they had been talking about some of the Welsh team and had targeted Scott and Craig Quinnell. They felt that they were the two weak links in the Welsh pack and were particularly vulnerable in terms of their discipline.

To this day, I am not sure whether the fax ever existed, nor do I want to know. But it was another masterstroke. Scott, Craig and a few of the other boys were incensed by what Graham had said and on the journey back from Old Deer Park to the hotel there was only one topic of conversation. From that moment, I knew we had a real chance.

We spent most of Friday talking about our game plan. Having watched numerous videos of the English pack, we decided that our new-look front row of Garin, Ben and Peter would target the English front row and put them on the back foot. In turn, that would prevent Lawrence Dallaglio from picking up on the front foot and breaking through our first line of defence. If we put them under pressure by stopping numbers eight and nine from functioning effectively, we could pressurise Mike Catt at ten. It didn't happen as often as we might have liked when it came to the game, but it certainly worked on the odd occasion.

Our Friday run-out at the stadium was extremely tense and, realising that the boys were getting quite anxious, Lynn Howells organised a Grand National sweepstake on the bus journey back to Kensington. I think mine fell at the second! It helped us relax, as did the race itself. We watched the Scotland–France game on television on the Saturday afternoon, expecting France to win, and then watched the National. I think Scotland's victory put more pressure on us to perform, if only to give them the championship at the expense of England. Nothing would be nicer. Having said that, I think the manner in which Scotland won made us feel that our victory in Paris had not been as good as we might have thought. It certainly put things into perspective.

The Saturday evening was quite special because after my captain's talk Ieuan popped into the hotel for a coffee. By that time I was feeling quite nervous, so to see someone of Ieuan's experience was very comforting. Both he and Jonathan Davies have been wonderful to me since I started playing for Wales and especially in the two years since I first captained the side against Italy. For someone like me who enjoys using others as a sounding board, it is nice to know that Ieuan and Jonathan are always there to lend an ear. I honestly don't think I would have got through some of the difficult times without them.

Although we had beaten France and Italy, the success was still overshadowed by the dreadful defeats against Scotland and Ireland. Ieuan knew the score and understood what I had been going through, both as a player and as a captain. We had spoken about the criticism from various members of the press and he agreed that it was hardly worth worrying about. That's all very well, but at the time it hurts.

I was glad that Ieuan had come in to see me but slightly concerned when he asked whether I had heard his BBC radio interview earlier in the week. I hadn't, so I asked him what he had said. 'I told the world that you will beat England, so go and do it.' With that little gem he left, and after taking my customary sleeping tablet I had an early night. It did the trick because by the time I got up on Sunday morning I was quite relaxed.

The day of the game can be very tedious indeed, especially with a four o'clock kick-off. Although there is plenty to think about, you spend the day kicking your heels, just waiting for the off. The players took breakfast in ones and twos and were visibly nervous. To combat that, Graham took us to St James's Park for a light run-out. Not only did it get us away from the hotel, it also enabled us to kill a bit of time and relax. The backs went through a few moves and I did a bit of kicking with Jenks. There was quite an audience and I started to feel the intensity of the situation.

We changed into our tracksuits after lunch and had a rub down and at about two o'clock Graham called his team meeting. As ever, he came in late. Dai Pickering, our team manager, always phones him when everyone is there and then Graham comes down from his room. It's a ritual. He strolls in straight-faced and then peels off his jacket before straightening his tie. Then comes the sermon.

By now, we had earned his respect as a team. Now we had to prove ourselves to England. He felt that they had no respect for us and that beating them in style was the only way we could change that. It took me back to Ian McGeechan's speech in South Africa. It was very moving and by the time he picked up his jacket and walked out the adrenaline was flowing and we were buzzing with anticipation and excitement.

The final hour and a half is always difficult and that is where Blackie comes into his own. He builds us up gradually but keeps the boys calm at the same time. Then, when it's time to fizz, he becomes very animated. He picks on certain individuals who he thinks are not totally focused. Often it's Colin Charvis. Colin is a great international forward but very quiet and Blackie doesn't like that. He wants to know that players are up for the challenge, so he picks on them. Ben Evans and Dafydd James are the same – and they get the same treatment.

By the time we got to within a mile of Wembley, the bus was engulfed by a sea of red jerseys and red-and-white scarves. That was when it really hit us. This game meant everything to the people of Wales and we had to win.

We got to the dressing-room and then had a stroll around the pitch, trying to gauge the conditions. The wind circulates at Wembley and any captain will tell you that it's important to get a feel of that before you go out for the toss. On this occasion, the breeze was blowing back towards the tunnel. Graham asked me what I was thinking of doing should Lawrence call incorrectly and I said that I wanted to play into the wind.

We had our warm-up with Blackie and the noise from the crowd was already ringing in our ears. Then Max Boyce and Tom Jones appeared on the touch-line and the whole place erupted. Although we hadn't completed our warm-up, I told Blackie that I wanted the players to go back to the dressing-room. You could feel the intensity and we needed to collect our thoughts.

The toss of the coin was crucial, or so I thought. So when Lawrence called correctly and decided to kick with the wind, I was inwardly pleased. I was also surprised at his choice, although once again I felt there was a certain arrogance in the decision. I felt that England believed they would crack us in the first half and close off the game before we had mastered the elements. I told the boys and that wound them up even more.

I suppose I had wound myself up too about all of this and before we got on to the pitch I was keen to put one over on Lawrence and the England team. Once the talking had stopped and the pre-match speeches had been delivered, it was time to go. The referee called us and the plan was for both sides to walk out together. We didn't budge. I was not going to allow England to share the noise that our supporters would make on our arrival. In our previous games at Wembley the two sides had always walked out together. Not this time. England finally realised that we were not coming out, so they left for that 45-second walk up the tunnel and out on to the pitch – on their own.

Once they were out of the way, I opened the door and led the boys out. It was a magical experience. The noise was incredible as we made our way towards the royal box for the anthems. The referee had informed the teams on which side of the royal box they should line up, so we made our way to the left where the Welsh flag was hanging. However, as we arrived at half-way, we realised that England were standing on our side in front of our flag. We told them to move and put a couple of balls down where we were supposed to stand. As we did so, Lawrence led his side in front of us and Richard Cockerill, whom we were not too fond of anyway, kicked one of our balls across the front of our line and gave a few of the boys a typically cocky smile. It was totally dismissive and very disrespectful. You can imagine my feelings when the final whistle went. A look of abject disbelief had replaced that arrogant smile and I loved it.

Remembering everything that Graham had told us, we knew it was crucial that we didn't gift them any early points. We had to take a hold on the game, retain the ball and try to stretch them if we could. We couldn't and, to give credit where credit is due, their defence was impeccable. Neil Back was like a man mountain. What's more, Dan Luger scored a try in the third minute, Howie and Gareth Thomas collided to give Richard Hill a try and Steve Hanley capped his first half of international rugby with a straightforward third try just before half-time. It was left to Neil to keep us in touch and, as has been the case on so many previous occasions, he came up with the goods.

Although we had not threatened England's line too often, we were still within touching distance and that gave us a great deal of confidence. At half-time, we were well pleased. They had thrown the kitchen sink at us yet of the two sides we were far more content with what had happened.

Graham gave us an old-fashioned roasting for playing too much rugby in the wrong areas and in the second half we changed our style to suit the game. Howie crossed for the first try, and with Jenks chipping away and England making so many wrong decisions, we always felt we were in with a chance.

The turning point came with ten minutes to go. Much to our surprise, Lawrence opted to kick for touch and not at goal. We stopped their driving line-out and after winning decent ball Colin Charvis was the recipient of a high tackle from Tim Rodber. The referee awarded us a penalty and Jenks kicked for the corner. I looked up at the clock and we were into injury time. It was our last chance, yet considering how many times we had tried and failed to break their first-up defenders, I was not exactly exuding confidence as Scott Quinnell took receipt of a flat pass from me and pinned his ears back.

The key moment was when he fumbled the ball. It seemed to put the English defence out of their stride. Gibbsy took the pass from Scott and smashed into their midfield, and I was screaming for him to go all the way. He broke the first two tackles and then a third before the twenty-two opened up and the try line beckoned. When he dropped over the line, I sprinted over and hugged him. I was close to tears, although I realised that Jenks still had to kick the conversion to put us in front for the first time in the game.

I was told by one of our replacements that a minute before the try a member of the English contingent had asked a steward which side of the royal box the players should go up to collect the trophy. When Gibbsy went over he must have had second thoughts. I went back over half-way and held my breath. I need not have worried, because Jenks put it straight through the middle.

It should have been game, set and match but there was still one more moment of madness and we could have lost it in the sixth minute of injury time. We were awarded a scrum and I told Scott Quinnell to hold it in while we wheeled through 90 degrees. The plan was to do that for a second time and then on the third occasion I would feed Neil, who would put it into touch. The referee went round to the other side of the scrum and as he did so Matt Dawson kicked the ball out of the back row. It was loose going back towards our own twenty-two, so I dived on it and held on for dear life. The referee told me to release and I just kept shouting, 'I have let go! I have let go! I can't roll away!'

It was a dreadful moment because he blew his whistle after a few seconds. I thought he was going to penalise me for holding on in the tackle. However, he gave England a scrum and that, at least, was a godsend. Now we had to prepare for the drop goal. The ball came out quite quickly and as Matt passed to Mike Catt, Brett, Jenks and I charged at him. He sliced the kick into Howie's hands and he marked it. There was just time to kick it into touch and then the whistle went. What a feeling!

I still can't believe that we won the game but that is what makes it so special. To see England with their heads in their hands was a wonderful experience. I will never forget the disaster at Twickenham but this certainly made up for that humiliating defeat, and I felt very fortunate to be part of the side at Wembley that day.

17. 'DON'T CRY FOR ME ARGENTINA'

A Perfect Start to a Perfect Summer

With respect, a summer tour to Argentina is not something to look forward to. The rugby is hard, as you might expect, the food is often shocking and the crowds, who love to hate you, can be very volatile, as the likes of JPR Williams will tell you from his experience of touring there in the 1960s.

The squad was obviously on a high after the championship victories over France and England but we were far from licking our lips in anticipation. What's more, the press did their bit to light the touch paper as usual, so by the time we set off from Heathrow, we knew all the gory details of what had happened on previous tours. An article with JPR in the *News of the World* explained how the side had been bombarded with rotten fruit, while the former England scrum-half Dewi Morris told of how a Union Jack had been set alight by the locals on the terraces during an England game. There was even a story about an Argentine player who actually died after a game against Wales. Although he had been ill and perhaps should not have played, I am sure I remember reading somewhere that Wales got the blame for killing him. However, when you have had your head split open by a stray boot and been punched on more than one occasion by an Argentine player, you realise that their rugby is a little different from ours.

- With the World Cup less than five months away and with Argentina booked as our first opponents in the competition, I suppose they were the last side we wanted to play at that time, especially on their turf. Fortunately, on this occasion, we had finished the previous season on a high and we travelled in much better shape. The victory over England, in particular, had settled a few scores and given the players a much-needed boost.

It had also been a particularly tough time with regard to our contracts. The WRU had replaced the old pay structure with a new style of contract and had requested us to sign way back at the beginning of the year. There was a great deal of scepticism amongst the squad members, however, and it took many a long meeting before we decided to sign on the dotted line.

The basic ingredients of the deal meant that the WRU was recognising experience and rewarding success. Instead of offering another flat-rate deal of perhaps £30,000 per season plus bonuses, they offered an appearance fee of £1,500 per man per match up to a maximum of £10,000 per season, a £5,000 win bonus for beating any level of opposition and an extra £75 for every cap you had won over your first five. I worked it out that for the first Test I would earn close on £8,500 if we won. Neil Jenkins was close on £12,000.

What concerned the players was the uncertainty. We understood the benefits of playing and winning but we were slightly reluctant to give up a guaranteed sum of money for a contract which could, if we got injured or were dropped, earn us nothing. As you can imagine, that concern increased after the defeats against Scotland and Ireland. If we continued like that we would certainly lose out. However, with the upturn in fortunes during the second half of the championship season, I felt that it was worth the gamble. I signed and so did the rest of the boys. For the WRU, who were being questioned on a daily basis by the local press, it was a definite plus.

With the contracts having been signed, the squad was able to concentrate on its one major aim – to win both Tests and to become the first country to achieve such a feat on Argentine soil. England and New Zealand might have won a series there in the '80s but no side had ever recorded a clean sweep. While I understood the degree of difficulty involved in achieving that, I was confident that we would probably never have a better chance.

Considering the result at Stradey Park earlier that season and the way in which our front five had been destroyed in the scrum, that might sound a bit strange. They were a very powerful side and had made it quite clear after the Llanelli game that playing in Argentina would give them a definite advantage. Graham told us in no uncertain terms that if we wanted a place in the history books we would have to play even better than we had done in the first half in Paris and in the second half against England at Wembley. That was the enormity of the challenge ahead. Argentine rugby has improved out of all proportion in recent years and we knew that having come so close in November they would really fancy their chances of reversing the outcome on their own patch.

The second objective, and perhaps more important in the long term, was to escape from Buenos Aires without suffering any serious injuries. We had already lost Scott Gibbs to a bruised sternum and a thumb injury prior to the tour, and considering the World Cup was fast approaching, we could ill afford any further injuries to key players.

Unfortunately, the omens were not good. I had never been on a tour where we had counted the same players on to the plane on the way home as we had on the way out. You can usually bet your last pound that somebody will have to go home with some ailment or another. So when the same 37 players returned on the Jumbo three and a half weeks later, I must admit to being somewhat surprised and, ultimately, relieved.

I think Steve Black deserves a pat on the back for that. There is no doubt that he nursed us through a very demanding tour with typical expertise. There were the customary bumps and bruises – and certainly a few bruised egos by the time we departed from Buenos Aires. However, on the whole it was a genuine success. It certainly vindicated Graham's decision to bring Blackie on board.

For the players I suppose there was one consolation – the actual length of the tour. We had the two Tests, a game against Argentina A and two other games against provincial opposition. In essence, it was an extended World Cup trial and nothing more.

From what Graham had said to us in the build-up to our departure, the players understood that he had a good idea of what his final 30-strong World Cup party would be. However, there were still a number of places up for grabs and players like Matthew Robinson, Nick Walne, Darren Morris and Arwel Thomas were all anxious to make a lasting impression.

On a personal front, I was obviously concerned about my own well-being. After all, the previous two summers had ended with me either coming home early or missing the final Test through injury. I didn't want this to be a case of third time unlucky. I was sick and tired of injury and I knew that if I suffered the kind of problem that I had in South Africa in 1997 I would almost certainly miss the World Cup. I don't think I could have coped with that.

Having left Cardiff in good spirits, we arrived at Heathrow and Graham immediately called the squad together. As organised as ever, he laid out the plan of attack for the entire tour and by the time we got on the plane everything had been covered, right down to the very last detail. I was more than happy. Graham had chosen three scrum-halfs – me, Dai Llewellyn and Rhodri Jones – and told me that I would not be involved in either of the midweek matches. I wouldn't even have to sit on the bench. That was just about right in my book. It was certainly a huge relief, because in South Africa in 1997 and again 12 months later I had been injured in the build-up to the Test. On this occasion, I would play against Buenos Aires in the opening game and then in the two Test matches. That was my lot.

Since Graham took over, the strength in depth of the squad has improved dramatically and that has certainly enabled him to avoid overloading key players. Whereas we used to have just 15 players and a few who could play at a push, suddenly there were 37 players who were justified in thinking that they deserved a place in the Test side. Whether every player would get a chance, I wasn't sure, but when we left that was a definite possibility.

Graham decided to rest Jenks, who was just getting over shoulder surgery, and both Quinnells for the opening game against Buenos Aires, who were the provincial champions. Arwel played at ten and Leigh Davies featured instead of Gibbsy, who had been left behind in Wales to undergo treatment and take a well-earned rest. His absence and the minor injuries to players like Scott and Craig meant that other players would have an early chance to stake their claim.

I know that Graham told the press that his team to play in the first Test would be selected on the evidence of the England game but I was not convinced. If that was the case, it suggested that Graham was prepared to allow certain players to take it easy in the first game, knowing that they would be an automatic choice to play against the Pumas. Not a chance. Graham has never once allowed players to take their foot off the gas. You do that at your peril.

Unfortunately, I don't think too many fringe players, like Arwel and Leigh, took their chance in that opening game. I must admit they were a good side and they prevented us from playing fast, fluid rugby. We failed to control the game and, to be honest, a lot of that was down to the fact that it was Arwel's first game under Graham Henry. He and one or two others had to take on so much information before the game about how and where we would play that it all became a bit too much.

Arwel's a lovely player and an individual who can crucify you on his day. However, you can't compare him with Jenks. Neil is so consistent; he's a conventional player on whom you can depend. He runs the game with far more control. In contrast, Arwel has a tendency to switch off during a game, and as a captain and a scrum-half, that's the last thing you want from your fly-half. Still, he did a good job as Jenks's understudy in the remaining games on tour and was perhaps a little unfortunate not to make the World Cup squad. After all, when Graham named his 30 there was only one natural choice at number ten.

The match against Buenos Aires was a frustrating one, the lead changed hands five times, Arwel kicked 19 points and we still lost 31–29. To be fair, we didn't deserve to come away from there with a win, regardless of the narrow margin at the end of the game. I suppose the only consolation was that we had wiped away a few cobwebs.

For Buenos Aires and for the national side, victory was the perfect tonic. For us it was a real disappointment. At that time, people back home and one or two of the supporters who had travelled out to watch had a genuine concern. They wondered whether our victories over France and England had been a flash in the pan. Had this defeat exposed real cracks in the side and were we perhaps not quite as good as some might have thought?

After all, the tour was unlikely to get too much easier. The locals had told us that Buenos Aires would probably provide us with the toughest test, although I was not so sure. Tucuman would be a physical and very competitive side, Argentina A would comprise players desperate to push themselves into contention for the second Test and the Pumas themselves were a strong side who knew what it would take to beat us. Or at least they thought they knew.

I was quite glad for the contribution of Craig Quinnell that night. He recalled a conversation he had had with Argentine scrum-half Augustin Pichot. Pichot was a former team-mate of Craig's at Richmond and he supported the view of the locals in Buenos Aires. He even predicted in the paper that Buenos Aires would beat us but that the Pumas would probably go down in both Test matches. Once the tour was over, I considered asking him to choose my lottery numbers!

When we got back to the hotel after the game you could sense a feeling of relief amongst the boys who had missed out on that first game. They knew that on Tuesday night, against Tucuman, they had a chance to put themselves in the frame. The so-called first team had underperformed, so the chance was there.

Training became very interesting after that. The senior players in the side for the Tuesday got together and realised that an opportunity had arisen from our defeat on the Saturday night. If they could play well then Graham might be tempted to make a few alterations in personnel for the second Test, if not for the first.

Playing up country against Tucuman was something that Graham had experienced ten years earlier when he had led a New Zealand touring party to South America. He too had read the horror stories in the papers and was determined not to subject us to any repeat performances. In the end, his preparation was spot-on. It was like a military manoeuvre. The players who were not involved in the game, and that included me, were whisked into the ground just before kick-off and were whisked away from their seats five minutes before the end to avoid any potential trouble. I must admit that although there were no flags burning on the terraces or fruit being hurled at the players, it was an experience to behold. We talk about partisan support in Wales but this was something else. The Welsh supporters call you names; these fans were baying for blood.

It was a strange game because we went 20 points up and then found ourselves 25–20 down just before half-time. However, we were clearly the better side and with Matthew Robinson in fine form we won 69–44. For Matthew, it was the perfect night. Not only did he score four tries but he played well too. Once again, Graham was in a corner with regard to Gareth Thomas, who had not played well against Buenos Aires but who had played a significant role in the victories against France (as a replacement), Italy and England. Should Graham stick with Alfie or should he reward Matthew, who, to his credit, had never once let Graham down? The next couple of days were spent wondering whether he would play safe or go for gold.

Because of our early departure from the ground, we were already relaxing back at the hotel when the rest of the boys returned. They walked in feeling like a million dollars, had a few beers and as good as said 'Point proven'. That was when the pressure came and Graham, despite all that had been said about picking his side on the evidence of the victory over England, dropped Alfie and went with Matthew on the right wing.

It was certainly a kick up the backside for Alfie and I spoke to him about it. I told him that while we all recognised him as a world-class player, he now had to go out, probably in the midweek game against Argentina A, and prove himself once again. He was very disappointed, especially having battled so hard to overcome a shoulder injury early in the year. However, it did send a message to everyone in the squad. Graham would not tolerate any loss of form or lapse in concentration in the months leading up to the World Cup. Gareth had been given his warning and the rest of the boys took heed.

The first Test of any series is crucial and with such a strong squad on tour, the preparation in the four days leading up to the game was absolutely perfect. The sessions throughout the week were superb and the plan of attack for the whole day was precise. It was just a shame that when it came to Saturday, all the hard work went out of the window – and through no fault of our own.

On any tour, you rely on the home union and various liaison officers to get the organisation and the timings spot-on. After all, for three weeks we were in the hands of the Argentine Rugby Union and the various local authorities and emergency services. On this occasion, we were let down badly and it could quite easily have changed everything. That is the fine line between success and failure.

The team hotel was about 45 minutes from the ground so Trevor James arranged a police escort to cut the journey down to close on 25 minutes. It was a decent idea considering the volume of traffic that builds up in Buenos Aires. Unfortunately, it didn't come off. We got on the bus and waited but the escort didn't turn up. We decided to go it alone but with so much traffic about it actually took us 50 minutes to get there.

Blackie was pretty annoyed by now because his role on match day is crucial. He needs us there, changed and out on the field in plenty of time to get the necessary drills done before we come back in for our final chat. Not only were we late arriving but also the officials at the stadium said that we were not allowed to warm up on the pitch. Blackie didn't kick up too much of a fuss at the outset because he had located a basketball court behind the dressing-rooms. That would be adequate for us. Unfortunately, when he asked for permission to use the area, the same officials told him that the court had been designated for the Pumas. It was shocking. Heaven help us if we ever go down that road and treat touring teams like that!

In the end, we were shown to a netball court on the other side of the ground. There was no shelter from the afternoon sun and it was a poor substitute. The sun was burning by that time but we had very little option. After all, we only had 20 minutes in which to get ourselves ready. I could imagine what was going on inside Blackie's and Graham's heads – they must have been livid. However, they never once allowed the players to see that. They kept their cool and told us to carry on regardless. Blackie convinced us that it would not affect us during the game.

After 20 minutes we were 23 points down and wondering where our next piece of possession would come from. I am not one to make excuses but missing out on the best part of our warm-up was crucial. I couldn't see any way back for us. The boys were leaden-footed and there was no spark. The Pumas were loving it; I am sure the officials were too.

It was a real test of character for us. We had shown what we were capable of achieving when trailing against England at Wembley but this was different. It was even harder. I kept telling the boys that our first job was to actually get the ball because the first 20 minutes had been spent chasing shadows. Secondly, we had to score at least once before half-time. Thankfully, we scored twice. Jenks kicked a penalty and then converted a fine try from Dafydd James.

Graham gave us a roasting at half-time and in the second half we were a different side. Brett Sinkinson and Chris Wyatt scored tries and we ran out winners 36–26. It was a remarkable turnaround and one in the eye for the

Argentine officials. It was also further confirmation that this Welsh side had bottle. I am sure that the side which lost at Twickenham the previous year would have folded.

The next few days were unbelievable. We had won fair and square for the second time in seven months, yet here we were facing accusations of cheating and foul play from at least one Argentine player. Nothing was said at the time but we felt it to be quite ironic. Graham and Lynn Howells had had a quiet word with the Argentine Rugby Union after one of the boys complained of eye-gouging but they had certainly not made a song and dance about it. We kept our complaint fairly low-key and didn't tell the members of our own travelling press. However, when I read what the Argentine players were complaining about, I wished we had shouted it from the highest mountain. The papers were full of quotes from Federico Mendez about our so-called illegal scrummaging methods. It was laughable, really, but confirmation that we had not only beaten them but also redressed the balance in the set-piece area. Whereas we had taken the November lesson on the chin, they were squealing like pigs.

Sadly, there are quite a few sides like that. When it goes well they can't say enough about the opposition. When it doesn't go so well they start bleating. I have very little respect for players when they go down that road and I must admit that at the time I would have given anything to have beaten them in the second Test seven days later.

We moved on to Rosario for the game against the A team and that was where the travelling nightmare began. We were told that there was no airport in Rosario so we would have to travel by coach. Most of us have done that before and it doesn't bother me that much. If nothing else, it's the perfect opportunity to get the card school up and running. On this occasion, however, I did have a few words to say about the arrangements. To start with, travelling for five and a half hours on a bus that I am sure must have been first registered in the late 1940s was hardly the best preparation for a match of such significance. I felt like Forrest Gump sitting in one of those old American-style yellow school buses.

Thankfully, we got there in one piece and I took an hour out to chat with Martyn Williams, whom Graham had chosen as captain for the two midweek games. Martyn is a quality player who had been treated quite harshly in previous seasons and I wanted him to feel as comfortable as possible with leading the side. He was a little concerned about speaking to players like Dai Young, Gareth Llewellyn and Jonathan Humphreys because of their experience. I told him how I had felt when I'd captained

Ieuan for the first time against Italy. It's difficult but you can't afford to be overawed.

In my eyes, Graham could not have chosen a better captain than Martyn. And, with respect to the others, I don't believe anybody would have led the side with such gusto. Okay, so they lost 47–34 to Argentina A, but once again there was a handful of decent performances, especially from the captain.

Now all that remained was the selection for the second Test and the game itself. Personally, I couldn't wait, because the rest of the tour, with the exception of the games, had been awful. The food was woeful, there was very little in the way of entertainment and the amenities were certainly sparse. Blackie tried his best to get the entertainments committee going but when they did organise a night out at the annual Buenos Aires festival, they got the dates wrong and we ended up downtown without a soul around.

Then there was the fishing party who arrived back late from a trip on the high seas. I stayed back at the hotel with Jenks to play snooker while a dozen or so players went out to try and catch a few fish. Once again the travel arrangements were not exactly precise and they ended up returning an hour late. It meant that Martyn's team meeting had to be put back an hour, which didn't go down too well, although there were members of the team management involved too. For some of the boys it was a good joke but I felt for Martyn. It was an important meeting for him as an inexperienced captain and there we were without half of the side and team management present.

Argentina made five changes from the first Test whereas Graham made just a couple, Matthew Robinson giving way to Gareth Thomas and Geraint Lewis coming in for Colin Charvis. I was sitting at the same table as Matthew and Colin during the team announcement and I felt a bit awkward. As a player, you always think the captain has had a major say in selection and I wondered what both Matthew and Colin were thinking. It certainly wasn't the case on this occasion. Graham and Lynn had made up their minds and I had not even been consulted. However, I did make it my duty to speak to both players later that day. In fairness to Graham, he had told Matthew and Colin before the meeting that neither would be in the side, which is the right way to go about things. I don't think there is anything worse than sitting in a room with the rest of the squad when the coach springs it on you.

I spoke to Colin on the bus back to Buenos Aires and he told me that it was the first time he had ever been dropped from any team. He couldn't understand the reasons why Graham had dropped him, yet he promised to fight his hardest to regain his place in time for the game against South Africa in Cardiff later in the month. I was delighted to hear that and didn't want to add any more. I wanted to tell him that, like Gareth Thomas's, his relegation was down to Graham wanting to issue a kick up the backside. Colin's contribution to the victories over France and England had been significant and in my eyes he was an automatic choice for the World Cup and for the upcoming games against South Africa, Canada and France.

Once again, it was Graham telling the players that nobody has a divine right to wear the Welsh jersey. So while we all felt that Colin would be back for the Springboks game, nobody would have placed a bet. If Graham felt that he would be better served playing Geraint against the world champions then he would do so. He certainly doesn't bow down to player pressure.

We were all desperate to get back to the relative luxury of the Buenos Aires hotel and to get on with the tour. However, the journey back could not have been any worse. The bus overheated half-way through the journey and we spent 45 minutes standing on the side of the road waiting for the radiator to cool down. We finally arrived in Buenos Aires some six and a half hours later and pretty pissed off.

What made it even worse was that when we arrived at the hotel, Jonathan Davies asked me why we had come by bus and not on the plane. When I told him that it was because there was no airport in Rosario he just laughed and said, 'What did we land on then, a motorway?' It turned out that there *was* an airport, so why didn't we use it? Whether it was the Union trying to cut costs, I don't know, but after suffering a pretty comprehensive defeat, being put on a bus like that was tantamount to rubbing salt into an open wound.

Having had a moan about the travelling arrangements, we got back down to business. The boys were mindful that only half a job had been done. We were also very aware of the fact that the players who had featured on the Tuesday against Argentina A, with the exception of Gareth Thomas and one or two replacements, were effectively off tour. They were relaxing and having a few beers while we were working towards the game. It is always a difficult situation.

Our team manager, Dai Pickering, had been responsible for cocking up the dates of the festival and we gave him a bit of stick. But in trying to redeem himself, he made things even worse. Realising that he had to keep the party together in those final few days, he planned a trip for a slap-up meal in a top restaurant. To me, a top restaurant means tidy grub: good chips, good sauces and plenty of it. This was anything but. For starters, we had black pudding which had been introduced to the frying pan but remained uncooked; for the main course, we had a piece of steak, or as I called it an eight-ounce piece of fat, and as an added bonus we had pig's intestines. Well, the look on the boys' faces was amazing. It was a total waste of a night and I felt sorry for Dai. He had spent ages organising the night and here we were, desperate to get out and find a McDonald's. I do like junk food and at that point I would have killed for a Big Mac, large fries and a Diet Coke.

There wasn't any point going back to the hotel for a meal because the food they served up there wasn't to the liking of too many players either. So we decided to do what we had done for much of the tour. A few of us, led by King Big Mac Peter Rogers, went out and had a couple of burgers just to fill our stomachs. Graham didn't interfere with our visits to McDonald's and Blackie didn't make a fuss either. What's more, there was one hidden benefit. If Graham had wanted to call a team meeting at short notice, he knew exactly where to come. One telephone call to McDonald's would have been enough.

Having learned our lesson from the first Test, we were far better prepared for the second. We organised our own way to the ground and made sure we had somewhere to warm up. It was important to get that right because this was our big chance to become the first side in history to enjoy a 2–0 series win over the Pumas in Argentina.

The first half was marred by a free-for-all, but having beaten them seven days earlier and read all the nonsense in the papers, we were ready for it. So when it did go off, the boys didn't stand on ceremony. One of their forwards threw the first punch and while I am not one to condone retaliation, I was mightily impressed with the way we handled ourselves. It sent a message to each and every one of their players. They wouldn't push us back in the scrum and they wouldn't knock us out. From that moment on I don't believe there was any doubt about the final outcome. The funniest sight was Dr Roger Evans trying to pull off one of their forwards as he tried to lay into Scott Quinnell. I am sure that Roger gave him one for the road as he grabbed him!

Although we led 9–8 at half-time, Graham had a go at us at the interval and said that unless we started playing with a bit more control we would waste this golden opportunity of rewriting the history books. Thankfully, in the second half, after Pichot had delivered a sharp punch to my cheek when referee Chris White wasn't looking, we made sure of that series success.

174

Once again, Jenks was immaculate, and despite conceding a late try, we held on to win 23–16.

Our scrum was awesome. We shoved them back on our ball and, considering what had gone on at Stradey Park in November, that was a remarkable achievement. I was very emotional at the final whistle because it was the first time I had ever won anything in a Welsh jersey. Obviously, I had finished on the winning side a few times, but I had never won a series or a championship. It was a wonderful feeling and I milked every moment.

To go to Argentina and win as we did was something special. I felt that it was further confirmation that Welsh rugby had negotiated another significant hurdle. To come home with the same players that had travelled out was a feat in itself. But that, as I mentioned earlier in the chapter, was down to Steve Black. His methods may be a little off-the-wall at times and I have to admit that a few boys have questioned his programmes. However, there is no escaping the facts. We took 37 players out to Argentina for a five-match tour and we came home with the same number and exactly the same faces.

The journey back was obviously very relaxing and once again the lads got stuck into the cards. I didn't let Ceri know then but by the time we landed at Heathrow I was planning a visit to my bank manager. I think I was about £500 down. I was determined to win some of that back before I got home, so the moment we got on to the team bus in London I called the card players together – Gareth Llewellyn, Mike Voyle, Neil Boobyer and one or two others – and dealt my first hand. By the time we arrived in Cardiff I was ready to tell the world of our 2–0 win in Argentina and of my rejuvenation as a card player. It might only be two or three hours door to door but in that time I had reduced my debt to just over £100. It was a good end to a very good tour.

18. A LEGAL SUBSTANCE

Creatine, Lawrence and the
Pressure of Professionalism

Nobody, with the exception of the *News of the World* staff, would have derived any great pleasure from reading how Lawrence Dallaglio had opened his heart to a reporter in a hotel room. I was in Argentina with the squad when the news broke but Ceri rang me straight away. The boys were absolutely gobsmacked. The story itself was shocking but, furthermore, Lawrence had allegedly admitted to taking drugs with two other British Lions players on the 1997 tour of South Africa.

While I knew that I was clean – and believed the rest of the squad to be clean too – there is always that feeling that supporters and other players are looking at you and wondering, 'Did he? Was he? Has he?' They are questions that, in my case, are answered with a definite no. What's more, I don't for one minute believe that Lawrence and/or any other player snorted, injected or swallowed anything illegal during that tour. If they did, well, it wasn't in front of me, nor was it spoken about between the boys. Normally, in such a tight-knit environment, gossip spreads like wildfire, especially something like that. Can you honestly imagine the boys keeping something like that quiet?

Unfortunately, the whole issue of drugs and performance-enhancing substances seems to have escalated in the time that I have been playing. And, sadly, Welsh rugby cannot claim to be squeaky clean. First there was Richie Griffiths, a South Wales Police centre who tested positive for steroids, and then there was Paul Jones, the Llanelli lock, who was caught and subsequently banned for taking a similar steroid, allegedly to speed up his recovery from a shoulder injury.

I have to admit that I was somewhat surprised at both players and concerned that the image of the game and of the leading players in Wales had been tarnished because of those two isolated instances. As I have said before, I am not one to preach to others and I don't like being preached to myself. However, I was given some spot-on advice when I first came into the game and I have passed on that information to many other young players who have suggested that taking steroids is a quick way to the top.

The advice is simple. Firstly, and most importantly, steroids, so I am told, do the body no good whatsoever in the long term. Secondly, it's cheating. It's as simple as that. I don't want to be associated with cheats and I don't want to cheat my way to the top either. If others do, then I would rather they seek out another sport in which to do it. Better still, get out of sport altogether.

Personally, I have never touched a needle, taken an illegal substance or spoken with anyone about the possibility of doing so and I never will. However, I have recently supported the product Creatine, which I have taken at regular intervals. I took it last season up until the South Africa game at Wembley and have taken it for the past four or five years. And until the medical precautions came about I had no concern. Whether I am worried about what has been said, I am not sure, but I have not taken it since November 1998.

Creatine is a substance that enhances strength, power and endurance and it works for some individuals like myself. My belief is that it works with people with high muscle mass. It is based on protein and taking two or three spoonfuls is like having four or five fillet steaks. The more muscle mass you have, the more Creatine you absorb. A body with less muscle overloads, the substance goes into the system and it can do damage to the liver. It is not, however, something I took without doing my homework. I talked to people and other users for a long time before I subscribed to it myself. I even spoke to medical people about it and was assured that there was no harm in taking it.

The results were first class. It helped to increase my speed and endurance and strength. What more could I ask for? It was legal and I felt good for taking it. One or two people have taken a dip at me for taking it, however, and I have been featured in the *News of the World* for supporting the substance. I can't see why people make a fuss – it's recognised as a legal substance by the International Rugby Board, so what's the problem?

As far as testing is concerned, well, nobody has been tested more than I have in recent times. I have been an international for four years and have been tested on ten or eleven occasions. Thankfully, apart from the time factor, I quite enjoy it. I know I am clean so my message is to come and test me whatever the day, week or month. In fact, with the increased number of tests being taken on an *ad hoc* basis, players who do gamble must be very foolish. Not only can steroids damage your body but they can also damage your sport. A banned athlete brings shame on himself, his club and, more importantly, his country and his sport.

If you are going to succeed in sport, there is no way that you can cut corners and believe you will get away with it. If you try you are going to get found out. That was probably why I was so shocked when I heard about Lawrence. Having got to know Lawrence on the Lions tour and having spent a lot of time with him, it hit me hard. I couldn't comprehend first that he would put himself in that position and second that anyone in his position and with so much to lose would be foolish enough to say such things, especially about the Lions.

I can categorically say that during the five weeks I was out there, we had one night out, after the victory over Western Province, and I was with Lawrence for all of that night. If anything was taken then I must be stupid. There was no sign of it, no talk and certainly no evidence. That still baffles me. To be quite honest, I wouldn't really know whether to smoke cocaine, sniff it or stuff it in my ear. But I think I would have known if it had been taken by others. Let's just leave it at that.

19. SPRINGBOK SLAUGHTER

The Day the Millennium Stadium Was Born

There is no doubt in my mind that when it comes to mind games, Graham Henry is the master.

We had successfully negotiated the tour to Argentina, winning the series 2–0 and becoming the first side to achieve that feat on South American soil. It was a physical examination more than anything else and the players were delighted when we finally arrived back at the Copthorne Hotel to meet our wives and girlfriends. At any other time, it would have been the signal to drive home, open the holiday brochures and roll out the trunks. However, on this occasion, there was the small matter of an impending game against South Africa at the new Millennium Stadium to concentrate the mind and wipe out any thoughts of a fortnight in the Caribbean.

Admittedly, the boys were tired, and some of the squad members asked why it was so necessary to have yet another game. After all, the summer would be tough enough as it was. With the World Cup kicking off on 1 October, our close season was anything but. There were games against Canada, France and the USA to think about and three training camps in north Wales, west Wales and finally on the Algarve in Portugal.

At the end of the previous season, I had had a moan about the tour to South Africa and said how pointless an exercise it would be. However, 13 months on, I was singing from a different song-sheet. While I understood that a few players were sick and tired of rugby and needed this friendly international like the proverbial hole in the head, I saw it as a golden opportunity to further confirm our rejuvenation.

The victories over England, France, Italy and now Argentina had proved that we were not the World Cup no-hopers that many had suggested we were after the championship defeats by Scotland and Ireland. However, there was still a point to prove. In my own mind, I was not convinced that we had finally turned the corner. Once again, it was my pessimistic side that was talking.

Our position, however, was straightforward. We had won five games on the bounce and the South Africans had problems. Henry Honiball, Bobby

Skinstad and Joost van der Westhuizen would all miss the game through injury while one or two others were not exactly at the top of their form. I saw a golden chance to secure a first ever victory over them and to send a timely message to the rest of the rugby world. Okay, so the critics would still focus on the injuries and an understrength South African side, but that mattered not a bit to us. A victory over the Springboks, whatever the circumstances, would be a wonderful start to our World Cup countdown.

What's more, we had a few points to prove. In Pretoria 12 months earlier, Nick Mallett had described us as one of the worst international rugby sides he had ever seen. And then in the autumn we had come to within an ace of beating them at Wembley. If that wasn't enough of an incentive to drive us through one more obstacle, what was?

On the previous 12 occasions that Wales had met the Springboks, there had been only one draw, back in 1970 at the National Stadium, and no wins. It was a pathetic record. In the four defeats since that red-letter day for Welsh rugby, we had conceded 201 points. In contrast, we had managed to notch up just 74.

Graham gave the squad a complete week off before calling us back the following Sunday to prepare for the game. It would be the first game played at the Millennium Stadium, albeit in front of a rather modest 25,000 crowd, and that in itself was something to shout about. The previous two years had been spent trekking up and down the M4 to Wembley. At last we would get the opportunity to play a home game at home.

Whenever we meet up at the Copthorne prior to a game, Graham always calls a senior players' meeting for the Sunday night to discuss the week ahead. It's quite informal but Graham likes to get his point across. It was during that meeting that Graham told us of his next master plan – once again the mind games were about to start. It was like a military briefing. 'It's simple, fellas,' he said. 'We can beat the Springboks and I think we will. But I'm not going to tell the press that.'

At the time we were all slightly baffled by what he would tell the press. But by the end of the meeting, and having listened to how and why we would end that 93-year wait to make history, we knew the score. 'I am going to tell the press and the media at tomorrow's press conference that the game is a hurdle too far for you. I'll tell them that there's no way we can win having just come off such an arduous tour to Argentina,' he said.

Without needing to look around the room, I could feel the various sets of eyebrows being raised. I think we were all somewhat taken aback by Graham's latest plan of attack. But as we have learnt over the past year or so, you don't question Graham, you just go along with him and give him the support he requests.

Graham said that he was going to lay it on thick and would obviously need us to adopt the same approach. If we were asked about our general well-being or about our chances of beating the Springboks, the party line was to be that we were tired and could well do without the game. Whether Graham had informed the WRU of his intentions, I don't know. However, it did seem a little strange that on the one hand, the WRU were beaming about the prospect of us playing at the new stadium, while on the other hand, the players and the coach in particular were saying that we would rather be spending quality time at home or on our holidays.

The press conference came and went without incident and the press left wondering just how many points we would concede this time. You could see a few of them mumbling. I hadn't been asked the question directly but, like the other boys, I just nodded and agreed with Graham when he said he would much rather see the players spending Saturday on the beach. There were one or two WRU committeemen at the conference and I tried to sneak a glimpse at their faces when Graham started talking. If they were inwardly fuming, they did a good job of hiding it.

Once we got out of the room and back to the real business of preparing for the game, we put on our other hats and faces. I have never suffered from schizophrenia but I did feel a little two-faced at the time. I was telling lies to some very well-respected journalists. But, as Graham has always said, the bottom line is winning and if we can do that by telling a few white lies along the way, who really cares? We certainly didn't.

Graham had spoken to me on the plane on the way back from Argentina and said that despite having dropped Colin Charvis for the second Test in Buenos Aires, he had no intention of leaving him out of the game against the Springboks. He thought that his decision to play Geraint Lewis against the Pumas would have given Colin a reminder that nothing is safe in international rugby.

There would be two other changes too. Scott Gibbs, who had missed the tour through injury, would return for Allan Bateman, who had deputised so well in Buenos Aires, while on the tight-head David Young would come back in place of Ben Evans. Well, at least that was the plan.

When we arrived at the Copthorne on the Sunday evening, Gibbsy had already spoken with our physio Mark Davies and Dr Roger Evans because he was still concerned about the injury to his sternum. Scott was actually in the senior players' meeting when Graham told us that he was unable to play because of the problem and that Allan Bateman would continue at inside centre.

To lose a player of Scott's ability for such a big game was a real blow, especially as he had made such an impact for the Lions in 1997. However, when you have a replacement like Allan Bateman to play alongside Mark Taylor, it certainly softens the blow. The two of them had played well in Argentina, although Allan was certainly not as comfortable at 12 as he was at 13. He made that clear to Graham but never once threw his toys out of the pram. Allan is not a player who sulks; he is a real professional who takes it on the chin and gets on with it. I only wish that all players would follow his example.

The sessions on the Monday and Tuesday were outstanding and for the few journalists who pitched up it must have seemed quite strange. We were supposed to be down in the mouth, wishing we were on the beach topping up the tan. Yet here we were, on top of our game and with everything working like clockwork. Having missed the opportunity to beat South Africa at Wembley, Graham was almost begging us not to make the same mistakes again. We had been close that time but on this occasion we had to take it all the way.

On the Tuesday morning, we arrived at training to find another seven players had pitched up to help us in the build-up to the game. It was at that session that the players started to feel the World Cup was near. Graham was due to name his World Cup squad shortly after the Springboks game, and while the 22 on duty against the 'Boks were almost assured of their places, there were another 15 from the tour to Argentina who were holding their breath. It didn't take a rocket scientist to realise what was happening. The seven who were asked to turn up and help us prepare would be the seven who would join us, along with Jason Jones-Hughes, in the final 30.

That brings me nicely to the farcical Jason Jones-Hughes affair. Jason was battling to prove himself eligible to play for Wales after the Australian Rugby Union had lodged a complaint regarding his eligibility. The ARU chief executive John O'Neill said that Jason was ineligible to take up the opportunity with Wales because he had played for the Australian Barbarians the previous year. At the time, that side was deemed to have been the official second team of the Wallabies, so Jones-Hughes was therefore a Wallaby and couldn't switch.

Well, that was a lot of nonsense. Firstly, I had never heard of a Barbarians side being classed as a second team, and secondly, if Jones-Hughes was being prevented from switching, what about the two Tongan players who

182

had allegedly featured in the same side and who were now in the Tongan squad? It smacked of double standards and I couldn't see that the ARU had a leg to stand on. Unfortunately, they took it all the way and if Jason had not been such a strong character he would probably have crumbled and accepted his lot. I remember him saying that if his bid to come to Wales failed, his career would be ruined. 'I will find myself somewhere between Wales and Australia, doing nothing,' were the words he used to me. I know that rules are rules but I questioned why another Union would put a player in such a position, especially after the International Board, following an appeal from Jason, had ruled that he could play.

So, with the 29 together for training, we stepped up our preparations and made good progress that week. If any of the players were still feeling jaded after Argentina, they certainly didn't show it.

The Thursday morning was spent training at the stadium and for many of us it was the first time that we had set foot on the playing area. We had had a quick look at the arena before we left for Argentina but at that stage it had been nothing more than a building site and we couldn't really get any feel for it.

This was unbelievable. To think that in a little more than three months this magnificent stadium would be full of 72,500 people, most of whom would be cheering us on against Argentina. Now, however, it was only half finished, and although we were grateful for the chance to get in there, it was an eerie feeling.

I think most of the boys agreed that it was time to take our hats off to Glanmor Griffiths. Most of us had read the papers and were aware of the criticism that had been levelled at Glan but he told us that it would be ready for the game against South Africa and he said that by the time the World Cup kicked off it would be complete. He was right on both counts, although I didn't see too many people eating humble pie on 1 October.

By the time we had taken in the surroundings, Graham had already given us a roasting. He had a few words with Colin Charvis and Dai Young, amongst others, and that set the scene for the session. It was time to get our heads together and forget everything else that was going on around us.

It worked a treat. We trained superbly well. What's more, come 9.30 the following morning, we turned up in the foyer at the Copthorne Hotel to catch the coach down to training and Graham told us to go back to our rooms, get changed and take the rest of the day off. That epitomises Graham Henry. When something needs saying, he is not afraid to say it, but when there is a chance to give a collective pat on the back, he will do so.

The training had been so good the previous day that Graham felt we deserved some time off.

I went into the car park with the forwards and did some line-out spotters while the other boys took a few hours to collect their thoughts, have a swim or a game of snooker or just relax in their rooms.

The Saturday was really odd. For the past couple of seasons we had endured a 45-minute journey from our hotel to a home international match at Wembley. This time it would be a matter of 15 minutes from door to door. It was a godsend and meant that at last we could relax back into our old pattern.

We left the hotel at four o'clock and had arrived at the stadium by quarter past. Unfortunately, we were told that there was a problem with the turnstiles and that the game would have to be temporarily delayed. It's not what you want at that stage of the proceedings but, once again, Blackie was brilliant. We were ready to go out at 4.54 as normal but had to come back into the dressing-room area to start all over again. Blackie told us that there was a five-minute delay, and although it was really a 15-minute delay, we didn't know until after the game. In his own inimitable way, he made the time pass quickly. Telling us that we had 15 minutes to wait would have had a negative effect and, as we have learnt over the past 16 months, the word 'negative' does not exist in Blackie's vocabulary.

Then came the moment. I walked out with the mascot, trying to calm my own nerves by asking him his life story. By the time we arrived on the pitch, I knew most things about him, most importantly the fact that he supported Cardiff. Good lad! He was as nervous as I was but we got through it together. Quite sad, really – a grown man being coaxed through the last few minutes before an international by a ten-year-old boy!

The reception the team received was fantastic. Although the ground was only a third full it was wonderful. The noise was unbelievable; the 27,000 Welshmen were making the noise of 127,000. If we had needed a reminder of what this game and the next few months meant to Welsh rugby, this was it. The fans had been through some terrible times with us over the past two or three years but they had stuck by us.

In the first 20 minutes we were as good as we had been all year and if we had taken our chances we could have been out of sight by half-time. Unfortunately, all we had to show for our dominance was a Mark Taylor try, four kicks from Jenks and a lead that was not as big as it should have been.

Graham was far from happy at the interval and although he was pleased with the commitment and endeavour we had shown as a side, he was not impressed with the way in which Jenks and I had controlled matters. I had experienced the wrath of Henry back at Wembley nine months earlier when he had told me to sit down and be quiet at half-time against the 'Boks, and I knew that I was about to experience it again. We had practised a lot of back-row moves to target the likes of Werner Swanepoel and Bram van Straaten but we hadn't really got into the right areas to carry out those instructions. Graham didn't see it like that, however, and he gave us a real blast. He looked at me and said, 'For God's sake, Rob. We have been practising these moves all week, so for goodness' sake, do as I say!'

Point taken. In the second half we had plenty of opportunities to work off the back row and eventually, thanks to quality ball from the forwards, we scored off one of Graham's planned moves called 'eight easy ten'. I was elated when Gareth Thomas went over but I chose not to look up at the stand where Graham was sitting. I could imagine the grin all over his face. Graham is not usually the most animated of people when things go right or wrong during the game but he loves it when a plan works. This was a case in point and he never let me forget that moment. He still goes on about 'that try' now.

Although Alfie's try gave us a cushion, I was still a little anxious. We had thrown away the game at Wembley the previous year, had almost lost a decent lead against the French in Paris and might have lost to England had Mike Catt's drop-goal attempt gone straight. What do they say? Don't count your chickens!

I had talked of that anxiety at half-time and told the boys that I didn't want us just to defend the lead. We had almost paid the price for doing that in Paris so we had to learn from our mistake. However, I knew that South Africa would throw everything at us at the start of the second half so we might have to spend a little more time knocking them down instead of running at them.

I was right. They came out with all guns blazing. It was like playing against a different side. They were ten times faster and harder and they were totally focused. Their problem in the first half had been one of over-confidence. I think they expected to win. They had been blasé in their attitude and it had backfired.

I think that is the downfall of some South African players. Although most of them are good lads, there are a few who try to bully you on the pitch, believing they are bigger, stronger and better. That had been the case in Pretoria the previous summer but it was certainly not the case here in our own back yard.

There were 15 minutes of intense pressure yet the boys fought fire with fire. Some people had doubted the strength of character within the Welsh side and claimed that when it came to playing against the 'big boys' – South Africa, Australia and New Zealand – we would be found wanting. This was another one in the eye for the critics. Our tackling was right out of the top drawer. Twelve months earlier we had fallen apart – but not this time. Scott Gibbs always tells us that we could be better in terms of our defending but on this occasion even he agreed that we had been very special.

Having survived that onslaught, we pulled ourselves together and went on to win the game 29–19 with Jenks finishing with another 19 points. It was an awesome feeling. I would even go as far as to say that the result flattered South Africa. Had it not been for a lapse in concentration which resulted in a late try for the Springboks, it would have been 29–12. That would have been about right.

We all milked the applause and I tried to imagine what this stadium would be like with 72,500 people inside. It wouldn't be long before I found out. The dressing-room was the place to be. All the hard work that had been put in in Argentina had paid off. It had sent a message around the world that we were no longer the whipping boys. Beating France and England had been good but this was very special indeed.

Thinking about what I would say at the press conference, I remembered what Graham had said at the gathering six days earlier about this being a game too far. I had a chuckle and then grabbed a shower while Chris Wyatt turned up the volume on his master-blaster. Whether I am showing my age or not, I don't know. However, I didn't recognise one song and I don't think too many others did either!

It was a strange press conference. The media room was not finished so we gathered in the stand. I knew the first question would be about Graham's comment and – surprise, surprise – it was. I smiled but didn't spill the beans. I just said that we had done well to win after such a hectic programme and that if it had been a game too far then we had exceeded our own expectations.

What was more pleasing, however, was remembering that 12 months earlier the Springboks coach Nick Mallett had described Wales as one of the worst international sides he had ever seen. Now we had beaten his side with some ease and I was desperate to hear his reaction. After he came into our dressing-room to congratulate us, I felt a little humble. Had he locked himself away and cried into his beer, I might have taken great pleasure in reminding him of his comments. But, to be fair, he was sincere in what he said and even told me that he was pleased to see me back playing after the injury I had suffered when with the Lions back in 1997. He finished his own press briefing by claiming that Wales could go on to win the World Cup. Whether he believed that, I am not sure. I think he was talking us up to hide the disappointment of having lost.

The person I felt most sorry for was Gary Teichmann. He had gone through a tough time in the summer and losing to Wales was going to put his position as captain in real doubt. The defeat would ultimately cost him that role and his position in the side.

I spoke to him after the game to commiserate with him just as he had done with me in Pretoria. In hindsight, he felt that he shouldn't have played. But that tells you something about the man. He felt that the game was crucial to South Africa and that with so many key players out already his withdrawal would create insurmountable problems. His decision to play, though, had certainly backfired.

I didn't spend too much time feeling sorry for the Springboks, however, because there was plenty of celebrating to do. It was the end of a long, hard summer and time for a break – and a chance to spend some time with Ceri, who by now was seven months pregnant.

20. ON CLOUD NINE

Megan and the Perfect Build-Up

The great Liverpool manager Bill Shankly once said that football was even more important than life or death. Okay, so we knew what he meant. However, I can speak from personal experience when I say that the gift of life is the greatest gift anyone can ever be given. In the final chapter of the book I will explain the reason behind that bold statement. But for the time being, I will concentrate on what for me was the most amazing summer.

I was still on cloud nine after the victory over South Africa and, of course, my mind was already concentrating on the World Cup build-up and 1 October in particular. However, at the same time there was the small matter of Ceri's pregnancy and the impending birth of our baby daughter.

During one of Ceri's scans earlier in the year, we had asked the nurse to tell us whether Ceri was carrying a boy or a girl. Like any other couple, we had listened to all the old wives' tales and taken a guess as to the sex of the baby. However, when the nurse confirmed that Ceri was carrying a little girl, we were both really excited. We spent the next few days thumbing through books trying to find a name. Eventually we decided on Megan and then set our sights on the due date of 19 August.

It just so happened that two days later Wales were due to play Canada at the Millennium Stadium in one of three World Cup warm-up games. The obvious question was raised by a few of the boys and I gave the obvious answer. Although one more victory would make me the most successful Welsh captain of all time, there was never any question of where I would be should Megan decide to hang on for 48 hours. In the end, though, it didn't matter.

The victory over the Springboks was my sixth successive win as captain, a record matched only by the late Billy Trew, the great Mervyn Davies and the legendary Phil Bennett. One more and the name of Rob Howley would move to the top of the pile. As I told the journalists at the time, I am not one to chase records and would far rather see the team winning than anything else. Unfortunately, I couldn't help but read the constant reminders of how no other Welsh captain had led his side to seven successive Test victories. While it never played on my mind, I just hoped that in the end I would be able to enjoy both experiences.

Graham Henry knew the situation but there was never any pressure one way or the other. And in the end it worked out just right, with Megan arriving 18 days early. Coincidentally, the 1 August birth was exactly 12 months to the day and hour after Ceri and I were married.

Having enjoyed a long-overdue break after the South Africa game, the squad returned to training in mid-July. As ever, Steve Black had compiled a comprehensive programme that would take us up to the World Cup. Just reading it made me tired. Although I had been a bit worried about spending so much time away from home during the pregnancy, Ceri was fine and the doctor was confident that she would go the distance and deliver just in time for me to rush off, wet the baby's head and then play and hopefully break the record against Canada.

I drove to the first camp in Brecon instead of taking the team coach, just in case, but had no real cause for concern. Blackie put us through our paces and it was a good few days. It was during that week that I met Andy Marinos for the first time. The Rhodesian-born son of a Greek with Welsh grandparents had arrived in Wales to sign for Newport and within a matter of days had agreed a two-year contract with the WRU.

Because of the problems surrounding the availability of Jason Jones-Hughes, Andy was invited to Brecon to meet the squad. He was told by Graham that he was on World Cup standby and would step into the squad should Jason lose his appeal against the International Board's initial decision to prevent him from switching nations. At that stage, I didn't get the chance to have a real chat with him, but from what Graham said, he seemed to be a decent lad who was very keen to prove himself capable at the highest level.

Because of Jason's plight, Andy joined the squad on his return to Wales in August and actually played against the USA on August Bank Holiday Monday. After that, he travelled to north Wales with the squad and must have thought that his chance would come when the Australian Rugby Union applied even greater pressure on Jason.

Unfortunately for Andy, the International Board upheld Jason's appeal and when Jason finally arrived on Welsh soil in early September Andy was released from the party and put back on standby. It was a cruel blow and not surprisingly Andy had to choke back the tears when Graham broke the news to him in Bangor. I made a point of speaking to him shortly afterwards but he was too disappointed to say anything more than 'I think my world is caving in'.

To his immense credit, Andy displayed the depth of his commitment to the cause by completing the training session that day, before returning to Newport in the evening. That impressed me greatly. Although his chance of playing in the World Cup had finally disappeared, he was still prepared to give his all. I am sure that he will return in the coming months. From what Shane Howarth has told me, his performances for Newport have already confirmed his ability.

The Brecon camp was tough, although, as ever, Blackie made sure that we had plenty of time to relax. We played a bit of football and water polo and even went down the pub to have a pint with the locals. It was the perfect way to introduce us to the final countdown.

I was on the way back from Brecon when my mobile phone rang. I checked the screen on my phone and realised it was Ceri. A slightly concerned voice at the other end said, 'Rob, I've had a few twinges and I think I'm going into labour.' Knowing that there was still the best part of three weeks before Megan was due, I dismissed her worries and said, 'Don't be stupid, the baby's not due until the 19th of next month.'

By the time I got home Ceri was still suffering, and at ten o'clock we decided to ring the hospital for some advice. The nurse told Ceri to take a couple of paracetamol tablets and to have a hot bath. They didn't think it was anything to worry about but said that we must ring again if we had any further concerns.

Ceri had a bath but the pain didn't ease. So, after phoning once again, we were told to get everything together and to make our way to the hospital. It was about 1.30 a.m. when we finally got there. We were both tired, albeit for different reasons, and could have done with a spot of shut-eye. Ceri was shown to her bed in a private room off the main ward, while I was given the option of a rather uncomfortable-looking chair in Ceri's room, or the hospital floor. I chose the latter but switched to the former when my back was in two pieces later that morning.

The nurses monitored Ceri throughout the night and when morning came I made my way home. I was like the proverbial spare part. Thankfully, I caught up with a bit of sleep before returning later in the day to see how she was. The next 24 hours seemed like 24 days. It was not what I had expected.

Because of the discomfort Ceri was experiencing, we spent most of the afternoon walking around the hospital grounds. We were told that the walking motion would ease the pressure on Ceri's stomach and would hopefully speed things up if she was going to give birth over the weekend.

I still hadn't got my head around the situation because my diary said 19 August. Fortunately, as I always remind Ceri, there was some decent television on that night and I was able to settle down in my chair to watch *Rocky IV*. Unfortunately, just as the crucial late stages were unfolding, the nurses came in and decided it was time for Ceri to depart for the delivery room. To this day I haven't seen the ending!

She got to the delivery room at about one o'clock and I thought it would all be over within a matter of hours, maybe even less. When the clock ticked past one o'clock on the Sunday afternoon, however, there was still no sign of Megan. That was when the doctor suggested that it might be wise if Ceri was to have a Caesarean. From what I could understand, Ceri's back and Megan's back were together, and although they were hoping that Megan would turn, there didn't seem to be much chance of that happening.

Ceri was exhausted by that time and although she wanted a natural birth, neither of us thought it was worth taking any risks. It was a worrying time although Ceri was fine and Megan's heartbeat was perfect. I don't let too many things get the better of me but because of the length of time Ceri had been in the delivery room, I must admit to feeling a little anxious. The baby was never in any discomfort, though, and the midwives were wonderful. Once we had given the go-ahead for Ceri to have a Caesarean, the anaesthetist explained what was going to happen. I was taken upstairs to get kitted out in a natty blue outfit with a hat and shoes while Ceri went to theatre.

I was always mindful that I wasn't going to watch, so I held Ceri's hand and stayed up at the other end. However, we didn't have too long to wait. Within a couple of minutes, Megan popped up into the air and the waiting game was over. Our daughter was born at 2.42 p.m. and tipped the scales at 6 lbs 3 oz.

Megan was taken away and that was when I turned to Ceri to help her through what was a difficult time. She had some internal bleeding and was by now in some discomfort. However, the next thing I remember was Ceri snoring. That was when I knew that everything was okay! I did the male thing by going out with the boys to have a few beers that night and to celebrate the wonderful conclusion to an incredible weekend. Everyone was elated and Megan and Ceri were both fine.

Unfortunately, as is so often the case, there was a sting in the tail. On the Monday night I went back in to visit Ceri and on the way to the hospital I got caught speeding. Some of the boys joked that I had never moved so fast in my life. At the time I didn't care, although I tried to explain to the policeman that my wife was recovering from a rather important operation and I was just a bit too keen to get there. It didn't help, so I coughed up and put it down to experience.

Ceri and Megan came home on the Thursday and although Ceri was unable to lift anything or drive for some time, she was far more comfortable at home and I was glad to see her there.

Graham had announced his plans to us some weeks prior to the game. The side to play the Canadians would be a mixture of first-choice and replacement players; the team to meet the French the following Saturday would be the side, barring injury, that would begin against Argentina, while the Bank Holiday game against the USA would be used to take a look at the remaining fringe players.

For the players involved in those three games, it would be the last chance to get a real feel of our new home. The stadium had shot up in the two months since we had beaten the Springboks and for the games against Canada and France we were told that there would be capacity crowds of around 52,000 and 62,000 respectively. I thought back to the South Africa match and remembered the noise that 27,000 people had made.

The crowd, as expected, lived up to all expectations and enjoyed our back-to-back victories. So did I. The first win made it seven on the bounce and the second meant that I had now led Wales to eight successive victories, dating back to that red-letter day in Paris on 6 March.

We were far from cohesive against Canada, however, and Graham had his say. But it did at least confirm that we were a side capable of playing badly and still winning. It was the same story against the French, although on that occasion we did improve after half-time and ended up playing some wonderful stuff. The fact that they clawed their way back to within a couple of scores was more down to our lack of concentration in the final moments. We took great pride in beating the French once again and felt that we had successfully blown away the summer cobwebs.

On the Monday, the players who had featured in the first two games offered to carry the water bottles for those who were playing against the USA. I remember when Jenks ran on to give Stephen Jones a bottle; he got a rousing ovation.

Once again we won, and although we understood that the 1 October game against Argentina would be rather more of an end-of-term examination than a mid-term test, we felt in good shape. For Ceri and me, it was the end of a wonderful summer and one that neither of us will ever forget. It was just a pity that the first few days of autumn couldn't bring with it such unbounded joy.

As far as the World Cup was concerned, the hard work had only just begun. Blackie had planned the two camps to north and west Wales and we knew that he would put us through it. We travelled north for four days and then, after spending another couple of days at home, it was off to Pembrokeshire.

It was during the camp in Bangor that Graham shared with me his major concern. As I have said before, the strength of the squad had improved greatly during the last 12 or 14 months and for the first time in a long time it was harder to get into the side than it was to get out. But still there was a headache. In certain positions – like fly-half and full-back – we were rather thin on the ground. Don't get me wrong – I think Stephen Jones and Neil Boobyer are fine players in their own right. But neither of them would choose to play in those positions, given the choice.

Graham was obviously concerned that if Jenks or Shane Howarth suffered an injury, we might face something of a mini-crisis. During a quiet moment in Bangor, he asked me how I would like playing with Mike Rayer as my fly-half. I didn't have a problem with that because Mike is a fine player. However, a part of me said it was like jumping out of the frying pan and into the fire. Mike is a full-back and has played all of his international rugby in that position. Yet here was the national coach looking for an alternative to Jenks and coming up with Mike.

That worry apart, the camp was a personal success and it was during those four days that I finally realised just what the World Cup meant to the people of Wales. I know that north Wales doesn't get too much top-class rugby but we were all somewhat taken aback by the thousands of supporters who turned up to cheer us on. I lost count how many hundred autographs I signed during that week and again in Pembrokeshire but my hand was sore by the time I got home!

Despite another blast from the ARU, Jason Jones-Hughes finally won his appeal and he joined us in Pembrokeshire, where he made an instant impression on Graham and Blackie. He was only 22 when he arrived at the team hotel – 23 when he left – but he showed a maturity beyond his years. Then, in Portugal, when the news filtered through that the ARU were supposedly considering legal action against him, he put it to one side like an old pro. We were very fortunate to have added another positive member to the squad.

The six days on the Algarve were as tough as they come. Graham and Blackie had us out three times a day in temperatures ranging from 22 to 29 degrees centigrade and they pushed us hard. However, it was a wonderful facility, hidden away in the resort of Vale de Lobo and away from the prying eyes of the locals. A few holidaymakers, most of them from Connahs Quay, did pitch up on the Saturday and Sunday but they didn't get away without lending a helping hand. The sight of me, Gibbsy, Jenks, three journalists, a cameraman and about nine bronzed tourists standing on the scrummaging machine was one to behold.

Sadly, when I got home, a few of the Cardiff boys told me that the television pictures from Portugal had shown us eating at a barbecue, drinking beer by the pool and playing football. I was a little annoyed by that because if the cameramen had spent their time watching the training they would have seen that we deserved a little rest. Anyway, the barbecue was on the Saturday night before our day off and the boys were allowed one or two beers. It was nothing more than that and was certainly not a regular occurrence. We trained hard, ate the right things, rested well and, when given the chance, enjoyed ourselves.

Having said all that, I must share with you my ten-minute stint on the putting green at the Barringtons sports complex, where we were staying. Neil Boobyer, Chris Wyatt, Stephen Jones and I decided to have a little competition for a few quid. By the time we reached the third hole, it was quite tight. I let Chris and Boobs go first and they putted quite close to the hole. It was my turn. I set myself up for the 50-footer and watched with a huge smile on my face as it struck the pin and plopped nicely into the hole. I felt like doing a lap of honour but with other golfers still to play I didn't want to step across their line. Now that would be a bit naughty, wouldn't it, Mr Lehman and co.!

The putting and the odd game of snooker came as a welcome break from training. It was hard and hot out there and we grabbed any time we could to relax. Graham and Steve were keen on that and felt that we were certainly in the right surroundings to do a bit of both.

By the time we had completed the programme and had arrived back home, we were ready for one last rest before the off. Ceri and I took it easy for a few days before I got into the car and headed for the Copthorne Hotel. It had been a long, hard summer but at last we were there. The opening game was a matter of six days away and we couldn't wait to get on with it.

But that was when everything went terribly wrong.

21. THE WORLD CUP

The Great Divide

I have always taken a great deal of pride in my performance on the training field, whether it be for club or country. I don't have a great deal of time for shirkers or for those players who dismiss training as an unnecessary exercise. So, as I fumbled my way through the penultimate session prior to Wales's opening game of the World Cup against Argentina, there must have been one or two rather sceptical journalists. Nobody said anything, but I'm sure they wondered exactly what I was up to.

If that was the case, they were not the only ones. As the session broke up, not a moment too soon as far as I was concerned, Graham Henry pulled me to one side and asked me to explain my rather pitiful performance. 'Is there a problem, Rob?'

I just looked him in the eye and nodded, trying desperately to hold back the tears. The truth was that my daughter was lying in the children's ward of the Princess of Wales Hospital in Bridgend, having been unable to breathe on her own less than 48 hours earlier. Neither Ceri nor I knew what was wrong with her and we wouldn't find out the results of a second set of tests until late the following day. Although Megan had made significant progress since we took her in early on Tuesday morning, I was still anxious about the long-term outcome.

There I was, face to face with the Wales coach, telling him that I had far more important things on my mind than the World Cup opener against Argentina which by now was just over 48 hours away. As I explained the situation to Graham, he told me to put everything else to the back of my mind. There are times in your life when sport pales into insignificance. I suppose that at that precise moment I was far from being certain about my availability for the game on the Friday. But I was desperate to keep it quiet and to act as though nothing had happened. It was proving rather difficult.

I had decided to spend the Monday night at home with Ceri and Megan because we had a day off the following day. The plan was to spend the whole of the Tuesday out with the girls, enjoying that last bit of freedom before we went into battle. But by the time I got home on the Monday, Ceri had already taken Megan to see the doctor. She had been a little concerned with her appearance and her temperature and so, as it's better to be safe than sorry, had taken her for a check-up. The doctor had put Ceri's mind at ease, however, and we settled down for a quiet night in watching television. It turned out to be anything but a quiet night.

Ceri fell asleep downstairs, so I took Megan up to bed, hoping to get a few hours myself. For about an hour I was unable to settle, aware that Megan was fidgeting and making some rather peculiar noises. Just to be on the safe side, I went downstairs to tell Ceri and we both went back upstairs to make doubly sure she was okay. It was then that we realised something was wrong. Not only was Megan grunting but she appeared to be struggling to get her breath, and if anything it was getting progressively worse. As first-time parents, we both panicked and decided that we were not going to take any chances.

By the time we were ready to go, Megan had deteriorated to such an extent that Ceri said she felt limp in her arms as she carried her to the car. We were both hysterical and I don't mind admitting that I probably didn't adhere to the Highway Code as I drove to the hospital.

I dropped Ceri at the door to Casualty, parked and then joined her in the hospital, where the nurses had taken over. We were both in tears but, to be honest, I think we both thought that the nurses would simply tell us there was nothing to worry about and that within a few minutes Megan would be back at home with us, ready for another feed.

Nothing could have been further from the reality of the situation. The nurse took Megan from Ceri's arms and rushed into a room where an oxygen mask was put over her mouth and nose. It was awful to see our eight-week-old daughter with a rather ugly-looking mask covering most of her face. I was struggling to stay with it, and when I heard the nurse say 'Come on, Megan, breathe!' I lost control and ran out of the room. I was no use to anyone. Ceri, meanwhile, was shouting out the answers to the questions being asked by the nurse such as Megan's weight and age, and I was grateful that at least one of us was in control.

I paced around outside until Ceri came out and said that the nurse had advised us to go for a walk as Megan had started to get a bit of colour back into her cheeks. They were certainly the words we wanted to hear, although the fact that nobody knew what was causing the problem meant we were still unsure as to whether we had done something wrong.

The doctor took some blood from Megan and then did a lumbar puncture to check for meningitis. I will never forget the bruises she had. It was terrible to see this tiny baby struggling just to stay with us, and both Ceri and I will be eternally grateful for the efforts of the consultant, Mr Trevor Jones, and the nurses.

Throughout the Tuesday Megan improved, and by the time I checked back into the team hotel later that night I felt a little better. However, although we were told that the meningitis test was negative, it would be another day or so before the results of the blood tests were known. Every thought possible was racing through my mind, but I didn't want to concern anyone else so I kept it quiet and hoped that I could keep my concentration during training. I couldn't, and Graham was the first to realise.

Because the game was now only two days away, I was not sure how long Graham could hold out before he took the decision out of my hands. It was obvious that in my current state I could not play. Graham had a word with our doctor, Roger Evans, and Roger said that he would try to speak to the consultant to see if he could help me understand what was going on. He later came up to my room and said that although the results had not yet come through, it was probable that an infection had been responsible for the initial breathing problems and that everything should be okay. They were treating Megan blind, but she was certainly responding and appeared to be heading in the right direction. When the results finally arrived the following day, I felt as though the weight of the world had been taken off my shoulders.

While it was far from being the best possible preparation for a game of such importance, I now felt that I could relax a little and make up for the pathetic performance I had given at training on the Wednesday morning. As most people know, I am a nervous person when it comes to games. However, on this occasion, there was no doubt that the distraction back in Bridgend had taken my mind off the game. For once in my life, I actually enjoyed the final preparations and the journey from the hotel down into Cardiff. The place was awash with colour and the city was absolutely jumping. So was I. Although my daughter was still in hospital, I felt comfortable with the situation and said to myself, 'This one's for Megan.'

Walking out on to the pitch for the games against South Africa, Canada and France had been something special, but to stroll out before the opening ceremony and to see the place full and with the roof shut was an unforgettable experience. The boys were so taken aback that Steve Black came on to the field and advised us to go back into the dressing-room. The pressure had been enormous in the build-up to the big day, and this unprecedented atmosphere was making it even worse. Blackie could see the players struggling to cope with the situation.

With Megan under observation in hospital, Ceri decided to go to the game and, like the rest of the players' wives, girlfriends and parents, was excited at the prospect of experiencing a day that would encapsulate everything Welsh. At the time, the players didn't know where the girls, mums and dads had been put, and although we looked up to the normal seats in the BT stand, we couldn't see them. However, by the time the game was over, all hell had broken loose and there were 50 or 60 very irate people.

I am not sure who was responsible, but the seats were at the bottom of the lower tier in the corner of the North Stand. Their view of the opening ceremony was masked by the choirs that stood at that end of the ground and their view of the game was blocked by the punters who kept standing up in front of them every time we got the ball. To add insult to injury, there was no pre-match function for them to attend. When the players were told how the girls in particular had been treated, we were livid. Peter Owens, the WRU assistant secretary, apologised to them after the game, although Gareth Thomas's mother took it upon herself to tell Graham Henry exactly what she thought.

I felt for Ceri because as an occasion it was wonderful. Unfortunately, or perhaps fortunately in Ceri's case, the game didn't quite live up to expectations and by the time half-time came around we knew we were in for another ear-bashing from the coach. We weren't wrong: Graham told each and every one of us that we were a total embarrassment to the Welsh public. After reading us the riot act and telling the boys to buck up, he finished by saying, 'You are playing as if you have a right to win. You have to earn that right. Now get out there and make up for that nonsense.' Thankfully, we did find a bit of form in the second half, and despite relaxing a little too much in the final 15 minutes, we won 23–18 and in doing so gave ourselves the perfect start.

But the day was far from over. First there was the rumpus over the family tickets and then, as the players were sitting in the dressing-room, Lynn Howells came over to me and said that Blackie had been taken to hospital after suffering a turn during the second half. The boys were obviously concerned and later that night I rang the hospital to see how he was. It was no surprise when the nurse told me that he had spent most of the night cracking jokes. When Blackie came to the phone, he said there was nothing to worry about and that after a blood transfusion the following day he would be 'as right as rain'. He was already planning his return to the hotel for some time on the Sunday morning. I laughed to myself – and then laughed again on Sunday lunchtime when he breezed into the Copthorne having just undergone a four-pint blood transfusion. Within an hour, the tracksuit was back on and Blackie was back in business.

By that time, Colin Charvis had been cited by the World Cup panel and was on his way to a 14-day ban. Roberto Grau, the Argentine prop who had been involved in the first-half fracas, got 21 days. To be honest, we were all a little surprised at the severity of the punishment. Colin was devastated and immediately apologised to the boys for the way he had retaliated. Eventually, and having taken advice, he appealed on the basis that the citing commission were wrong in stating that he had gone back a second time to retaliate. Unfortunately, he lost that appeal at Twickenham and we would not see him again until the quarter-final.

Colin knew that he had let himself down by retaliating, but what annoyed me was the fact that so many other incidents had gone unnoticed and unpunished in the game. Peter Rogers had his ear bitten in the opening minutes and needed treatment and Garin Jenkins had been gouged, an act that was clearly caught on camera by a local photographer. The picture in the paper was absolutely frightening – Garin's eyes were being used like the holes in a bowling ball. But nothing was done. On the one hand, Colin and Roberto were being castigated for a rather tame dust-up, while on the other hand, an act of gratuitous violence was being overlooked. The only good thing that came out of Garin's experience was that we now had a new nickname for the man previously known as 'Roundhead'. He quickly became known as '10-pin head'.

The citing procedure took a hammering in certain areas of the press and on this occasion I was on the side of the press. It seemed obvious to me that Colin and Roberto had paid the price for being involved in the opening game. Had the incident occurred in any other game in the tournament, they might have escaped punishment. There is no doubt in my mind that Colin's retaliation should have gone unpunished and that the yellow card for Grau was sufficient. When you think what others got away with in the tournament, it did seem a touch unnecessary to hand out such harsh penalties.

With Colin out of the Japan game and with Graham keen to make one or two changes, the side that faced Japan barely resembled the team that had taken us through the summer months unbeaten. However, regardless of who was playing, the target was to win by scoring 60 points. The World Cup rules stated that if three nations were tied on the same number of points at the end of the group games, the criterion for qualification would be the number of points scored.

We achieved our target, although once again our first-half performance left a great deal to be desired. I was pleased to score my seventh try for Wales and was delighted that I had played well before giving Dai Llewellyn an opportunity to play the final 20 minutes. With two wins from two, we knew that victory over the Samoans would be good enough to ensure automatic qualification for the last eight – and a quarter-final game against the Wallabies in Cardiff.

Nobody had reckoned on Argentina beating Samoa at Llanelli the following day, but the upshot of that result was that it was now quite possible that three teams would finish level on points. If we lost against Samoa and the Pumas defeated Japan on the Saturday, we would be involved in a three-way tie for the top spot. But if Japan won that game, we would finish second by virtue of having lost to Samoa. It was complicated – unless, of course, we won the Samoa match.

The absence of Colin and subsequently Craig Quinnell through injury meant that we were a couple of ball carriers light for the game. Against the Samoans that was always likely to be a problem. Scott Quinnell is one of the game's very best in that area, but I was a little anxious about his ability to take on the workload that ordinarily would have been spread between the three of them. In the end I was proved right.

Because of his relationship with the likes of Pat Lam and Va'aiga Tuigamala, Graham was obviously anxious that we got this one right. Getting it right meant combatting the Samoans' strength by taking the ball away from the contact area. Having seen their pack being demolished by Argentina, we were also relatively confident that our scrum would dominate. We were right about that, but wrong in so many other areas.

At 12–3, everything was fine. However, the Samoa coach, Bryan Williams, had worked us out. We wanted to play a kicking game, probing the corners and forcing the Samoans to restart from their own twenty-two. Unfortunately, they dropped Brian Lima and Tuigamala deep and used fly-half Steve Bachop as another sweeper along with the full-back. They nullified our game plan and very quickly got the better of us. Scott Quinnell, Gibbsy, Jenks and I failed to take the game by the scruff of the neck and by the time we had lost the ball out of the back of the scrum in the final minute we were 38–31 down and heading for an anxious wait.

Nobody admitted it at the time, probably because we didn't want to give the press any further fuel to throw on to the fire. However, we made two crass errors that day and they cost us dearly. Thankfully, Graham has made it clear to this side that individual rollickings are pointless and counterproductive. If somebody makes a mistake, we take a collective roasting. After all, it is very rare that one man is solely to blame.

The try that Samoa scored from our line-out just before half-time was the result of a breakdown in communication. And for those who blame Garin for missing his man, don't. Garin threw it on a sixpence; it was the perfect delivery. Unfortunately, the call code was messed up. Chris Wyatt should have gone back, but he thought the call was to go forward. Let's leave it there and accept that people make mistakes.

Secondly, the first of Steve Bachop's tries could have been averted had we defended the move as we had done on 20 or 30 occasions in training. We knew the call and we knew how to defend it. On this occasion, however, we didn't carry out the simple instructions. At this level a mistake like that invariably costs you seven points. We had played straight into their hands and now we had to rely on Argentina beating Japan but not scoring 69 points in the process. That was the only way we could go through to the last eight and stay in Cardiff.

Graham was devastated by the result and admitted to us the next day, after chatting with Va'aiga, that the Samoans had anticipated the way we would play and reacted accordingly. Va'aiga told Graham that he and Pat Lam had gone to see Bryan Williams the previous day to tell him how they thought Graham would approach the game. In effect, they rumbled us and got their just reward. I think that hurt Graham more than the result itself.

It had always been Graham's intention that we would celebrate our victory over Samoa by taking the wives and parents to the Le Monde restaurant in Cardiff for a slap-up meal and a drink. Well, that was Plan A. Having lost, we reverted to Plan B. That entailed a pool recovery period back at the team hotel and then a chance to invite the girls up to see us for a drink later that night.

Although the guys were absolutely stunned by the result, we didn't see any real benefit in crying over spilt milk. We thought the best way to forget what had been a mediocre display and a poor result was to get a few beers down us. I am not sure why Graham told the press conference on the following Tuesday that he didn't believe defeat hurt us as much as it did the Kiwis, but perhaps it was because we had chosen to drown our sorrows rather than go to our rooms and reflect. In fact, at 9.45 p.m. he actually told us that the bar was closing and that there would be no more drink.

The senior players were far from happy and we made our feelings known. It wasn't a case of needing a drink, but we didn't think Graham was doing the right thing. In the end, he took us away from the girls and into an adjoining room to have a chat. He was obviously less than pleased with the day's events, although in the end he said that the bar would stay open and it was up to us whether we carried on drinking. I stayed with Ceri and we did have a couple, but it was no more than that. After all, our World Cup was far from over at that stage and I am not the biggest drinker the world has ever seen. However, it was an opportunity to spend a bit of time with Ceri and to try and forget about the rugby for an hour or two.

The next couple of days were spent analysing the performance and watching the Pumas beat Japan without ever threatening our position at the top of the group. While in hindsight it might have been better to have finished third, we were quite happy to be staying in Cardiff to play Australia at the Millennium Stadium. That had always been our aim, and although we had done it the hard way – a typical Welsh trait, really – we had achieved that first step without suffering any serious injury. What's more, Colin Charvis would be back for the Aussie game and that would be a significant boost.

Graham had a plan for the game against the Wallabies, although we couldn't have envisaged what would happen later in the week. In the end, it didn't really do us any favours, although finding a sheet of paper in the David Lloyd fitness centre in Cardiff on which was written the moves and calls for the Wallaby side was at the time seen as a definite stroke of luck. We had studied the video of the Wallabies very hard indeed and when Graham called me to say that he had been handed this sheet of paper I couldn't believe it. The only problem, however, was that the calls did not seem to coincide with the moves on the sheet. Their plan to defend our line-out was there in black and white, but we were not too sure what they would do in each of the six areas of the field in terms of attack. Graham suggested that Alun Carter, the WRU analyst, could take away the moves and calls and try to match them up by watching a video of Australia's pool games. That idea must have been shelved, because Graham never even mentioned it to the players. Furthermore, I did wonder whether the paper, with Jason Little's name on the top, had been left there on purpose.

The Wallabies proved throughout the World Cup that they are as good now as they were when they lifted the trophy at England's expense in the 1991 competition. For us to beat them it would take a superhuman effort. We would have to get everything right; there was no margin for error. There was certainly no room for complacency.

Much of the week leading up to the game had been spent reading how Graham and Rod Macqueen, the Wallaby coach, were playing mind games.

It was no surprise to us to learn that Graham had told the world that we had very little chance of winning, but to hear Rod Macqueen joining in was a little surprising. Having said that, with such a wait between games, the press were simply running out of things to write about.

The fact that it was raining on the day of the match certainly brought a smile to our faces, although we felt that we would still have to play better than we had done at any stage in the tournament to get anywhere near a victory.

George Gregan's early try was certainly a killer blow, as was the injury to Dai Young just before half-time. Dai is a good friend of mine and I know how hard he had worked to recover from the calf injury he had suffered the previous season. Later that night, Dai was in tears when he realised that he would have to spend the next couple of months on the sidelines. The front-row union doesn't always admit to things like that, but it just shows Dai's feeling for the game. Out of all the forwards I have ever played with, I think Dai would have to be the best.

To see Ben Evans coming on to the field certainly gave us great heart, however, because if there is one position in the side where we do have genuine strength in depth it is on the tight-head. Ben had kept Dai out of the side earlier in the year and had a real spring in his step as he packed down for the first scrum. Unfortunately the Wallabies, probably on the advice of Alex Evans, had been coming across on Dai Young earlier in the game and I suppose they targeted Ben in that initial scrum. Not surprisingly, the scrum was quick to go down and Colin Hawke immediately penalised Ben.

I went straight up to Colin to ask what the problem was. He told me that his touch judge had come in and he was not prepared to talk about it at that moment. At the next stoppage I made it my business to ask David McHugh, the touch judge who had allegedly caught Ben taking down the scrum, what had gone on. He told me that he had not seen anything and had not attracted the attention of Colin. Not knowing what Colin Hawke had told me, he said that the decision must have been made by the referee. I was livid. All I wanted was a straightforward answer to a straightforward question so that I could tell Ben and Garin where it was going wrong. I never got one.

As far as Colin's performance was concerned, I have to say that it didn't have any real bearing on the result. However, I didn't think he had the greatest game, and when the final try was given after a clear knock-on, two or three of the boys told him in no uncertain terms what they thought. I think the words of one of the boys even came through on the feed from Colin's mike. They certainly picked it up in the television studio. However, I'm sure Colin knew he had made a mistake. I was just happy that it was not a crucial error that had cost us the game.

We had taken some stick in the tournament for our style of play and our execution, but on this occasion I don't believe we could have done much more. We lacked the Australians' skill and pace and simply have to accept that we are still not as streetwise as players like David Wilson, Tim Horan and George Gregan. The southern hemisphere superpowers have been performing at this level and just below for as long as I can remember. When I spoke to John Eales after the game I asked what he would do after the World Cup. He said they were going to have a rest before preparing for a domestic season next year that would include the Super 12. For us, it was back to a domestic league that, while vastly improved, is in no way comparable. With respect, playing against Dunvant and Caerphilly is not exactly like playing against ACT, is it?

The one thing we do have on our side is the support of the nation. I know that we do have our moments and that we are sometimes too parochial for our own good. However, for the four games at the Millennium Stadium we attracted close on 300,000 people. What's more, the players were taken aback by the crowd's response to us after the game. There might have been a few tears and a few ifs and maybes, but as a collective the supporters were wonderful. I think we are very fortunate.

I thought before the World Cup began that we could do better than we did overall, but I don't believe we should underestimate the power of the Aussies, the All Blacks and the Springboks. They are bigger and better than us and we have to work tirelessly into the new millennium if the gap is going to close. At 10–9 against Australia I felt we were still in it, but equally I felt that if push came to shove they would find another gear. That is the difference.

Before the competition started, I honestly thought that a northern hemisphere side could win the event. While it hurts me to admit as much, I thought that side would be England. However, I was wrong. I have no doubt that the gap is closing but, believe me, there is still a distance to travel before we can justifiably claim to be on an even keel.

As for the competition itself, well, I will look back on those four weeks as the best in my rugby life. What an experience, what an event. And, in the words of Max Boyce, 'I was there'.

APPENDIX

Rob Howley's Career Record

INTERNATIONALS FOR WALES (UP TO 23 OCTOBER 1999)

1996

England	Twickenham	Lost	15–21
Scotland	Cardiff	Lost	14–16
Ireland	Dublin	Lost	17–30
France	Cardiff	Won	16–15
Australia 1st Test	Brisbane	Lost	25–56
Australia 2nd Test	Sydney	Lost	3–42
Barbarians	Cardiff	Won	31–10
France	Cardiff	Lost	33–40
Italy	Rome	Won	31–22
Australia	Cardiff	Lost	19–28
South Africa	Cardiff	Lost	20–37

1997

USA	Cardiff	Won	34–14
Scotland	Edinburgh	Won	34–19
Ireland	Cardiff	Lost	25–26
France	Paris	Lost	22–27
England	Cardiff	Lost	13–34
Tonga*	Swansea	Won	46–12
New Zealand	Wembley	Lost	7–42

1998

Italy (captain)	Llanelli	Won	23–20
England (captain)	Twickenham	Lost	26–60
Scotland (captain)	Wembley	Won	19–13
Ireland (captain)	Dublin	Won	30–21
France (captain)	Wembley	Lost	0–51

Zimbabwe (captain)	Harare	Won	49–11
South Africa (captain)	Wembley	Lost	20–28
Argentina (captain)	Llanelli	Won	43–30

1999

Scotland (captain)	Edinburgh	Lost	20–33
Ireland (captain)	Wembley	Lost	23–29
France (captain)	Paris	Won	34–33
Italy (captain)	Treviso	Won	60–21
England (captain)	Wembley	Won	32–31
Argentina 1st Test (captain)	Buenos Aires	Won	36–26
Argentina 2nd Test (captain)	Buenos Aires	Won	23–16
South Africa (captain)	Cardiff	Won	29–19
Canada (captain)	Cardiff	Won	33–19
France (captain)	Cardiff	Won	34–23
Argentina – WC (captain)	Cardiff	Won	23–18
Japan – WC (captain)	Cardiff	Won	64–15
Samoa – WC (captain)	Cardiff	Lost	31–38
Australia – WC (captain)	Cardiff	Lost	9–24

* Denotes replacement
WC – World Cup

Total: Played 40 games; 7 tries
Record as captain: Played 22, Won 15, Lost 7

BRITISH LIONS

1997 tour to South Africa

BARBARIANS

2 appearances: v. New Zealand, 1993; v. Australia, 1996

CLUB CAREER (UP TO 23 OCTOBER 1999)

Bridgend Rugby Club

1990–91	Played 24 games; 4 tries
1991–92	Played 22 games; 9 tries, 1 conversion
1992–93	Played 24 games; 9 tries, 9 conversions, 6 penalties
1993–94	Played 16 games; 6 tries, 1 conversion
1994–95	Played 29 games; 7 tries, 1 conversion, 1 penalty, 1 drop goal
1995–96	Played 20 games; 2 tries, 2 conversions, 1 penalty
Total	Played 135 games; 37 tries, 14 cons, 8 pens, 1 drop goal

Cardiff Rugby Club

1993–94	Played 5 games
1996–97	Played 23 games; 14 tries
1997–98	Played 20 games; 6 tries
1998–99	Played 18 games; 6 tries
Total	Played 66 games; 26 tries